Research Series on the Chinese Dream and China's Development Path

Drawing on a large body of empirical studies done over the last two decades, the *Research Series on the Chinese Dream and China's Development Path* seeks to provide its readers with in-depth analyses of the past and present, and forecasts for the future course of China's development. Thanks to the adoption of Socialism with Chinese characteristics, and the implementation of comprehensive reform and opening, China has made tremendous achievements in areas such as political reform, economic development, and social construction, and is making great strides towards the realization of the Chinese dream of national rejuvenation. In addition to presenting a detailed account of many of these achievements, the authors also discuss what lessons other countries can learn from China's experience. This series will be an invaluable companion to every researcher who is trying to gain a deeper understanding of the development model, path and experience unique to China.

More information about this series at http://www.springer.com/series/13571

Quanxi Gao • Wei Zhang • Feilong Tian

The Road to the Rule of Law in Modern China

SSAP

Springer

Quanxi Gao
Institute for Advance Studies
in Humanities and Social Sciences
BeiHang University
Beijing, China

Wei Zhang
People's Prosecutors Office Beijing
Chaoyang District
Beijing, China

Feilong Tian
Institute for Advance Studies
in Humanities and Social Sciences
BeiHang University
Beijing, China

ISSN 2363-6866 ISSN 2363-6874 (electronic)
Research Series on the Chinese Dream and China's Development Path
ISBN 978-3-662-45636-1 ISBN 978-3-662-45637-8 (eBook)
DOI 10.1007/978-3-662-45637-8

Library of Congress Control Number: 2015930201

Springer Heidelberg New York Dordrecht London

Printed on acid-free paper

Springer-Verlag GmbH Berlin Heidelberg is part of Springer Science+Business Media (www.springer.com)

Series Preface

Since China's reform and opening began in 1978, the country has come a long way on the path of Socialism with Chinese Characteristics, under the leadership of the Communist Party of China. Over 30 years of reform efforts and sustained spectacular economic growth have turned China into the world's second largest economy, and wrought many profound changes in the Chinese society. These historically significant developments have been garnering increasing attention from scholars, governments and the general public alike around the world since the 1990s, when the newest wave of China studies began to gather steam. Some of the hottest topics have included the so-called "China miracle", "Chinese phenomenon", "Chinese experience", "Chinese path" and the "Chinese model". Homegrown researchers have soon followed suit. Already hugely productive, this vibrant field is putting out a large number of books each year, with Social Sciences Academic Press alone having published hundreds of titles on a wide range of subjects.

Because most of these books have been written and published in Chinese, however, readership has been limited outside China – even among many who study China – for whom English is still the lingua franca. This language barrier has been an impediment to efforts by academia, business communities and policy-makers in other countries to form a thorough understanding of contemporary China, of what is distinct about China's past and present may mean not only for her future but also for the future of the world. The need to remove such an impediment is both real and urgent, and the *Research Series on the Chinese Dream and China's Development Path* is my answer to the call.

This series features some of the most notable achievements from the last 20 years by scholars in China in a variety of research topics related to reform and opening. They include both theoretical explorations and empirical studies, and cover economy, society, politics, law, culture and ecology, the six areas in which reform and opening policies have had the deepest impact and farthest-reaching consequences for the country. Authors for the series have also tried to articulate their visions of the "Chinese Dream" and how the country can realize it in these fields and beyond.

All of the editors and authors for the *Research Series on the Chinese Dream and China's Development Path* are both longtime students of reform and opening and recognized authorities in their respective academic fields. Their credentials and expertise lend credibility to these books, each of which having been subject to a rigorous peer-review process for inclusion in the series. As part of the Reform and Development Program under the State Administration of Press, Publication, Radio, Film and Television of the People's Republic of China, the series is published by Springer, a Germany-based academic publisher of international repute, and distributed overseas. I am confident that it will help fill a lacuna in studies of China in the era of reform and opening.

Xie Shouguang

Preface

There are many reasons that the Opium War in 1840 was chosen to be the starting point of China's modern history. The encounter of the East and the West set off such fundamental changes that Qing Dynasty reformist minister Li Hongzhang exclaimed (they) "hadn't been seen for three thousand years". The war ushered in a period that, in the Chinese collective consciousness, is associated with military defeats, land cessions, war reparations, and humiliating treaties. The staggering cost both in the form of human lives and territorial loss inflicted a deadly blow to the old, ailing empire. While it opened the eyes of ignorant Manchu rulers to the fact that China was not a "heavenly kingdom and superior country", it also left a searing scar in the minds of the common Chinese people, for whom, the prospect of their country being turned into a Western colony would henceforth be a constant nightmare. Determined to thwart fate, the elites of the Chinese people strived to institute one after another reforms. In the process, ideas were conceived and social experiments were carried out, with the utmost goal being transforming China into a strong modern state – a theme that would recur in the subsequent 170 years. Even today, this transformation is still in progress and we are standing in the middle of a journey of national self-redemption and rejuvenation. Born out of the need of self-preservation, such a hardship-ridden journey, leads towards integration of the unique Chinese civilization into the world order, a feat that will be accomplished with much creativity and self-adaption.

Rather than a natural continuation of its traditional form, China that undertook changes "unseen for three thousand years" should be viewed in the context of the unprecedented transformation which turned the country from a classical society into a modern one. This is also the reason why the late Qing dynasty reformists were in a situation very different from their predecessors. In history, China had seen several reforms that set off immense changes: Shang Yang's Reform, Northern Wei Reform, Wang Anshi's Reform and Zhang Juzheng's Reform, to name a few. In a broader sense, Confucius' authoring of *Spring and Autumn Annals* and Deng Zhongshu's reinterpretation of Confucianism can also be viewed as reforms in view of their social implications. However, the reforms that we are talking about are distinctly different, both in terms of thoroughness, unprecedentedness and the influence they exerted on China's over a century-long modernization.

Since the Opium War, especially the First Sino-Japanese War, China had become integrated into the world order so that it could no longer be regarded as the organic, self-developed classical society that it once was. Thus it would be wrong to view the near-modern Chinese history as another dynastic cycle, or a phase of spontaneous development rooted in China's own culture and tradition. The social changes, as the Chinese thinkers of the day such as Li Hongzhang realized back in the day, were indeed "unseen for three thousand years". In response to the changes, a new consciousness, as a result of increasing exposure to the Western influence, took shape. It would spur China to adopt Western notions and institutions. Succession of dynasties had become a thing of the past; the rigid sinocentric world order that places an irrevocable distinction between *Hua* and *Yi* (Translator's note: The Central Kingdom and Barbarians) was rendered obsolete. Desperate situation demanded desperate measures – to save the nation from the onslaught of the West, China was sent onto a route of reform that would span the next century, a time when turbulence coexisted with transformation, opportunity arose from crisis, death followed by rebirth.

Worldwide, China's modernization is rather special in the sense that other nations descended from the great ancient civilizations such as Ancient Greece, Rome, Egypt and India had all but perished by the modern time, whereas the Chinese was the only one that preserved a civilization of over three thousand years long. However, this historical bequeathal cut both ways – for one thing, it made China's transformation towards modernity fraught with setbacks and stagnations. Yet with the national survival at stake, there was no other choice but to cut off the past, to reshape its spirit, to replenish its energy, and fight for survival – which is the logic that has dominated China's modernization. Commenting on this period of history, later day historian Yeo-Chi King said "China's order of civilization faced unprecedented challenge in the mid-nineteenth century. This challenge came from the modern Western civilization that came in front of China and other eastern Asian countries in the form of imperialism and colonialism. People like Li Hongzhang and Yan Fu were aware that China was in the throes of the greatest transformation since Qin Dynasty… to put it simply, it is about how China responded to the provocation from the West, its conception of modernization, as well as renewing and developing its own traditional civilization."[1]

For China, the word 'modernity' has three layers of meanings. The first mainly concerns with instrumental aspects and material conditions, i.e. living standards, means of production, etc. These constitute the most basic or technological layer of modernization. Following the Opium Wars, the best Chinese thinkers began to realize that China must modernize itself to survive as a civilization; they had henceforth engaged in efforts to institute reforms to promote the modernization. Examples of the early-stage modernization efforts include coastal defense plan composed by

[1] See Yeo-Chi King: *Construction of China's Modern Civilization – On China's Modernization and Modernity*, part of *Economic Democracy and Economic Liberty* edited by Liu Junning, Shanghai Sanlian Bookstore Press, 1998, Pp. 42–43.

Wei Yuan, the Westernization Movement to build a "strong" and "prosperous" country, Sun Yat-sen's *Strategy of State Building*, Mao Zedong and CPC's "Overtake Britain and America" Movement, and the Four Modernizations Campaign, Building Well-off Society Campaign in the late twentieth century. Underlying these phenomena, there is a strong consensus – that China must be turned into a modern state. This rather elementary understanding of modernity has been a major driving force throughout a century of modernization.[2]

On top of the basic layer, there are notions, values, perceptions, as well as intellectual debates that formed public opinion and social values. While the public had relatively little problem accepting the instrumental modernization, modern social values and notions proved to be a hard sell. The Chinese people's reluctance to forsake their values and embrace Western ones is reflected in the popular notion "Zhong Ti Xi Yong" (Translator's note: Chinese foundation and Western practical application). Another example is the recent debates concerning the merit and demerit of the American development model vis-a-vis the Chinese one. Such a divide among the public would contribute to a concatenation of historical events, with outcomes not always desirable. The Chinese thinkers of the day were well aware of the divergence. Examples can be found in debates over the Confucian dichotomy of Hua and Yi, Wei Yuan's writings on maritime sovereignty, Westernization Movement, Constitutionalist Movement, Hundred Days Reform, May 4 Movement, Xinhai Revolution, the Soviet-style Communist Revolution, as well as Socialism Construction that spanned over 60 years. These events raised questions that not only concern the technological, but also the conceptual. In fact, one of the central questions this book will try to answer is why the strong consensus and remarkable progress in terms of the instrumental did not happen when it came to the conceptual.[3]

The answer lies in China's own tradition – the third layer. Modernity, a concept deep-rooted in the Western tradition, was wedded to Western cultural institutions. They were inseparable with nation states, capitalism, and commercialism, and some significant historical events such as Industrial Revolution, technological revolutions and reforms of Christianity had all left deep marks. Although over the course of 300 years, the Western modernization experienced many setbacks in its own right, the problems they experienced, unlike ones faced by China, are ingrained in their own culture, hence despite the setbacks, modernity always triumphed and renewed

[2]To read more about the distinction between modernization and modernity, see Qin Xiao's *Contemporary China: Modernization or Modernity*, Social Science Academic Press, 2009; *On China's Modernity Solution* by the same author, Social Science Academic Press, 2010. The modernist concept of material progress deeply influenced China's choice of its economy model (such as prioritizing development of heavy industry in post-1949 era) and its constitutional spirit (build a "prosperous and strong" state). In terms of the former, read Lin Yifu's *China Miracle: Development Strategy and Economic Reform*, especially the second chapter, Shanghai People's Press, 1999; the later, see Chen Duanhong's *On Constitution as the Basic Law and Advanced Law,* Beijing University Law Journal, Issue 4, 2008.

[3]See Tang Degang's *70 Years of Late Qing (I): A Review of China's Social Culture Transformation*, Yuanliu Publishing House, 2003.

itself – as a result, we see that modernity in the West has in many ways been transformed into post-modernity.

Things are different for China. Not only it had a late start, modernity being a product of a foreign civilization, it was borrowed, imposed as a result of its association with the West and many characteristics indicate China's modernization was a passive response to external provocations. For the Western civilization, from its inception until the twentieth century, modernity had gone through a process of transformation. All institutions and values, such as constitutional monarchism, sovereignty, individual liberties, representation democracy, free will, conception of order and civilization, the relationship between state and citizens, between human beings and nature, between politics and religion, had all be changed drastically. In the twentieth century, a new development emerged – post-modernism emerged as a counteraction to modernism. All the crises notwithstanding, we should see that the modernization in the West is rather spontaneous and logically coherent, while the same cannot be said for China.

Given the "provocation-response" nature of the Chinese-Western interaction, it seems only natural that the concept of modernity, rooted in the Western tradition, did not resonate with its Chinese audience. As a latecomer, China's modernization needed more than importing Western technology, ideals such as "science and democracy", capitalism, socialism, justice, liberty, rule of law, etc. It was critical for China to decide what kind of modernization it wanted, and to do what in different time, in what fashion. Unfortunately, during the century-long modernization, we saw little cool-headed, self-reflective thinking in this regard. This inadequacy has much to do with the reality that today, a healthy and stable modernity has yet been fully implemented. In fact, revolution and radicalism were chosen at multiple historical crossroads and dominated China's modern history. Such a pattern is quite obvious throughout the history.

Let's begin with a review Hundred Days Reform. At the first glance, the theory Kang Youwei and Liang Qichao advocated seems to be a new development of the traditional Confucianism with a bent on political innovation and reform. However, upon a closer look, it became plain that Kang and Liang's new theory differs greatly from traditional Confucianism in meaningful ways. Most importantly, some of the central ideas were borrowed from the West. Not only their inspiration for the reform was derived from the Western civilization, their endeavor to reinterpret Confucian doctrines is essentially "disguising" Western revolutionary radicalism as Chinese Confucianism. In doing so, Kang expressed his vision and aspirations regarding modernity. In fact, the whole reform can be regarded as an expression of the Chinese civilization's aspirations to renew itself under the pressure of survival. Almost the same took place in Japan, which inspired Fukuzawa to put forward his "Leave Asia and Join Europe" theory – Asia refers to the Chinese tradition, while Europe stands for Western civilization and modernity. Therefore the Hundred Days Reform should be regarded as a manifestation of which way should China pursue – the traditional Chinese way or the modern Western way. The same question was later put in front of Sun Yat-sen and the communist revolutionaries after him. These revolutions might have differed from the Hundred Days Reform, but they shared the same radicalism – all insisting that a modern China can only be brought about after the old one was destroyed.

But why did China showed a strong preference for revolutionary radicalism to milder alternatives? Of course, there was the great national bitterness as a result of the Western subjugation. When ancient Chinese civilization was confronted by the Western powers, when the very question of its cultural survival was at stake, little wonder that the Chinese elites, aware of the gravity of the situation back in the day, opted for extreme means compelled by the belief that such measures were the most effective. Many of them sincerely believed that only through radical measures, a fate of subjugation and slavery could be thwarted; they also believed that China's problems could be solved at one stroke. Driven by such a view, they endeavored to lift China's international status, trying to help China to deal with the West on equal terms. Given the intensity of sentiment and urgency, it was done with great haste. Yet with the benefit of hindsight, we know that despite all the bloodshed, regime changes, and tyrannies, and over century-long modernization, a healthy and civilized state remained unaccomplished. One may argue that today China has emerged as a world power, but one should not overlook the costs paid for it – individual dignity, liberty, traditional virtues and morality, all having been sacrificed to some extents. Ever since the May 4 Movement, radicalism attained mainstream recognition with the public who grew increasingly fed up with anything traditional. Such sentiment heightened during the Tutelage Era, and later the Cultural Revolution. Even today, the specter of radicalism has not gone yet. In spite of the long process of modernization, a sound legal and moral order to provide better justice and moral guidance for the modern Chinese people has yet been established.

We need to look beyond the national bitterness and contemplate why this form of modernity was chosen and why did this form of modernity that we chose degrade, mutate and finally led to undesirable outcome. Is revolutionary radicalism the only way to achieve it worldwide? During the 170 years, is revolutionary radicalism the only driving force? Or were there any other that were overlooked or suppressed, yet nonetheless vital and legitimate? To put it simply: During four centuries of Western modernization and over one century of Chinese modernization, is revolutionary radicalism the only solution? Is revolutionary radicalism the only source of legitimacy for our society and institutions? The answer is obviously negative.

In fact, in the Western society, revolutionary radicalism is only one alternative, and has been proven to be a "twisted" one. Conservatism, which opposes revolution and radicalism, remains mainstream. Worldwide, modernity has two different traditions: the Anglo-American rationalist and gradualist approach, whose principles shaped the Britain and United States, two bases of conservatism. Without their steadfast championing of conservatism principles, which have been the guiding values since the seventeenth century, the world order as we know it today would have been inconceivable.

There is no denying that even within the tradition of conservationism, revolution sometimes could not be avoided. England, for example, had Glorious Revolution, while the United States had American Revolution, yet overall, these conservative revolutions differed from the radical ones – they are more restrained and their contradictions were resolved within the political institutions; highly critical of themselves, these revolutions sought to terminate themselves as the ultimate goal. We call such trait revolutionary counter-revolution, which leads to a revolution ending with revolutionary principles written into the constitution, thereby achieving peace and constitutionalism, as happened in England and America. Here we can see that what conservatism conserves is not the old feudalist institutions, but revolutionary values. With conservatism, ravages of revolution were contained, a stable state with sound legal system emerges in its wake, whereas in a radical revolution, such outcome is often unattainable. This does not mean, however, these conservative societies have difficulty in renewing or improving themselves; on the contrary, renewal and improvement were deeply ingrained in conservative constitutionalism tradition, and played a critical role in their social progress. So the difference between the two is whether the extreme radical means can be restrained. In case of conservative constitutionalism, revolutionary means would be put in cold storage once the revolution succeeded and counter-revolution will take over to complete the transformation from extreme political condition to an everyday one.[4]

The revolutionary radicalism tradition stemmed from the French Revolution, further developed through the later German Revolution and Russian Revolution. This route to modernity lays its emphasis on constant destruction of old institutions. It posited that only through destruction of the old can the new be established. What it overlooked is the dialectics that new will become old, hence will also need to be get rid of one day. Without a brake, which a conservative revolution can provide, destruction cannot be stopped until complete annihilation. In such a process, even the ideals the revolution once upheld will be reduced to what Strauss called "nothingness". Hence we should see that "construction through destruction" is a form of sophistry. Destruction is destruction; it does not necessarily entail construction. No peaceful modern society was constructed according to this pattern. Fortunately, radicalism is just one option in the West and never gained mainstream recognition. Although at certain points, its influence was strong enough to contend with conservatism – the French – Russian tradition could not compete with the conservationist Anglo–American tradition in terms of effectiveness in constructing a stable social order. However, even today, the two contradicting tendencies still coexist in Western conservationism, resulting in paradoxical contradiction between the pacifist ideals championed by the British and American constitutions and their imperialist hegemony designs.

China as a latecomer, faced problems very different than the Western countries did centuries ago. In China, conservatism and conservatives had weak legitimacy from the beginning. Radicalism was the dominating force throughout much of the

[4] For more about political and constitutional jurisprudent analysis of Revolutionary Jurisprudence and Counterrevolutionary Jurisprudence, read Gao Quanxi's *On Revolutionary Jurisprudence*, Beijing Post-graduate Journal, Issue 1, 2010; *The Secret of American Politics—Reviews From the Perspevtive of Political Philosophy,* Strategy and Management, Issue 5 and 6, 2010; *Revolution, Constitution and China Constitutionalism*, Beijing University Law Journal, Issue 2, 2010, Beijing University Press.

modern history. This is compounded by China's choices at some historical crossroads, which, to a good measure, prevented China from building a healthier and more rational form of modern society in line with conservationism. On the other hand, China's modern history is not completely devoid of the influence of conservatism. One can say that the influence of conservatism was weaker, but it remained alive and resilient, and even during the worse times was not absent.[5]

Since conservatism focuses more on incremental improvement and gradual change, it is less noticeable, thus often neglected by the grand narratives, which preferred wars, political struggles, constitutional changes, major diplomatic incidents, etc. Society, even when revolution was at its most intense, could not be reduced to a shell of abstract ideas. It is still a complex body of morals, sentiments, traditions, and individual initiatives. After the establishment of People's Republic of China in 1949, especially during the Cultural Revolution, individual initiatives seeking social-improvement experienced great difficulty; however, even in the harshest times, certain elements of conservationism were preserved. Gu Zhun (1915–1974), economist who witnessed radicalism at its worst during the heyday of Cultural Revolution, acutely sensed a tidal change of public sentiment from radicalism towards gradual improvement and heroically championed a "transition from idealism to empiricism".[6] Gu's is just one of the examples the Chinese intellectuals did not submit themselves in spite of harsh conditions, but consciously seeking to preserve a sense of conservationism. Today, decades after Deng Xiaoping's Reform and Opening-up, which launched the country onto the route of market economy, remarkable progress was achieved with respect to building a civil society. Although a systematic institutional reform that could have established these values had yet been implemented, China has at least transcended the old revolutionary discourse and been advancing towards a more rational and healthy future.

Two questions need to be clarified before we go further to establish legitimacy for this counter-revolutionary conservatism in the context of China's modernization. First, conservatism in modern China is not a continuation of traditional feudalistic dynastic politics; actually, reforms of such nature are beyond the scope of this book. Although traditional China had experienced great social changes, such as the dynastic change of Qin replacing Zhou, Han replacing Qin, or ideological changes, such as Confucianism replacing Taoism as the governing philosophy, Dong Zhongshu's reinterpretation of Confucian classics, or political reforms such as Wang Anshi's Reform, no matter how profound their implications may be, these changes fall into a different category. The legal, political and academic conditions that traditional "conservatism" relied on were no longer there after China's defeat in the Opium War. The conservatism that this book addresses refers solely to modern conservatism,

---

[5] See Gao Quanxi, *The Constitutional Moment: On the Imperial Edict of the Manchu Emperor`s Abdication*, Guangxi Normal University Press, 2011; The Chinese constitutionalists, represented by local gentry class, played a great role in stabilizing local political order and preserves autonomy, which shows the social influence and political power of the Chinese conservatives. See Zhang Ming's *Xinhai, A Rocking China*, Guangxi Normal University Press, 2011.

[6] See Gu Zhun's *Gu Zhun Anthology*, Guizhou People's Publishing House, 1994.

which is different from the aforementioned form of "conservatism" mainly due to its legitimacy. Modernization of the U.K and the U.S.A, especially the former, though experienced republican radicalism momentarily, retained strong ties with tradition. For that reason, Glorious Revolution is sometimes regarded as a restoration of the old dynasty. One example is the Whig history, which portrayed British history as a consistent whole without the kind of upheavals that China experienced in late Qing dynasty. However, reality was hardly as harmonious as the Whig history portrayed. Otherwise, it would be hard to explain books such as *Leviathan*, revisionist view on Glorious Revolution and the emergence of Whig history itself. That, however, should not prevent us from admitting that modernization in Britain and America was less abrupt than in France and Russia.

China's conservatism cannot be modeled on the British model given the great gap between its modern state and classical state. The incompatibility of the two to some extent justified a French-style radical revolution to introduce an institutional overhaul. At a time when possibility of self-developed modernization from the old system exhausted, Western radicalism arrived in China as an inspiration. Yet the question remains: what to do after the revolution. How to treat tradition and revolution are but two sides of the same coin. If a country cannot treat its revolution in a reasonable way, it is unlikely to treat its tradition in a reasonable way. Czar Nicholas II was an example of a monarch that intransigently rejected revolution and insisted on traditionalism, and he was annihilated with his reign. The same question is also faced by China. If radical revolution has the way, the only way to treat tradition is criticism, denial, and even smearing. Destruction is to be praised; "poor and blank" is a preferable because "the best picture can only be drawn on a piece of blank paper" (translator's note: this is believed to be a Mao Zedong quote). Although such way of thinking dominated much of China's modernization, it was barren soil for concepts such as liberty, constitutionalism, democracy, and rule of law.

Is there a way to reconcile the traditional and the modern, to develop a form of conservatism that safeguards the revolutionary ideals? As we said, revolution, its rational side notwithstanding, requires someone to pull the brake to save it from self-perpetuation. It can only succeed when revolutionaries can be highly critical of themselves, and actively transform themselves into a constructive counter-revolutionary force. If revolution is all about destruction, and laws cannot take hold, then the role of lawmakers has to be taken up by other forms of counter-revolutionaries other than revolutionaries themselves. Law is different from revolution in the fact that it is a safeguarding force and it does not reject tradition. This is not to say that constitutionalism is subordinate to tradition for its attitude towards tradition is one of equal dialogue and selective adoption. The post-revolution relationship of the old and the new should not be one of disconnection and antagonism. However, following one after another revolutions, which spanned over a century, China has not produced a voluntary "restoration" by the revolutionaries that brought China back to the path of conservative development, which barred a gradual and spontaneous improvement from happening. By revolutionary "restoration" we mean to bring things from extreme revolutionary mode back to normal state. When revolution succeeded, old institutions were abolished, it is time for people to shelf the spirit of revolution and let constitution take over and the normal social order to recover. In this sense, restoration is not about the revival of the old, but a rather sympathetic reconciliation between the modern and the old. The major Chinese revolutions failed to achieve this objective; as a result, the governments built by them were often unstable. In spite of much bloodshed in the name of revolution, a modern state that upholds rule of law failed to be brought on. In comparison, the claim to immortality of the English Glorious Revolution and American Civil War lies in the fact that both of them achieved a "revolutionary restoration". As a result, when military actions ceased, victory was shared by both sides. The ashes of the war dead from both sides entered the shrine and celebrated as heroes – reconciliation was thus achieved. By the same token, for China, the best way to measure how successful a revolution is should be whether the "revolutionary restoration" was accomplished. This approach should also be applied to measure the success of modernization. There should be no more revolutions except those that seek self-termination. We pay homage to our revolutions, praise their glory, though we are not to destroy the order and life that we enjoy today for another one. What we should do is to use tradition to relieve the pain caused by revolutionary radicalism, by doing so, when looking back at the 170 years of great change we will be able to appreciate the Chinese modernity better.

These are the reasons justifying the writing of this book, which is an effort that seeks to examine the modern judicial reform from late Qing Dynasty onwards. By combing through the historical relics, we hope we can connect the dots and show the direction towards modernity and identify the causes behind victories and failures alike. We hope by such a book, we can help people appreciate a healthy and rational road towards modernization, thereby help ourselves to find a way out of the mist, and resolve the legacy left by a century worth of revolutionary radicalism.

The reason that this book chooses rule of law as the entry point is because establishing a modern judicial system is a main objective of the first wave of social reforms in late Qing dynasty. This can be seen in the popular slogan of the day: Bian Fa Tu Qiang – Change Law to Become A Prosperous State. Noteworthy is that the rule of law here refers to a modern political state and structure based on the principle of constitutionalism. Rule of law includes both political institutions formed under extreme conditions that lasted into non-extreme conditions, as well as political and social order formed under the non-extreme conditions. More importantly, it proposes a set of procedures that can smoothen the transition from extreme politics to everyday routine one. In European history, rule of law and related institutions were established gradually over the course of centuries, during which Europe experienced Renascence, Reformation, and Enlightenment, development of capitalism and capitalist revolution. Constitution is the most important condition as well as the core of modern rule of law institution. It is installed with an aim to protect individual's rights from government's violations by restraining the latter's power. Rule of law not only constitutes the mainstream Western political form, but also shapes its political culture and social form, which in turn facilitates its development, and through its global expansion, achieved world domination. Hence whatever differences between late Qing constitutionalist movement, Xinhai Revolution, Republic of China, and People's Republic of China, they shared one thing in common, which is that all of them attempted to build a strong and modern China by establishing a modern political form. The transformation since Hundred Days Reform is a history of effort seeking to install constitutionalism in China in response to Western provocation. This concept of China's rule of law development entails bringing China up to the standard of international mainstream political and legal civilizations, rather than resisting them.

To view the Chinese modernity from the perspective of rule of law, we need to answer questions that concern the acceptance of modern rule of law concept in China, steps that have been taken to improve its legal system, and construction of a modern and healthy rule of law framework. Up until 1978 when the Reform and Opening Up was launched, all efforts with a view to achieve the above-mentioned objectives had failed to achieve these objectives. The Hundred Days' Reform was purged, their leaders banished, or executed. Later, KMT revolutionaries abolished China's first constitution, putting an end to the Constitutionalist Movement. Then Yuan Shikai usurped republic and declared himself emperor, before his sudden death plunged China back into anarchy. During the period, the Chinese people had nothing but the name of a constitution with no real rights given to them. A ray of hope shined briefly when the CPC joined KMT in their anti-Japanese effort, but then collapse legal. In 1949, China's status as an independent nation was finally secured, but its judicial construction suffered great setbacks due to the ensuing political turmoil. In 1978 when the Party sought to rectify its policies, the Chinese legal development stood close to where it started in late Qing dynasty. Reform to make China a strong nation was again the public consensus. Measures were taken to restore democracy and rule of law. The "socialist market economy" was recognized and written into the constitution. A consensus was formed among the country's leadership that rule by law as well as a robust socialist democracy are vital to this form of economy. Legal development was given high priority, leading to the establishment of the most fundamental norms of the public law and private law. Rule of law was constitutionalized, with specialized clauses dedicated to protecting human rights and right to private property. All of these pushed China's legal development to a new height.

That is not to say that the mission of China's legal construction has been accomplished. Neither can we claim China's modernization has succeeded, or flaunting the so-called "China Model" or "China Experience" as great contribution to the world. Some may argue that aside from national independence, at least when judging by economic development and social welfare, China achieved dazzling growth. But has it met the targets that we set a century ago? Today as a result of globalization, we have been integrated deeply into the modern world order; however, when measuring by social and political development levels, we are still in an early stage of modernization. This assessment also applies to the development of modern political institutions – values underpinning modernity such as liberty, rationality, individual rights, as well as institutions like market economy and democratic constitutionalism have not been fully implemented. China remains on its way towards becoming modern state. Achievements that we have made, such as independence and economic growth, are the basics. When it comes to the conceptual and spiritual aspects, few things truly remarkable have been accomplished.

The problems that we try to solve over the past 170 years corresponded to those that were faced by Western countries in the seventeenth to nineteenth century. While we are solving the problems that the West had solved hundreds of years ago, we must be aware that we are in an era drastically different from theirs. Challenges come from two fronts: While we are still on our way in building a modern nation state according to the principles of liberty and democracy, which the West spent centuries to accomplish, we are seeing the trend is shifting to "denationalization". The flaws of modern states underpinned by civil liberty, democracy and constitutionalism and international order constructed according to these principles are becoming more and more pronounced. Thus, while we are still on our way towards modernity, we also need to cope with the post-modernity challenge. For example, the legitimacy of modern nation state has been weakened with the rise of globalization. Moreover, our 300 years of political and historical burden did not always make things easier. To handle it requires us to be prudent and balanced in decision-making, so that we can retain our Chinese characteristics while joining the world order, find a balance between modernity and pluralism, unique tradition and universalism, indigenous resources and Western institutions.

To sum up, not only the China's legal modernization has not achieved full success yet, the risk of regression remains; not only the so-called "China Experience" or "China Model" not worth of bragging about, we should apply more caution and prudence; not only a long-term vision is needed, we should also be prepared for the complexity of the challenge that future may present. With these in mind, the book endeavors to draw a sketch of the evolution of China's legal modernization, in doing so, providing a coordinate system for the future reforms. We hope by a review of the past 170 years and especially the latest 30 years of constitutional and legal reform, to identify the shortcomings of revolutionary radicalism, but we also intend to do so without denying the legitimacy of revolutionary radicalism. We are looking for a modern conservative way that can ease revolutionary radicalism without negating the historical roots and national grievances.

Beijing, China

Quanxi Gao
Wei Zhang
Feilong Tian

Acknowledgments

After a relatively short gestation period, the *Research Series on the Chinese Dream and China's Development Path* has started to bear fruits. We have, first and foremost, the books' authors and editors to thank for making this possible. And it was the hard work by many people at Social Sciences Academic Press and Springer, the two collaborating publishers, that made it a reality. We are deeply grateful to all of them.

Mr. Xie Shouguang, president of Social Sciences Academic Press (SSAP), is the mastermind behind the project. In addition to defining the key missions to be accomplished by it and setting down the basic parameters for the project's execution, as the work has unfolded, Mr. Xie has provided critical input pertaining to its every aspect and at every step of the way. Thanks to the deft coordination by Ms. Li Yanling, all the constantly moving parts of the project, especially those on the SSAP side, are securely held together, and as well synchronized as is feasible for a project of this scale. Ms. Gao Jing, unfailingly diligent and meticulous, makes sure every aspect of each Chinese manuscript meets the highest standards for both publishers, something of critical importance to all subsequent steps in the publishing process. That high-quality if also at times stylistically as well as technically challenging scholarly writing in Chinese has turned into decent, readable English that readers see on these pages is largely thanks to Ms. Liang Fan, who oversees translator recruitment and translation quality control.

Ten other members of the SSAP staff have been intimately involved, primarily in the capacity of in-house editor, in the preparation process for all the Chinese manuscripts. It is time-assuming work that requires attention to details, and each of them has done this, and is continuing to do this well. They are, in alphabetical order of their surname: Mr. Cai Jihui, Ms. Liu Xiaojun, Mr. Ren Wenwu, Ms. Shi Xiaolin, Ms. Song Yuehua, Mr. Tong Genxing, Ms. Wu Dan, Ms. Yao Dongmei, Ms. Yun Wei and Ms. Zhou Qiong. In addition, Xie Shouguang and Li Yanling have also taken part in this process.

Ms. Liu Xiaojun is the SSAP in-house editor for the current volume.

Our appreciation is also owed to Ms. Li Yan, Mr. Chai Ning, Ms. Wang Lei and Ms. Xu Yi from Springer's Beijing Representative Office. Their strong support for the SSAP team in different aspects of the project helped to make the latter's work that much easier than it would have otherwise been.

We thank Mr. Mu Xiaoliang for translating this book.

Last, but certainly not least, it must be mentioned that funding for this project comes from the Ministry of Finance of the People's Republic of China. Our profound gratitude, if we can be forgiven for a bit of apophasis, goes without saying.

Social Sciences Academic Press
Springer

Contents

About the Authors

Quanxi Gao is Dean of the Institute for Advanced Humanistic Studies and Sociology of Beihang University. He is also a Professor of Law and received his Ph.D. in Philosophy.

Wei Zhang is a prosecutor working at Beijing's Chaoyang District People's Procuratorate. He received his Ph.D. in Business Administration.

Feilong Tian is Assistant Professor at the Institute for Advanced Humanistic Studies and Sociology of Beihang University. He holds a Ph.D. in Law.

Chapter 1
Inception: From Hundred Days Reform to Xinhai Revolution

1.1 Historical Background of the Encounter of the East and the West

China's encounter with the West in mid-nineteenth century set off changes that had "not been seen for three thousands years". These changes, including the Opium War, and later, the First Sino-Japanese War, jolted the Qing dynasty onto a course of modernization and ushered in China's near-modern history. China's defeats in the wars set the tone for the period of history, which to this day is still remembered with much bitterness. But imperialism and colonialism were not all the enemies that China faced; a stronger foe was feudalism from its own past. Together, the two forces defined the objectives of China's modernization: national survival, people's liberation and individual wellbeing. In comparison, the West, which experienced the same process centuries before, shared similar yet different objectives in their own modernization: individual liberty, nation state and citizen's wellbeing.

China modernization, centuries behind the West's, didn't occur as a result of its own decision. A strong element of nationalism and collectivism distinguishes it from the West's. In the West, collectivism had little influence in the process; instead, individualism was the inspiration for many who rose against the feudal lords. Notwithstanding the difference, both China and the West sought increase of national wealth and building modern state-building as their objectives, although to achieve them, the two took a different routes and assigned different priorities to individual liberty and legal system.

As we said, a fundamental difference between China and the West is that for China, modernity is an export rather than something grown from its own tradition. Unlike in the West, China was deprived of the chance to walk itself out of its feudalistic tradition and form a modern sovereign state of its own accord. Given such historical context, we would conjecture that China's modernization is a response to external provocation posed by a powerful alien civilization. We would also like to mention John King Fairbank's "stimulus-reaction model", which is highly pertinent

Q. Gao et al., *The Road to the Rule of Law in Modern China*,
Research Series on the Chinese Dream and China's Development Path,
DOI 10.1007/978-3-662-45637-8_1

when applied to the circumstances that China was under. To sum up, China, after experiencing Opium War and the First Sino Japanese War, had been jolted onto a course of modernization, a process more a response to external provocation than a spontaneous development.[1]

However, a mechanic understanding of the provocation-reaction conjecture should be avoided. As a civilization, China had proved itself a resilient, vigorous, and responsive one. If it merely reacted to the provocation passively, it wouldn't have developed modernity so rich yet distinctly Chinese. Thus we conjecture that the Western provocation only served as a catalyst. It was through this catalyst, the Chinese civilization was spurred to tap into its fountain of life and take initiative to recreate itself. When we look into the origin of China's modernization, we see that the modernization process began as a passive reaction, yet as it developed, it would finally be transformed into a positive recreation.[2]

Given the reasons provided above, Chinese modernity was developed indigenously and spontaneously, rather than purely the consequence of a concatenation of events led by external forces, or a work of passive imitation. This conclusion led to the birth of this book, which is in the main an effort to examine the Chinese modernity from a Chinese perspective. Readers should not be led to think that we are denying the obvious, that during three thousand years of history, China failed to transform itself into a country that that is structurally similar to the modern West; neither should the book be seen as an attempt to trivialize the profoundness of the great impact of the China-West encounter. We acknowledge that modern China is an outcome of historical events set forth by the encounter, whose influence we are still living under. On the other hand, we want to remind readers that China didn't perish under the impact; instead, it triumphed in transforming itself into a modern state, which is the ultimate proof of its robustness.

Evidently, the Chinese civilization suffered staggering losses during this phase of history, at points, tittering on the brink of complete collapse, however, in the end, it thwarted the fate that many other ancient civilizations met: It neither perish or became assimilated. Instead, it recovered and renewed itself. As the clash between China and the West intensified, the danger for China to perish became graver; fact is that the clash between the East and the West over modernity is a theme throughout China's entire modernization process.

One question that many would ask is how did China perceive their dealings with the West? It is evident that this relationship was not an equal one. For China, its road towards modernization was paved by humiliation and bitterness. Its opponent held great advantage both materially and intellectually. Such an asymmetric relationship between China and the West led to the collapse of the order, though we acknowledge that without the sudden descent of the West, there would probably have never been a modern China.

---

[1]See Teng and Fairbank, *China's response to the west: A Documentary Survey*, 1839–1923, Cambridge: Harvard University Press, 1954, p. 1.

[2]American scholar Paul A. Cohen criticizes this "challenge – response" diagram overlooks China's spontaneous reform impulse. See his *Discovering history in China: American historical writing on the recent Chinese past*, Trans Li Rongtai and others. Linking Books, 1991, p. 1.

Two things are of note when it comes to the inequality between China and the West. First, from the perspective of the traditional Chinese civilization, the West posed a strong challenge to its sinocentric world order. Followed by China's military defeats, its tribute system collapsed. It was forced to open treaty ports and judicial extraterritoriality had to be granted, concessions, de facto enclaves were established in coastal cities, to the detriment of the Chinese sovereignty and national pride. In the eyes of the West, China was an uncivilized country; therefore International Law didn't apply to their dealings with the country. For them, the Chinese people were no different from other people that they conquered, were unenlightened barbarians; only those that met their standards and shared their Christian faith were worthy of the international law and equality. For over a century, the guideline that West adopted in its dealing with China was a colonist and "uncivilized" one. Hence China's modernity was not cultivated by civilized and equal dialogue, but grounded in war and struggle. Worth nothing that Western view of Chinese being barbarians were reciprocated to certain degree, the difference is that China happened to be the losing side, hence was forced to accept the West-dominated world order. If humiliation has any positive use, it prompted the Chinese people to reevaluate themselves and fortified their resolve to implement reform.

Neither military defeats nor social turmoil was new for China. In history, it had experienced many peasant wars, nomadic tribal invasions, and coup d'états. But the wound that Opium War opened was new. As mentioned before, the encounter between China and the West made China modernize itself, instead of building another dynasty. The conception of Chinese superiority, which is deeply wedded into the traditional Chinese culture and value system, used to be its guideline in handling diplomatic relationship and had achieved great success in handling the nomadic tribes. Although China was ruled by alien ethnic groups a few times, its core political institutions had been preserved, until the Opium War.

All foreign invasions China had experienced heretofore are within the purview of "old order". Over the decades following the Opium War, the Chinese elites were dismayed to find that the old doctrines concerning foreign diplomacy no longer worked. Now humbled by a string of military defeats, the Chinese were forced to reevaluate the situation, and began to see the advantage their opponents brought into the conflict. The response went through stages over time; first they focused on the instrumental – faster ships and more powerful cannons; later, as they lose their arrogance, they began to embrace Western cultural constructs such as science, religion and philosophy, though their anxiety also grew in the process. A great change "unseen in three thousand years" is indeed happening.

The West that the late Qing dynasty faced was a West that had undergone the "change unseen in three thousand years" of their own. Modernization being a global phenomena, it not only affected the West. The outcome of conflict between the modernized West and pre-modernization China is almost certain from the beginning. After a string of failures, China licked the wound and started its own modernization. For China, one of the earliest civilizations, for thousands of years, stability was the norm with little change. Now facing the challenge from the West, it was forced to reevaluate its own tradition and make adaptions.

China's modernization developed along two directions. First is its increased knowledge of the West, which had expanded from firearms to judicial, political institutions, philosophies and religion, as a result, understanding of the Western conception of modernization and modernity considerably deepened. The other direction is China's attitude towards its own tradition, life styles, means of production, rituals and political ideas, which also went through changes. A consensus slowly took its shape. This trend is manifested in some of the great intellectual writings of the time, from Huang Zongxi's Ming Yi Dai Fang Lu to Wei Yuan's World Records, to Li Hongzhang and Zhang Zhidong's Westernization Movement, all these people were examining the Western world while reevaluating China's own tradition, and tried to find a way to reconcile the two in the process of the turbulent progression of the world history. During this period, China's knowledge of the West increased. They originally regarded the Western culture as "barbarian", gradually came to recognize its legitimacy, and grew to recognize their right as an independent civilization. Gradually, it also realized that the Western powers, when dealing among themselves, followed certain codes and rules known as the international laws.

Such realization sent the Chinese into a legitimacy crisis. When it became evident that it would be futile to resist the Western powers using the traditional ways, many began to regard reform as the only recourse. As mentioned previously, the reforms that China undertook in history, however influential they might be, were of a different type from the one at hand. When we talk about reforms, not only the Hundred Days Reform is an example of a new school of reforms, so are the Constitutionalist Movement and Xinhai Revolution. All of them sought to rectify the Chinese political and law system and reestablish their legitimacy, in doing so, lay the foundation for China's modernization.

Three major reforms were launched in the wake of Opium War: Hundred Days Reform, Constitution Movement, and Xinhai Revolution. All these reforms carry strong modernizing overtones, and were revolutionary in essence. The difference between them is the first two were conservationist revolutions that sought to rectify the old institutions, whereas the later was a radical one that tried to overthrow the old regime. When we look at these three movements one by one, it is evident that each one is more radical than the previous one. Such tendency would be even more pronounced in later social movements. From Monarchy Constitutionalism, to Citizen Constitution, from Racial Revolution to Five Ethnic Group Joint Government, from Political Revolution to Yue Fa Jian Guo (Constitutional State-building), we see a profound, modern radicalism pattern underneath the three movements, which foreshadowed more social and political turmoil that would come.

1.2 Hundred Days Reform

On June 11, 1898, Guangxu Emperor issued Decree on Sate Affairs, which marked the official start of the Hundred Days Reform. Over the next three months until September 21, the emperor issued more decrees that covered a wide range of subjects – politics, economics, to culture and education. Although these decrees were progressive in their outlook and extensive in scope, they were not thoroughly implemented. With the exception of Hunan province, where the policies were carried out to a fuller degree, most provincial level governments chose wait and see. On September 21, Dowager Empress Cixi resumed regency and Guangxu Emperor was put under house arrest in Yingtai at Summer Palace, while orders were put out to haunt down masterminds of the reform including Kang Youwei; six were captured and executed. In total, the Hundred Days Reform lasted 103 days.

Enough ink has been spilled trying to identify the causes of the failure. Some scholars believe that the Dowager Express and her anti-reform coalition were too powerful when compared with the reformists. Although the later has the support of a pro-reform Emperor, they had no real political muscle to contend with the Empress and her cronies. Some blamed Yuan Shikai[3] for leaking the reformists' secret plans to the Empress, but they overlooked the reform's fundamental defect. Their great nobility and patriotism notwithstanding, from the onset, the reform suffered for being excessively radical. Such radicalism was not ended with the failure of the reform; on the contrary, it persisted and continued to inspire new generations to carry on with the Chinese modernization cause.

The Hundred Days Reform was not a randomly incident. In a sense, it was an extension of the Westernization Movement that preceded it. Following the Opium War, reform had become the national consensus. Similar to the Hundred Days Reform, Westernization Movement was another manifestation of this consensus. A surgical reform, which refrained itself from touching the existing political institutions, would have short-term benefit. Such benefit, however, is bound to diminish with passage of time. Situation demanded a thorough overhaul. Such demand was echoed in a flood of new books beating the drum for reform prior to the Hundred Days Reform. Among them, Feng Guifen's *Xiao Ban Lu Kang Yi*, Zheng Guanying's *Grave Words in a Prosperous Age*, Guo Songtao, Wang Tao's *Tao Garden Anthology*, Xu Fucheng's *Advice on Foreign Affairs*, Chen Zhe's *Politics during Peace Times*, He Qi, Hu Lihuan's *Truth on New Politics*, Chen Zhi's Book on *Book of Yong*, Ma Jianzhong's *Shi Ke Zhai Chronicles* were most influential. All these reflect the mounting reformist sentiment prior to the Hundred Days Reform. When describing the necessity of transition from economic reform to institutional reform, contemporary scholar Yan Fu's view is highly pertinent: "To change A, B has to be changed, to change B, C has to be changed."[4]

If Westernization Movement ignited the public's hope over the country's future, the initial optimism would fizzle away with the defeats of the Sino-French War and subsequent First Sino Japanese War. Skepticism and disillusionment rose in its stead. According to latter-day historian Wang Rongzu: "Before the Hundred Days

[3] More on Hundred Days Reform, see Tang Degang's *70 Years of Late Qing Dynasty*, vol 3, Shanghai Social Science Academy Publishing House 2003; Mao Haijian's *Wuxu Reform Historical Facts*, Shenghuo-Dushu-Xinzhi Joint Publishing 2005; Huang Zhangjian's Wuxu Reform History Study (two volumes), Shanghai Book Store 2007.

[4] Ibid., p. 634.

Reform, the reformist sentiment has been building up for four decades, but the new way of thinking hadn't gain a solid recognition among the public. Reform had yet become the spirit of the era." "The trigger of the Hundred Days Reform is China's defeat in the First Sino-Japanese War, which led to widespread popular discontent. Petitions were staged by scholars and civilian organizations such as Qiang Xue Hui (Group of Strong Nation Studies) and Bao Guo Hui (Group of Protecting the Country) emerged. By the time of Hundred Days Reform, China had been seeing increasing danger of collapse. The consequence is that the Reform was born prematurely. What prompted this reform is sentiment rather than mature reasoning.[5]"

Wang Rongzu might be right in that the public was not ready for such a stormy reform, however, the sense of crisis and the patriotism the defeat inspired was also evident, and to a great extent compensated the lack of "spirit of the era". When news came that China relinquished Taiwan and paid 200 million liang of silver in war reparations to Japan, Liang Qichao wrote an article, urging China to wake up from its dream. Only when viewed against the historical background that we can appreciate why the reformists call for reform resonated so strongly among the intellectuals. Aside from Guangxu Emperor and his teacher Wong Tonghe, provincial governors such as Zhang Zhidong, Liu Kunyi, Chen Baozhen were also supportive of the reform. Li Hongzhang, a leader of the Westernization Movement, exclaimed his admiration for Kang Youwei, saying that he did what he always wanted to do but didn't. Even extreme traditionalists such as Yin Lin expressed a view to the effect that he was fine with a mild reform.

Consensus in favor of reform strengthened as a result of China's defeats in the Sino French War and First Sino Japanese War. If the reformists could obtain the support of moderates, and avoid antagonizing the vested interests, took a gradualist approach, then the Hundred Day Reform might succeed. However, Kang Youwei and the other leaders decided to pursue a radical route, both in theoretical level and specific policy level. Not only did they fail to ally with the moderates, they even antagonized the invested interests, led to an anti-reform coalition. Thus the reform is doomed from the beginning.

Kang Youwei took a very innovative approach to form the foundation of the Reform. His method is often summarized as Tuo Gu Gai Zhi or "adapt the classics to guide the present". To form the legitimacy of the reform, Kang wrote two books: *Exposing the Fabrication of New Studies* and *On Confucius's Reformism*. In the books, Kang asserted that all the Confucius' theories are expression the saga' positive views on reform[6]. By such an interpretation, Kang hoped that he could form an ideological common ground with the non-reformists. He believed what he did was to inject a new spirit into the old theories and turning them into revolutionary ones, in doing so, establishing legitimacy for the reform. Kang's approach was clever; he translated Western notions, such as constitutionalism, parliament, in the Confucian language, which is the reason that the reform should be treated as a revolution

[5] See The Reform Movement in Modern China: Constitutional Reform and Modernization, ed. by Institute of Modern History of Academia Sinica in Taipei, 1982, p. 36.

[6] See Xiao, Gongqin. 1995. Re-reflection on Hundred Days Reform – On cultural roots of early political radicalism. *Strategy and Management*, Beijing, issue 4.

because it promoted modern notions. The notions underlying Kang's theory include: progressivism, benevolence, liberty, and equality, democracy, and constitutional monarchism. Such an interpretation of Confucianism was a far cry from the mainstream interpretation back in the day.[7]

Contrary to his expectation, Kang Youwei's New Confucianism deepened rather than bridge the gap between reformists and moderates and traditionalists, which should and could have been avoided. Kang planned to invoke the authority of the ancient saga to provide a theoretical, or rather, theological, justification for his reform, to win over the bureaucrats, only to alienate them further more. Kang's theories were disparaged not only the traditionists but also the moderates such as Zhang Zhidong, one of the brains behind the Westernization Movement and erstwhile supporter of the Reform. Kang and his disciples initially adapted Confucianism to suit their Reform agenda, yet they failed to envisage the stiffness of opposition. Are Kang's two books a legitimate development to the traditional Confucianism? Theoretically, I tend to say yes. However, when it comes to outcome, it is evident such a strategy did more harm than good. It led to widespread skepticism and confusion regarding the reform, and alienated some potential allies. Kang thought he could use his theories to persuade the Confucian scholars to join his reform, only to be dismissed as blasphemy. As latter-day historian Xiao Qingong observed: "It was a fatal mistake, a classical example of good intentions caused perverse outcomes."[8]

Kang Youwei and reformists unrealistically expected that their lofty goal could be achieved at one stroke. With such optimism, the reformists deliberately challenged the mainstream values of the day. As a result the Reform was a very ambitious plan that covers many different sectors ranging from culture, education, economics, military to social customs, politics. Many didn't see the light of the day, among them, declaring Confucianism the State Religion; establishing Department of Confucianism and Church of Confucianism; adopting a dating system that starts with the year Confucius; formulating a constitution; establishing parliament, granting equal legal status to servicemen as well as civilians; equality between Manchurians and Han Chinese; emperor as the commander in chief of the military forces; changing the reign's name to Wei Xin (note: meaning Reform); relocating the capital city to Shanghai, etc. Kang once boasted: "Europe and America spent three hundred years to reach its current status. Japan spent thirty years to imitate and reached its current levels. For China, with its vast territory and massive population, ten years will be sufficient." Such an assessment was evidently unrealistic, and overlooked the scale of challenge and the complexity of the task. In practice, many of reformative measures were impossible to implement because what they demanded far exceeded what social conditions could provide back in the day. Hence, in either theory or practice, radicalism was a fatal failing.

As later-day historian Yu Yingshi said, "Hundred Days Reform is the first attempt in China's Modern history, it ended tragically."[9] The Reform was doomed from the

[7] Ibid. p. 63.

[8] See Xiao Gongqin: *Re-reflection on Hundred Days Reform – on cultural roots of early political radicalism*, Strategy and Management, issue 4, 1995.

[9] See Yu Yingshi: *Wuxu Reform Rereading*, 21st Century, issue 2, 1998.

beginning when Kang Youwei and his comrades invested their hopes on a puppet emperor. In addition, the measures were rather fantastical and out of touch with reality, often impossible to implement. Despite these shortcomings, the effort is significant for it was the first attempt trying to establish modern political institutions in China. In this sense, we should treat Hundred Days Reform as the start of China's legal system reform. Although by today's standards, its failing is evident, we have to view the issue in light of the dire situation back in the day. When viewed in the context of China's hundred years journey of modernization, we see that the failure of the reform prompted new generations of revolutionaries, which would be increasingly radical in their outlook and practice. In this way, the Hundred Days Reform is the harbinger of China's over century-long of radicalness.

1.3 Late Qing Constitution Movement

The two conflicting forces – revolution and tradition which joined hands in the Hundred Days Reform, parted their ways after its failure and led to two different routes. One led to the Late Qing Constitutionalist Movement, and the other resulted in the 1911 Xin Hai Revolution. Both of them should be regarded the offspring of the Hundred Days Reform, as well as responses to the conflict between China and the external world.[10]

To recap, during the time between Hundred Days Reform and Qing Emperor's Abdication, China's legal system reform forked in two directions. One is the Constitutionalist Movement aimed at accomplishing modernization through a moderate reform; the other being the revolution led by Sun Yat-sen, who sought to overthrow Qing dynasty's rule through armed rebellion and build a modern democratic republic. The gap between the two hasn't been closed even today. We also see that during China's century-long modernization process, revolutionary radicalism was the dominating force; notwithstanding its achievement, its dominance has caused certain negative outcome. However, even when revolutionary mood was at its highest, the moderate reform was never stifled; on the contrary, it maintained an active presence during China's revolution-replete history and finally triumphed. As we said, the failure of the Hundred Days Reform, who obtained its procedural legitimacy by the endorsement of the emperor, was responsible for increasing radicalism in its wake. Many former reformists, disillusioned, joined the cause of the revolution, which gradually gained mainstream recognition, and demonstrated its greater destructiveness than any peasant rebellions.

The Boxer Uprising triggered another round of foreign invasion. Following the fall of Beijing in 1901, Qing Dynasty rulers rushed to announce a reform. Until 1912, during a decade, Qing government implemented an all-encompassing reform that is grand in scale. Supported by the constitutionalists, steady progress was achieved. Unlike the Hundred Days Reform, this time opposition was much weaker. Unfortunately, with the outbreak of Wuchang Revolt, this reform was halted.

[10] See Zhang Pengyuan: *Constitutionalists and Xinhai Revolution* (preface), Jilin Press Group Ltd. p. 1.

All this begs the question: Why ten years of political reform, especially the constitutionalist efforts, failed so completely in bringing about a modern political system, instead, only fastened the fall of the dynasty.

In the wake of the Hundred Days Reform, the Revolutionaries and Constitutionalists completely parted their ways and went about to pursue their own politics. The camp of constitutionalists now had forked into two branches. One, led by Kang Youwei and Liang Qichao, leaders of the Hundred Days Reform that were on exile abroad, who continue to exert great influence, mostly among overseas Chinese. They spread their ideas through publications and rallied considerable support, including social dignitaries such as Zhang Jian, Yang Shouqian and other members of the gentry class. After 1901, the gentries constituted the main base of support for the constitutionalist reform cause. The other branch is within the government, represented by high officials such as Zhang Zhidong, Duan Fang, Yuan Shikai, who tried to follow the models of Japan, Russia, and Britain, and establish constitutional monarchism, which they regarded as the only way to transform China into an independent nation and stem the grave crisis. As the crisis deepened, the two forces converged, leaving Qing rulers with no recourse but to commit to reform.

Prior to Beijing's fall in 1901, the Dowager Empress and Guangxu Emperor fled the capital city. En route to Xi'an the emperor issued a decree, announcing the commencement of Constitutionalism Preparations. Once the situation stabilized, the Qing government sent five ministers to Europe in 1882 to study Western constitutionalism as Japan did. The next year, these ministers returned. The reports they submitted to the emperor highlighted three benefits of constitutionalism: 1. Secures the throne; 2. Alleviate overseas pressure; 3. Settle internal disputes. Yet the ministers also suggest that the implementation of constitutionalism should not be rushed, stating that the Qing government "should express our commitment quickly, though the date of implementation should be decided later". They cited the example of Japan, which announced constitutionalism in 1881, and formed its parliament eight years later in 1889. They suggested that China should make a similar schedule. It was until September 1, 1906 that the Qing government issued a decree announcing a bureaucracy system reform: "To undo the past wrongs and clarify accountability, we will conduct a reform on the bureaucracy system... Once the reform is completed, reform should also be carried out in other sectors – judicial system, education system, finance, national defense, police, and public political education. Once all of these have been accomplished, the constitutionalist reform will commence. All subjects and officials of His Majesty should spare no effort in the reforms. After an evaluation in a few years, the government will decide the specific date of constitutionalist reform based on the results." Thus the first step towards political reform was made. In two years, more decrees would be issued that provided more specifics regarding to the reform both at the central level and lower level administration. In August 1908, shortly after Dowager Empress and Guangxu Emperor died, four reform decrees were issued that outlined the design of constitution, parliament, election process, and other tasks to be completed during the 9 years' run-up to the final implementation of the constitutionalism.

However, the Qing government's commitment to the reform cause is half-hearted. With much reluctance, it released *Nineteen Tenets,* including *Outline of*

Imperial Constitution. The motive behind the move could be self-preservation and protecting the vested interests, to whom, the prospect of a constitutional monarchy didn't have much appeal. Given this lack of commitment and enthusiasm from the royal family, the process was excruciatingly slow. So much so that later-day historians often argued as to whether the Qing royal family should be given credit for actively promoting China's constitutionalism. Compared with the royal family's lack of commitment, the Constitutionalists outside the royal court showed greater eagerness. Led by Kang Youwei, Zhang Jian, Tang Shouqian, Tang Hualong, they were the backbone of constitutionalism. Although the constitutionalists prefer a conservative and non-violent alternative to revolution, they shared the revolutionaries' goal of building a new state. Due to the "old bottle for new wine" nature of their approach, the Qing constitutionalists earned a unique place in the Chinese modernization. Worth-noting is that unlike the revolutionaries demanded expulsion of the entire Manchu population from China, the constitutionalists were unwavering in their demand that Han Chinese and Manchus should be treated equally, both should be regarded as the citizens of the new country.[11]

Debates were protracted between the two sides over state building, especially over how to cultivate a politically aware and active citizenry and the form of the new government. Although both shared the same utmost goal, namely building a modernized China, they have distinct differences. Between the two approaches, I personally prefer the constitutionalists' approach, which would have involved less risks and closer to the ideal, not to mention its adherence to humanitarianism would have spared much bloodshed. Unfortunately, this path didn't get chosen. Much of the blame was on the Qing royal family. Unwilling to accept the constitutionalists' terms, their dedication to the constitutionalist effort was weak. With the dynasty, with its glorious days behind it, irreversibly heading towards destruction, the Manchu ruling class overall displayed little moral courage. Neither had they showed much political initiative since the demise of the resourceful Dowager Empress Cixi. The *Outline of Imperial Constitution*, which initially inspired high hopes, failed to deliver its promise and further deepened the mistrust and antagonism between Manchu and Han officials. As a result, many of former constitutionalists joined the revolution.

The *Outline of Imperial Constitution* was so generous with the Qing royal family that it was close to recognizing the emperor's despotism: "The Great Qing Empire is immortal ruled under one family who will lasts ten thousands of generations. Its emperors, who should be treated with utmost reverence, is divine with inviolable dignity." According to the *Outline*, the emperor had the power to convene, dismiss parliament, replace the entire bureaucratic system, command the military forces, declare wars, issue martial law, confer aristocratic titles, and override judicial rulings. Hence as a constitutional document, the *Outline* could hardly qualify as a modern constitutional monarchist documents for it gave the emperor almost unchecked, near-absolute power. Yet even for such a backward constitution, the royal family demanded nine years of preparation. Although during the preparation

[11] Ibid.

period, some progressive policies concerning judicial reform, education, regional autonomy, were implemented, overall, the achievement of this bureaucracy system reform was limited. Although the emperor's decree stipulated that the Manchu officials and Han officials would be treated equally, in practice, Manchu ministers took seven seats in the cabinet, Han ministers took four, in addition to a Mongolian minister and a Han Jun Qin minister (Note: naturalized Manchu who was originally Han). In the past, Manchu and Han officials were equal in number, now the balance tilted in favor of the Manchus, especially considering the Mongolian and Han Jun Qi ministers were always ready to yield to their Manchu colleagues, leaving the Han Chinese ones a minority with less than one third seats. As a result, the cabinet was ridiculed as the "royal family cabinet". In addition, the Ministry of Defense was staffed only by Manchus; among them, Tie Liang, a Manchu aristocrat, was appointed to be the War Lord. Under Tie Liang's directive, all armed forces now took orders directly from the Ministry and Han Chinese general Yuan Shikai was forced to hand over his command for four brigades of New Imperial Army. In 1907, Zhang Zhidong, governor of Huguang Region (Hunan province and Guangxi Province), and Yuan Shikai, governor of Zhili Region (Beijing and Hebei province), were promoted to ministerial positions in the central government, thus two of the most powerful ministers were relieved of command of the military forces.

Like the Qing constitution, the Japanese Meiji Constitution, replete with feudalistic traits, could not be regarded a modern constitution – which is the reason why it was chosen to be the model of the Qing *Outline*. There is little wonder the Qing ministers who were sent abroad to study Western constitutions, had good impression of the Japanese model. Zai Ze, leader of the five ministers, in his letter to the emperor, wrote that Japanese constitution not only preserved the monarchist state form, but dedicated 17 provisions to ensure the power of the emperor.

The 9 year-long preparation, often criticized for showing the Qing government's lack of willingness to commit to reform, is not entirely negative; considering the deep-rooted tradition that the reform is up against, the longer the transition lasted, the greater chance the reform might have. The real problem, instead of how much power should the emperor be allowed, or how long it should take to implement the constitution, is the ruling group's sincerity, or whether they are willing to yield to the expectations of the public. The emperor was well aware of it. In a decree, he wrote "Exhaustive research will be conducted, constitutional policies should be implemented, power transfer will be undertaken, and politics should be disclosed to the public." "The essence of constitutionalism lies in solidarity between the high and the low, hence the royal family and the commoners alike should dedicate themselves for public good, to forsake personal gains and devote to common good." However, such words were not matched with deeds, to the detriment of the credibility of the government. Compounding to the lack of trust is tension between Manchu population and the Han Chines. Had the Qing royal family been a Han Chinese one, then the constitutionalist movement would have a chance. That the ethnic origin of the Manchu ruling class was different from the majority of their subjects is a problem that is quite unique to China, for neither of the Japanese reform, Russian reform, nor British reform, had that problem.

The Revolutionaries were resolute in building a political platform that would exclude the Manchu ruling class. Their revolution, they insisted, was a "racial" revolution for one of its central goal is to expel the barbarians. The barbarians actually referred to more than the ruling class, but the entire Manchu population. The revolutionary doctrine held that only when the five million Manchus were gone, could 400 million Chinese achieve real constitutionalism. This radical view was not shared by the constitutionalists and moderate reformists, who still counted the Qing ruling group as an ally in the common cause of constitutionalism. At home and abroad, debates went on over how the Manchu ruling class should be treated. To the constitutionalists, the emperor was not only the emperor of five million Manchu population, but the entire 400 million Chinese regardless their ethic origins. However, they also hoped the Qing government could call off the discriminative policy and treat all ethnic groups equally. Such an enlightened view was initially approved of and written into the *Outline*. However the Qing government showed little intension to honor it, as Manchus continued to receive favorable treatments. This is corroborated in the formation of the cabinet, where the Manchu ministers occupied far more seats than the Han Chinese ministers. Such an arrangement was widely regarded as a breach of the *Outline*, caused great public discontent, especially among the Han Chinese officials and gentry class. Protests and petitions were launched in multiple provinces; people demanded that the preparations should conclude and parliament to be formed immediately. This turn of events would prove to be a turning point for the revolutionaries, who exploited the situation and gained immense popularity among the public.

Many social elites who were originally supportive of constitutional monarchism abandoned the cause because of the Qing government's obstinacy; they instead grew sympathetic towards and even joined the revolutionary cause who followed the politics of expelling the Manchus. As the date that the government designated for implementing constitutionalism approached, the public mood was also changing. Revolution gained remarkable influence; finally, with the success of the 1911 Revolution, and Southwestern provinces' subsequent declaration of independence, Qing's rule in these regions collapsed. The swift development of events prompted Regent Zai Feng to issue a new constitutional document – the *Nineteen Tenets* on November 2, 1911. The *Tenets* was a milestone in China's constitution history. Compared with the *Outline*, the *Nineteen Tenets* was more realistic as a constitutional monarchism constitution and more effectively restrained the power of the monarch as well as the cabinet by designating the Parliament as the source of state power. Thus *Tenets* is closer to the British constitution than the Japanese one.

Judging purely by content, the *Tenets* is a sound piece of constitutional text, yet it never had the chance to develop into a fully functional constitution, for it would soon be abolished by the revolutionaries. Today's scholars debated over whether the Tenets is a political ploy of the Qing dynasty to survive the crisis or a sincere effort to install constitutionalism. Yet sincere or not, the constitution text has value in itself. In fact, few political reforms were proactively made to forestall crisis, most were made to respond to external pressure, hence one shouldn't be too harsh in criticizing the Qing ruling group's passivity. What matters is whether the constitutional document was successfully implemented; worldwide, ample examples indicate that passive constitutions can serve the people. The tragedy of the *Tenets* was also a tragedy for the Chinese people. With the collapse of the Qing government, this excellent piece of constitutional text was thrown into the historical dustbin. One can't help but wondering what if there were no revolution, and the development along the path of constitutionalism continued, then China would have been a very different place. Its constitutionalism, obviously, would have attained a higher achievement. However, such thinking is flawed for overlooking the fact that the Tenets wouldn't have been passed in the first place had not because of the revolutionaries' steel resolve and willingness to sacrifice. Although this sort of what-ifs had little value in serious history study, scholars should have the courage to admit that aside from passion, courage and will, aside from reason and prudence, timing and luck played an incredible role in deciding the outcome of history.

Generally speaking, the Tenets is the culmination of the Qing constitutionalist movement. Originally seeing constitution as an expedient to preserve power, the Qing dynasty's understanding of constitutionalism improved over time. Yet, this route would be cut short by the eruption of revolution, which had henceforth taken center stage in China's state-building.[12]

The late Qing constitutionalist movement that took place during the space of 1901 and 1911 is another version of the Hundred Days Reform – both are top-down reforms, through which the Qing government tried to stem a deep crisis. The difference is that the later met far weaker opposition than the predecessor, which is to a great extent due to increasingly exacerbated crisis at home and abroad. These changes forced the Qing ruling group led by Dowager Empress Cixi to accept the idea of reform at a moment when their survival was at stake. Despite their unwillingness and lack of sincerity, the fact the reform was initiated by the rulers themselves accorded it with certain amount of legitimacy. Although its value is discounted by the fact that it was a passive response to the external factors, we should recognize it as a legitimate effort to promote constitutionalism in China. Neither should we overlook that the Boxer Uprising and the foreign invasion that it set forth inadvertently removed the opposition force of the reform from inside the ruling group –a significant factor that the later Constitutionalist Movement went further than the Hundred Days Reform.

Despite the possibility to have developed into a successful moderate reform, the constitutionalism failed to live up to its potential. A reform can be seen a form of self-renewal of legal and political legitimacy. The late Qing constitution movement is such a reform for it not only seeks to introduce a dynasty, but also a modern China, in this regard, it is richer in measures when compared with Kang Youwei's design. Despite its shortcoming as a response to external pressure, it was a blueprint that was spontaneously drawn by the Qing government, which whose scrutiny, development from nine years preparation, to the three year preparation, to the final announcement of 19 Tenets, some progress was accomplished, which makes it a

[12] See Gao Quanxi, *The Constitutional Moment: On the Imperial Edict of the Manchu Emperor`s Abdication*, Guangxi Normal University Press, 2011.

constitutional monarchist reform that is in many ways comparable with the British "Glorious Revolution".

Can a modern political form be developed from a feudalistic tradition? The British Glorious Revolution is an example of achieving such end through a reformist moderate revolution. Almost the same was achieved in Japan through Meiji Reform, which the Qing ruling group tried to imitate. Hence special attention is advisable to the so-called constitutionalist movement, whose nature we would conjecture as "putting new wine in an old bottle" – it sought to establish a constitutionalist monarchy, i.e. change the political form while retaining the appearance of the old political form, yet to retain it by injecting into it a new legitimacy. Had this succeeded, a non-violent gradualist path towards China's modernization would be provided. As we already know, the constitutionalist is a result of external influence. This is quite common worldwide. Without external influences, most reforms in history wouldn't have happened. Internationally, to survive a crisis was what motivated Britain and Japan to undertake their constitutional monarchist reforms. Given the two successful examples, implementing a constitutionalist monarchist reform is the best option available to Qing dynasty, but why did it fail?

With the benefit of hindsight, we may say that Qing government's effort came too late. In addition, much had changed since Hundred Days Reform at home and abroad – the tension between Han Chinese and Manchus got worse, the public sentiment had shifted in favor of revolution. The revolution promises more than what a constitutionalist reform can do, such as the revolutionaries demanded the Manchus to be expelled, which would be unimaginable for the constitutionalists. However, today when we look back at the history, knowing what we know, we can better appreciate the late Qing constitutionalist movements' merits, which makes us lament that such a good opportunity had passed by.

1.4 Xinhai Revolution

The failure of the Hundred Days Reform left a gap that would be filled by Xinhai Revolution. The Revolution, under the leadership of Sun Yat-sen, sought to bring about a constitutional democratic republic through armed rebellion. To achieve such an objective, the revolutionaries deemed it necessary to severe all ties with the old dynastic feudal system.

In the narrower sense, Xinhai Revolution refers to a series of uprisings that took place in the space between October 10, 1911 and January 1, 1912, the day Sun Yetsen took office as the President of Republic of China (ROC). About this revolution, later-day historian Tang Degang provided an account: "In the summer of Xinhai Year, Sichuan's railroad riot broke out, the Qing government ordered the garrison stationed in Hubei to be dispatched to Sichuan to dispel the rebellion. Many soldiers refused to leave. Some of them were members of two revolutionary organizations, such as Wen Xue She or Gong Jin Hu – both would play a critical role in the organization of the revolution. When the deadline came, the soldiers mutinied and seized command." However, the Xinhai Revolution was much broader than such a brief account.[13]

As an alternative modernization route, Xinhai Revolution is inseparable with its specific historical background; like the constitutionalist reform, it too should be regarded as a response to the unprecedented encounter between the East and the West. This route was set forth after the constitutionalist movement failed to achieve the desired result. In comparison, revolution in Chian had a humbler beginning but gradually gained upper hand in competition with the reform route. Many revolutionaries were former reformists, that includes the leader Sun Yat-sen himself. Sun once wrote a petition letter to Li Hongzhang in defense of Hundred Days Reform. Later, the failure of the reform led Sun to conclude that the Western conception of modernity is not compatible with the Chinese traditional political form – the old bottle can't be used to keep the new wine, and to introduce modernity in China, the Manchu ruling group must be unseated. At that time, anti-imperialism had yet become a theme in revolution; the revolution was exclusively about dethroning the Manchu emperor. This is why during the early stage of the revolution, many thought it was an anti-Manchu rebellion.

Sun Yat-sen and his comrades didn't find any use in revising the Confucian classics. Instead, they renounced the traditional political form. They also differed from the constitutionalist who tried to preserve and protect the Manchu monarchy, in their unwavering effort to unseat the Qing government. While the constitutionalists counted on Qing ruling group to redeem their promises about constitutionalism, the revolutionaries had no trust in the later. The ethnic problem was for the constitutionalists a triviality, whereas for the revolutionaries, it was a major goal of their revolution. For the revolutionaries, if the Manchus were sincere in their commitment to constitutionalism, it only made them a cannier foe. This is corroborated by the revolutionaries' assassination attempt against the Five Ministers who were sent abroad to study constitutionalism. Naturally, Sun Yat-sen's revolution is a radical departure from what had been seen previously. It was the first major political movement sought to empower the public and showed no reconciliation with the ruling class. They sought to replace the old legitimacy with a new one, which is neither based on mystic forces of "heaven" or divinity of monarchs, but the sovereignty of "people".

To recap, two things distinguish the revolutionaries from the constitutionalists: different degrees of racialism and whether they saw violence as necessary and justified means to achieve their ends.[14] This is corroborated by the revolutionaries' rhetoric "Only revolution can bring about constitution, no constitution can be implemented without a revolution. Qing government can't implement constitution, only the people can."[15] However, their jingoism turned out to be a limiting factor to their

---

[13] Ibid., p. 176.

[14] See Chen Xiqi's *Sun Yat-sen Chronology*, Zhonghua Books, 1991 p. 80.

[15] See Jiang Yongjing's *Revolutionary Party's Criticism of the Late Qing Constitutionalist Movement – Min Pao and Xin Min Cong Pao's Analysis of Constitutionalism Debate*, published as part of the anthology *Chinese near modern reform,* Central Research Institute Near Modern History Institute, 1982, Pp. 125–133.

own cause, neither could it accomplish the desired result. In spite of the fact that Manchu aristocracy lost their power, and China returned to the hands of the Han Chinese, things didn't improve; on the contrary, the internal fights among the Han Chinese political leaders only worsened the situation.[16]

Moreover, the revolutionaries tried to install a democratic political system largely based on the American model. However, despite their best effort, such a model proved to be rather incompatible[17] with China's reality, for it demanded more than the country could provide. Hence the revolutionary is regarded as overly opportunistic and idealistic.[18] More importantly, over a decade leading up to Wuchang Revolt, the consensus was formed among the public as regards the future of the country was weak. The vision of the revolutionaries, like their predecessors of the Hundred Day Reform era, was not one widely shared by the public. This contributed to the revolution's frustration, aside from apparent military organizational weakness.[19]

While the revolutionaries were plotting their revolts, the constitutionalists were not sitting idle. However, with the death of Guangxu Emperor, and especially Dowager Empress Cixi in 1908, China was deprived of a strong political figure. Although Regent Zaifeng, the de facto national leader, vowed to carry on with the

[16] See Ma Yong's *Transcend Revolution and Reform*, Shanghai Sanlian Bookstore, 2001, p. 67.

[17] After Revive China Society was established, Yang Xianyun, Sun Yat-sen were increasingly enamored of American political institutions. In what appeared to be an imitation of the US government, they introduced "building a federal government" as one of the objectives. They two even had a quarrel over who should be the "President". When the Eight Power Coalition force conquered Beijing, the emperor and dowager empress went on fight incognito, the governors of Southeastern provinces intended to form an American-style Republican government and elect Li Hongzhang to be the President. Li agreed. The plan was aborted after the emperor made a public appearance in Xi'an. In 1903, revolutionary Zou Rong wrote in his *Revolutionary Army*, in which he suggested that the new China should be called Republic of China, and suggested that China should have a central government to handle all state affairs, and that every province should elect a senator and the senators who would elect a provisional president and a vice president - this also shows the influence of the American political model. In 1905, when multiple revolutionary parties formed China Alliance Committee, the organization borrowed the American's separation of three powers design–Sun was the Prime Minister, Deng Jiayan was the Judicial System leader and Wang Zhaoming was the Parliament leader. See Tang Degang's *Late Qing 70 years: Yuan Shikai, Sun Yat-sen and Xinhai* Revolution, Yuan-Liou Publishing Co., Ltd. 2004 Pp. 156–157. However, in actuality, this model was not observed strictly. According to Tian Tong, who was secretary of China Alliance Committee's enforcement department: "For a clandestine organization, over-complicated procedures were the last thing that we wanted … due to the difficulty, some comrades suggest the three department to hold a joint-conference together. Since then all important matters were decided by the joint-conference and the judicial department and supervision department never exercised independent power again." In March 1907, Sun Yat-sen left Japan after taking Japanese funding. For such a significant event, it is surprising that no meeting was held. See Tian Tong's *China Alliance Committee's Foundation,* quoted from Tang Degang's *Late Qing Dynasty 70 years – Yuan Shikai, Sun Yat-sen and Xinhai Revolutio*n, Yuan-Liou Publishing Co., Ltd. 2004 Pp. 219–220.

[18] See Ma Yong: *Transcend Revolution and Reform,* Shanghai Sanlian Bookstore, 2001, p. 78.

[19] Wang Rongzu: On Hundred Days Reform's failure and thought elements, published as part of the anthology *Chinese near modern reform Central Research Institute Near Modern History Institute* 1982, p. 34.

constitutionalist cause, at the age of 26, the regent lacked neither the political skill nor ruthlessness to push forward the reform. His failure to coordinate different fractions of political forces turned out to be the last straw to the empire.

Even Sun Yat-sen admitted that luck played a big role in the revolution's success, saying that the success of Wuchang Revolt was "accidental".[20] Such a view is not merely modesty considering that the revolution was like a baby prematurely delivered into a hostile world. Now the Qing government was removed, the revolutionaries realized that they didn't have the ability to restore the order, without which the revolutionary ideals couldn't be implemented.[21] Xinhai Revolution, along with the democratic republic that it established, was such a departure from the traditional dynastic political models, that it had no historical parallels. Its goal was to establish a modern republic through revolutionary violence, hence differed from Hundred Days Reform and late Qing Constitutionalist Movement. The republic, judging by its form, is a democratic republic that upholds the principle of "consent of the governed", hence is different from neither monarchism nor constitutional monarchism. Yet deep in their hearts, Xinhai Revolution shared much common ground with the Hundred Days Reform and the late Qing constitutionalist movement. The Hundred Days Reform didn't seek to bring China back to its classic past; neither was Constitutionalist Movement trying to revive traditional dynastic politics. They were all essentially revolutionary and tried to establish a new legal authority in the modern sense. The difference is that Hundred Days Reform and Constitutionalism Movement both sought to use a moderate improvement approach and avoid provoking ethnic antagonism, and use constitution as a tool to restrain monarchy's power and build a modern state. Had China developed along these routes, then the outcome may be closer to those of Britain and Japan.

Different from the other two, Xinhai revolution sought to build a democratic republic. It purported to have a racial revolution, a national liberation movement. In terms of specific measures, it insisted on armed rebellion. Although the ethnic factor was expedient, the revolution only achieved a superficial victory as the new system that it established after much bloodshed didn't last. In fact, we see that despite its triumph over the late Qing constitutionalists, Xinhai revolution failed to build a stable, sustainable republic. Given what happened in its wake, such as warlords waging wars amongst themselves, restoration attempts, as well as the introduction of party rule, it is hard to argue that the revolutionary approach was not a major cause for such an unfortunate outcome.

---

[20] Sun Yat-sen: State-building Strategy, Sun Yat-sen Anthology, People's Publishing House 1956, p. 208.

[21] Ma Yong believes that "Revolutionaries had fallen into a trap typical of revolutions – they were convinced that only revolution can save China and disregarded all alternative solutions; on the other hand, the Qing government had been in a very passive position, and lacked the capacity to lead, or maintain a stable social order and social movements, as a result, the Qing government lost too many opportunities, during the process, disappointed and antagonized the revolutionaries furthermore. As a result, China can only forge ahead along the road of revolution". See Ma Yong's *Transcend Revolution and Reform,* Shanghai Sanlian Bookstore, 2001, p. 73.

This is not to deny the significance of Xinhai Revolution. Despite all its shortcomings, Xinhai Revolution removed monarchism and at least in form, returned the power to the people, by doing so, ushered in a new era of political and legal modernity. For that it deserves the credit as the start of democratic politics and rule of law in China. While the revolutionaries vowed to build a nation of the people, today, we are still in the middle of this journey towards this goal they set over a century ago. Of course, the revolution was dismissed as "a bourgeois revolution" by CPC, which introduced new ideals such as communism, yet we should still acknowledge that it was a historical culmination, which gave a huge impetus to China's modernization. But modernization is not an end in itself, the end is to establish social and judicial order and maintain it in a non-revolutionary way. After Xinhai Revolution, China would see waves of new revolutions; none of them accomplished what they alleged to, which is roughly the same goal that Xinhai revolutionaries set. Generations of Chinese people would be inspired by the idea of revolution, but the country can't thrive because of passion alone, rule of law needs to be built on something more solid. Instead of criticize or exalt casually, maybe a better attitude would be sit down and learn some lessons from this revolution.

Given the short intervals between Hundred Days Reform, Constitutionalist Movement and Xinhai Revolution in the late Qing, we group them together as the initial effort to construct a modern China under the great impact of the Western civilization. When looking at them in the context of modernity, the Hundred Days Reform is conservative in form and radical in substance. Similarly, the Constitutionalist Movement and Xinhai Revolution can also be regarded as extension of the Reform. They are essentially appeals for a new political legitimacy and a new state form. The difference is their approaches to realize the goal. The Hundred Days Reform sought to launch a revolutionary "reform" in a "legitimate" way, i.e. a reform that is in accordance with the law. It failed to achieve that aim due to strong resistance and its own radicalness. The late Qing Constitutionalist Movement is the monarchist dynasty's spontaneous effort to update itself, but due to its failure to handle the "racial" problem, incorporate the revolutionary forces, last but equally important, the bad timing. Yet despite all its shortcomings, and the abrupt end after the outbreak of the revolution, it proposed a valid new road towards China's modernization. Xinhai Revolution, which claims to be a "racial" revolution, succeeded to establish a new legal system, whose implication to China's rule of law is nothing short of profound. Yet due to its failure to handle the transition from the traditional society to a modern one, it created a condition that would send China into more extreme forms of revolutions. In addition, to address warlords' manipulation of the constitution, party rule system was introduced. Both would cause many setbacks to China's legal construction. An overview of the events would reveal convincingly that each of the three movements demonstrated greater radicalism than the predecessors. During the period, there are many different ideas trying to exert influences, yet none of them borne fruit, which is truly lamentable.

Chapter 2
Failed Legacy: The Early Days of the New Republic

The success of Wuchang Revolt in October 1911 opened a new chapter for the Chinese history. With the abdication of Qing emperor, and the establishment of the republic, China was given a great opportunity to form a sound modern government. However, notwithstanding its five thousands of years of glorious civilization and all the trials and tribulations, this country yielded itself to brutal forces, letting itself to be dominated by warlords with strongest military power. Up until Northeastern warlord Zhang Xueliang vowed allegiance to the revolutionary government in 1928, leading to national unification, for over a decade, a whirlwind of political incidents were staged: Second Revolution, Yuan Shikai Seizure of Crown, State Protection Movement, the Manchu Restoration led by general Zhang Xun, Constitution Protection Movement, South North Separation. During the timeframe, six constitutional documents were produced; among them, three were formally promulgated. However, none truly lived up to their names and failed to generate a substantial effect, politically or socially. Although monarchism had been put to an end in China, a stable social order failed to take over while China continued to be mired in chaos and anarchy. As a popular saying of the day says: "the barbarians were easy to kick out, the Republic is hard to build."

Now ROC had been established, the revolutionaries were given an opportunity to exercise democracy and republicanism that they championed, yet for over a decade, not only a modern legal system failed to take shape, neither was political normalization been achieved. Worse, the state power of the Republic fell into the hands of a handful of former generals. Over time, the public confidence in the Western democratic institutions diminished; finally China was sent onto a different course, one that promised cure to all the ills of western democratic politics, yet in actuality sent China further astray.

Q. Gao et al., *The Road to the Rule of Law in Modern China*,
Research Series on the Chinese Dream and China's Development Path,
DOI 10.1007/978-3-662-45637-8_2

2.1 *Provisional Constitution* and Its Limitations

By the time of Wuchang Revolt, the late Qing Dynasty had already been a leaky ship loaded precariously with three thousands of years worth of antiquated institutions. Although the traditionalist forces, from the Manchu royal family down, made a strenuous effort to keep it afloat, its downfall was precipitated by three forces – the Western powers, the revolutionaries, and the constitutionalists. These forces, whose influences ebbed and flowed as they competed each other, brought onboard different methods, objectives, and agendas as regards how the reform should be undertaken, how constitutionalism should be achieved, and how the new state should be like. Together, they formed the background against which China's first constitution would come into being, leading to China's first "constitutional moment" in the aftermath of the success of Xinhai Revolution, especially Wuchang Revolt. The three forces, especially the two domestic ones, had henceforth dominated the Republican China's constitution making alternately. Revolutionary constitution-making, Republic of Five Ethnic Groups, constituent right, Parliament, provincial self governance, federal system, the Chinese people, modern state, presidentialism and parliamentarianism, citizen's rights – all these new concepts, previously unknown to the Chinese public, flourished during the republic era, and were fodder for heated debate in this extraordinary time.

It is important to point out that as arbitrary as history sometimes is, with its intensions often mysterious, there are patterns. Traditional constitution scholars often tried to see the creation of the modern Chinese constitution and its "constitutional moment" using the "revolution – state building" paradigm, in doing so, they often overlooked the contribution of counter-revolutionary forces – for instance, the constitutionalists – in resisting revolutionary radicalism; they often take a textualist view in understanding the ROC constitution, which often led to failure to acknowledge the constitutional significance of *Qing Emperor's Abdication Decree*. The *Decree*, which epitomizes the spirit of the Chinese constitutionalism. is different from any such decrees in China's history. Its unique significance lies in that such a decree that facilitated the reform effort, hence greatly contributed to China's political transformation and the birth of a republican constitutionalist state – the Republic of China. It also saved the country from a complete collapse of order, which many traditional monarchist regimes experienced when their rules were toppled by rebellion. Here we will not delve into details, suffice it to say that the *Decree* echoes the revolutionaries' political demands and is a cornerstone of the ROC judicial legitimacy established by Xinhai Revolution; however the revolution didn't bring about modern constitutionalism in China, at least from a political-constitutional point of view, and we are going to examine why.

Enough ink has been spilled over the ROC Provisional Constitution, yet few scholars from either side of the Strait, regarded the formulation of the document as the first "constitutional moment" of China's First Republic. Surrounding this document, there are many debates of constitutional jurisprudential implications. Many scholars have been bickering about the merits and demerits of a parliamentary system as opposed to a presidential system, the debates that took place in the parliament, military prowess of the South and the North, government personnel reshuffled, the beginning point of China as a nation state and constituent power, political positions of Sun Yat-sen, as well as Beiyang marshals' control of the parliament. The majority of the study barely scratched the surface, with methods usually limited to recitals of constitution provisions and institutions. Yet in recent years, a remarkable change took place – academia from both sides of the Strait began to shed their ideological shackles, as a result, many inconsistencies in witnesses' accounts were exposed. But we should be aware that constitution study can't be replaced by constitution history study. The task of identifying the merits and demerits of Xinhai Revolution can't be trusted entirely on historians. After all, constitution study is an independent discipline, with its own application and focus. That is not to say that historical study and sociology are not important; what I want to stress here is that we need to acquire a new "enquiry awareness" in our evaluation of the constitutional implications of historical events, their contribution to China's modernization from the angle of constitutional jurisprudence.

ROC is a direct outcome of Xinhai Revolution, or more specifically, Wuchang Revolt, however, this significant fact was not recognized in neither the Provisional Constitution nor Provisional Government Organization Outline, hence, at least from a texualist point of view, we can say the constitution failed to account for the "revolutionary state building" nature of the republic. Since 1895, when Sun Yat-sen first organized the revolutionary party of Revive China League, and set the revolutionary goal as "expel barbarians, restore real China, build a republican government", the revolutionary cause's target of overthrowing Manchu's rule through armed rebellion had received great support at home and abroad and aroused great public solidarity. Up until the Wuchang Revolt, Sun Yat-sen and his revolutionaries had carried out more than ten revolts; among them, the better-known ones are Guangzhou Uprising, Huizhou Uprising, Huanggang Uprising, and Anqing Uprising, Huanghuagang Uprising. During the decade long struggle, the revolutionaries demonstrated great willingness to sacrifice. Finally Wuchang Uprising accomplished the task of putting over 200 years rule of Manchus to an end, hence one can't emphasize Xinhai Revolution's significance enough. In terms of constitutional study, it is without dispute that the Xinhai Revolution is a state building revolution, and ushered in the constitutional moment of the Republic of China.

The guideline of "expel barbarians, restore real China" may sound politically incorrect by today's standard, it nonetheless played a significant role in overturning the rule of Manchu autocracy. Yet after the task was shifted to state building, such political appeals turned out to be counterproductive. Had the revolution did what they promised – "expelling the barbarians", it could have easily been just another dynastic change. Well aware of the risk, the revolutionaries transcended their narrow jingoism by proposing a more inclusive political structure where five major ethic groups all had equal rights, therefore, putting the modern republican ideal into execution. In his *Declaration of Provisional President* on the New Year of 1912, Sun Yat-sen declared: "...the essence of the country is its people. The country's territory includes every inch of soil inhabited by Han Chinese, Manchus, Mongols,

Hui and Tibetan peoples. It population consisted five ethic groups including the Han Chinese, Manchus, Mongols, Huis, and Tibetans, who will be unified as one people." Of note is that in the declaration, Sun acknowledged the nature of the state building revolution of Xinhai Revolution. This point was further stressed by Sun later: "the Provisional Government is a government of the revolutionary era. For a decade, the revolutionaries, with utmost dedication and purity of will, bravely faced challenges that had never been taken before; if we can uphold this revolutionary spirit, we will be unstoppable. In this spirit, we will establish a Republic of China. Only when we fulfill this duty, then the Provisional Government can be free from blames." The speech, beaming with revolutionary rhetoric, set the tone for the later *Provisional Constitution*, which was promulgated shortly afterwards and formed its political-logical legitimacy.

The Qing ruling group, whose legitimacy rests on the divinity of monarchy, could not tolerate such revolutionary rhetoric. Naturally, they branded the revolutionaries as "traitors", their uprisings "treasonous" and sought to repel them with great ruthlessness.[1] Given the situation, part of the purpose of the *Provisional Constitution* was to justify the revolutionary cause and clear its name as a "rebellion", thereby forming its legitimacy as a righteous way to build a new state. Moreover, the constitution is also a step to put a stop on the revolution, "replacing revolution with a constitution", to end the bloodshed and stabilize the social order.

Revolution is by definition a form of violence; but it is a special, self-perpetuating violence through constant denial of the status quo, creating a condition that in Hegel's words – a "vicious infinite regress". In terms of its role in the constitution making process, revolution is the efficient cause, neither was it the formal cause, or final cause. That is to say that its contribution to the downfall of the old empire notwithstanding, revolution should be put into cold storage once the state was constructed and constitution was announced, otherwise, the reality could easily be what late Qing dynasty scholar Zhang Taiyan quipped: "the revolutionary army rises, the revolutionary party disappears". Zhang's observation revealed an inherent paradox of revolutionary state building and revolutionary constitution making. On one hand, the constitution needs to justify revolution that brought it into being; on the other hand, it needs to terminate and prevent new revolutions. This inherent paradox was not only evident in China's constitution making, had also in America and European countries. Some revolutions were followed by smoother transitions, which transformed the revolutionary extreme politics successfully into an everyday routine politics, but most failed to achieve this condition, while they destroyed the older order, it fell short of creating a new one to replace it.

Those who participated in the Republican constitution making had little awareness of such a paradox. Their mindset shows in the *Provisional Government Organization Outline*, the prototype of the later *Provisional Constitution*. The

[1] Although Qing Dynasty issued in September 9, 1911 Permission to Organize Parities and Pardon Decree, which pardoned the revolutionaries' rebellion behavior, however, this Pardon Decree is no longer in the purview of traditional dynastic legal system, but more in line with the monarchist constitutionalism legal tradition, that is embodied by the Abdication Decree that came soon after it.

Outline had no preamble or overview, but started directly by describing the function of the Provisional President and Vice Provisional President (chapter I), and the parliament (chapter II). In the description of the Presidential Election, *Outline* stipulates that "the Provisional President would be elected by senators appointed by provincial governments. The candidate who wins over 2/3 votes will be elected as the Provisional President." The second chapter delineated the workings of the Parliament: "The Parliament consists of senators appointed by provincial governments." Although *Outline* is regarded as a constitution, due to the haste, its scope was limited to laying out the most fundamental principles upon which the national provisional government would be built. Given such provisional nature, we should not be too harsh in criticism. As it turned out, the *Provisional Constitution* that came after it is very different from the *Outline*, and should be regarded as the first constitution of Republic of China. Overall, *Outline* met the requirements for a modern constitutional document for having outlined the fundamental institutions and fulfilled the public's expectations.

Most constitution scholars and constitution historians tend to pore over the provisions regarding the presidential and parliamentary systems, government power allocation, and the arrangement regarding the new officialdom when they study the two constitutional documents. Enough ink has been spilled on these respects and some achievements have been made. However, when judging from the pure political-constitutional angle, it is plain that these questions were not the most fundamental that one can ask about the Republican era constitutions. They are just peripheral questions while the essential ones should be those that are related to the revolutionary state building. To use German constitution theorist Carl Schmitt's words, the questions are often rather "constitutional law questions" rather than "constitutional questions". Fact is that the *Provisional Constitution* is full of this kind of the later ones and they haven't been fully explored. Here are some examples that concern the constitution's modern state building respect. The *Outline*'s first act defines the nature of the modern China as a commonwealth of the people, and stipulates that the state is people's state, a people's republic, one in which people have constituent power. Here two brand new concepts, namely "Republic of China", and "the Chinese people", never seen before, appeared. In Act II, it says: "The sovereignty of the Republic belongs to its people". This introduced another concept, and a new right as well, which is "sovereignty". Through these provisions, the Republic was brought into life, or in another word, the state organized by the Chinese people has become sovereign; it also made clear that the sovereignty belonged to the Chinese people, hence reflects the principle of "sovereignty belongs to the people". The third and the fourth act respectively define the territory and governing right. We see that collectively, the four acts completely built the framework of a modern state, hence determined the nature of the ROC, the rights of ITS people, the territories and the governing right.

Although the P*rovisional Constitution*'s *General Principles* section laid down the fundamental principles, it has certain shortcomings. Chief of all is that the *Outline* was formulated under the assumption that the country was under a regular political condition, thereby failed to acknowledge the reality that the Republic was in an extreme political state, as well as in the middle of the first "constitutional moment" and "state-building moment".[2] When we examine the starting points of modern states, regardless their geographic locations, this "constitutional moment" was often brought about by successful revolutions, hence how to reflect this revolution in the constitution, written or unwritten, to a good measure determines how successful the constitution would be, and shows the political maturity of the particular country. In this regard, one has to say that the founders of the Republic, including politicians, military leaders, intellectuals, other social elites, and especially, the revolutionary leaders, displayed little awareness.

That is not to say that the *Provisional Constitution* didn't have enough words in its description of the revolutionary state-building ideal; on the contrary, it did a competent job in this regard, in certain way, better than the some Western examples. The American Constitution, for instance, had a very brief Preamble, which mainly elaborates on the division and allocation of state power. Its "Bill of Rights" was introduced into the constitution in 1791 through amendments. In comparison, the *Provisional Constitution*'s General Outline has four sections, seven chapters, including People "People", "Parliament", "Provisional President and vice President", "Ministers", "Court of law". Collectively, they formed the foundation of the Republic as a modern state. The shortcoming lies in the fact that it was shaped by the revolutionary logic and principles, thus didn't actively endeavor to create an inherent "counter-revolution" mechanism, without which the constitution couldn't be stable. As we mentioned previously, a revolutionary state entails two levels of implications: revolution and revolutionary counter-revolution. To bring revolution to cold storage requires more than the effort of the revolutionaries themselves, but also their opponents, in China's case, the constitutionalists (including the Qing government and gentry class Constitutionalists) – to be more specific, political figures such as Duan Fang, Yuan Shikai, Zhang Jian, and Liang Qichao, who should be involved in the constitution making process. Had that been successful, the Republican constitution would have been more representative and have greater authority. However, the revolutionary regime ignored possibility of reconciliation. Although the armistice was signed, and military hostilities ceased, such reconciliatory spirit wasn't extended to the making of the constitution. Had the constitution making been more reconciliatory, it might have served to unify two major political forces, and bring the "revolutionary counter-revolution" to execution. As for the dispute over the presidential system and parliamentary system, it was just a symptom of this fundamental problem, though many scholars disregarded the fact by focusing on the seemingly impeccable text of the constitutional documents.

Aside from the above-mentioned issue, there is also the "people" problem. In this regard, *Provisional Constitution* failed to provide a proper definition of the relationship between people and state. The concepts of "people" and "Republic of China" were referenced a few times, yet no proper explanation was given. The *Outline* states that the Chinese people are the makers of the constitution, but in what

[2] See *Gao Quanxi's Western Early Modern Thought History and Its China Questions*, Dushu, issue 4, 2010.

way? In this regard, the *Provisional Constitution* went a step further than *Outline*, which focused more on the government's power, especially administrative power, whereas the *Provisional Constitution* accorded greater significance to the concept of "the people", including enunciating in its First Article that the Republic was created by the Chinese people. The second article stipulates that the sovereignty of the ROC belongs to its people – the Chinese people. The third defines the territory of ROC: "the territory of the Republic of China includes 22 provinces as well as the Inner and Outer Mongolia, Tibet and Qinghai regions"; it also defines its citizenry as "people who resided in the Chinese territory". Moreover, it dedicated the entire Chapter II, including a total of 11 provisions, to address the topic of "people", their political rights such as equality, freedom, and obligations such as paying tax and military service. Through this detailed specification of people, we can see "consent by the people" principle and "safeguarding the rights" principle are observed. The reason that the *Constitution* is regarded as the most significant constitutional texts in the Republic of China era is because it established the principle that people are the only source of state sovereignty; they are also the owner of the state. This is groundbreaking – after 3,000 years of history, for the first time the phrases such as "Chinese People's Republic" and the "Chinese people" were written into the Chinese constitution. This makes the *Provisional Constitution* significant both for China's constitutionalism as well as constitution study. In addition, *Provisional Constitution* specifies people's social and political rights, in a way that are reminiscent of Western civil rights bills, both demonstrating great progressiveness. Overall, *Provisional Constitution* is a competent modern republican constitution.[3]

However, the *Provisional Constitution,* for all its monumental historical significance, failed to provide a convincing solution to carrying the principle of "people's constituent power" into execution. The root of the problem lies in the constitution's evasion of a "revolutionary counter-revolution" role. According to the logic of the *Provisional Constitution,* the legitimacy of republic is derived from the fact that Xinhai Revolution is a people's revolution. In the process of creating the republic, a modern citizenry, namely the Chinese people had been created; this modern citizenry was expected to exercise the constituent power, as well as the power to build a modern state, namely, the Republic of China. But how did "the people" come to be? How do they organize the state, how can they exercise their sovereignty, and other political rights? Hardly anything was given.

Here I have two questions, namely where are the "people", and how did people "make constitution". For the first, it is evident that people and the People's Republic can't be assumed *a priori*. Instead, they must be created through strenuous effort and went through trials and tribulations. The process of creating the "people" took place on three levels. First, it is a process of discovering and exercising liberty and other rights, in doing so, the traditional subjects of monarchies would be transformed into modern citizens. Examples can be found in Late Qing scholar Yan Fu's writings,

[3] See Qiu Yuanqiu, Zhang Xibo's *History of ROC Laws*, Capital Normal University Press, 1997; Yan Quan's *Failed Legacy – China's First Parliamentary Constitution* 1913–1923, Guangxi Normal University Press 2007.

which provided a profound elaboration on "boundary of community and individuals", "individual liberty".[4] Secondly, the change of the collective identity. Once the segregation policy of Manchus was abolished, and a new government participated by "Five-Ethnic Groups" was enshrined by the constitution, the way the Chinese people perceive themselves also go through a change. The forces that facilitated the change include constant struggle against the Manchu despotism, a modern state building effort under the guidance of emerging modern nationalism, different from the traditional dynastic rebellion. Thirdly, suppression of individualism. Now the Chinese people had been transformed from the subjects of monarchies into modern citizens through a radical revolution, the tension between individual freedom and demand for collectivism intensified, finally individualism, which had never been fully developed, was suppressed by the "people's collectivism". To recap, through transformation of the subjects into a modern citizenry, a modern China, Zhonghua Minguo, or People's Republic was accomplished.

The double tasks of "state building" and "citizen renewal" were also faced by the Western states. In fact, this topic was explored by Hobbes in length in *Leviathan* and *On Citizen*. It was evident that both the British Glorious Revolution and the American Independence Revolution were conscious of the problems, and took measures to solve them; evidence can be found in the Declaration of Independence and Constitution of United States.[5] As for the legitimacy of a state-building revolution, often in the form of the revolutionaries' justification for their cause, such topics were thoroughly discussed by Sun Yat-sen, Huang Xing and Zhang Taiyan during the process of formulating the declaration of Chinese United League and other revolutionary documents. Moreover, large number of debates over related topics had been undertaken between the revolutionaries and the Constitutionalists led by Kang Youwei.

The idea of building a new Chinese citizenry has dogged the Chinese modernization throughout much of its duration. The *Provisional Constitution* had not much

---

[4]Yan Fu's *On the Division Between Public Powers and Individual Rights* was translated from John Stuart Mill's *On Liberty*, and it has greater enlightenment implication than most translation. Yan coined many new Chinese words and added his own commentary, to inspire people's awareness of individual rights and liberty. See *Yan Fu Anthology*, Zhonghua Books, 1986, Huang Kewu's *The rationale of liberty: Yan Fu's understanding and criticism of John Stuart Mill's liberty thinking*, Shanghai Book Store Press, 2000; Xu Jilin: *Shi Huaci's commentary on China*, Xinxing Publishing House, 2006; Chen Yongsen's *An Attempt to Bid Goodbye to The Identity as Monarch's Subjects,* China Renmin University Press, 2004.

[5]I previously pointed out that a "Leviathan moment" is an inevitable stage in modern state building process. It contains two seemingly contradictory yet unified themes, namely the State Sovereignty and the Sovereignty of the Individual. See Gao Quanxi's *Political Constitutionalism and Judicial Constitutionalism*, part of Gao's *From Constitutional Politics to Normal Politics–Politics, Law and Other Things of Our Times*, China Legal Institution Press, 2009; also see Otto Gierke's, *Political Theories of the Middle Age*, Boston: Beacon Press, 1958, p. 87 (Gierke believed that state sovereignty and individual sovereignty are two central principles of all social structures and their relationship remains the focus of many modern state political theoretical disputes); J. Plamenatz, *Man and Society: Political and Social Theories from Machiavelli to Marx*, 2nd, New York: Longman, 1992; Kong Xinfeng's *From Natural Man to Citizen* – Hobbes Political Thoughts Reinterpretation, Phd. thesis, Beijing University.

explicit elaboration in this regard. The problem is that whether and to what degree do our constitution makers and judiciary adhere to the spirit, therefore carrying the concept of people into practice. Had it been done, the "Chinese people" could have served to soften the animosity between Presidentialists and Parliamentarians; it could have checked Yuan Shikai's ambition and prevented wars over constitutional dispute. In reality, the "Chinese people" idea was often disregarded and the people concept in the *Provisional Constitution* is not a lively and vigorous one, but an empty sham. In comparison, the British "people", albeit never printed, and American Constitution's "We the people", had achieved far greater effect, and carried far greater authority and effectively kept the anti-constitutional elements at bay. In their constitutions, the people are truly upheld and became true constitution makers.

My second enquiry is how did the people make constitution. After the government organization method was released, the provisional government announced the National Congress would be convened within 6 months to formulate the constitution, which was delayed. At that time, peace talk between North and South was still ongoing, the emperor was about to abdicate, Yuan Shikai was to be the new Provisional President. Later, the senators publicized a resolution urging that the formulation of the *Provisional Constitution* to commence immediately. On Feb 7, 1911 the parliament convened, following two rounds of revisions, 32 days later on March 8, the *Provisional Constitution* was passed. On 11th, the *Provisional Constitution* was formally promulgated by the Provisional President. Given the great haste, the public didn't get a chance to participate in the constitution-making process. After the provisional constitution was released, the senators planned to reconvene in 6 months to make the former constitution. Experience worldwide indicates that it is common that a provisional constitution is enacted before it is replaced by the formal version; there is no standard answer as to whether the constitution should be made by an independent constitution-making commission or the parliament, which gives certain flexibility to how the constitution-making body was organized, as long as they fulfill the requirements. But it must be pointed out that an interim constitution-making organ or the formal parliament, the process of constitution-making, even a provisional one, is distinctly different from regular legislation. Modern politics and constitution study distinguish constituent power from constitutional rights, as well as constitution making from constitutional law making. That is to say, the creation of constitution, even a provisional one, differs in nature with the creation of regular laws, even they were decided by the same parliament. The making of a constitution is grounded in people's sovereignty and people's constituent power whereas regular legislation were made by the parliament consisted of people's deputies, entrusted to make state and governmental laws. Evidently, the former concerns a "constitutional moment" or "state building moment", hence falls into to the purview of extreme politics, while the later is just daily practice of people's constitutional rights, thus fall into the category of daily routine politics.[6] Later, constitution-making process, originally scheduled to last 6

[6] See Sieyès's *On Privilege: What is the Third Estate?* Feng Tang, trans, The Commercial Press, 2004; Carl Schmitt's *Constitutional Theory,* Liu Feng, trans, Century Publishing Group, 2005; Gao

months, turned into years. As a result, the constitutional moment was stretched to about the first decade following the establishment of ROC, so was the transformation of the country from extreme political state to daily routine political state.

Many scholars attributed the protracted constitution moment to realpolitik factors, such as superior military power of the antirevolutionary forces, internal struggle within the revolutionaries, clashes between different leaders' vision, institutional and personnel changes, squabbles over parliament seats, fractional fights, dispute over presidential system against parliamentary system, Presidentialists against the Parliamentarians, fight over the quota for parliament seats, and reevaluation of new and old congressmen, etc. The significance of these questions notwithstanding, they were not central questions regarding the ROC's constitution-making. They are more constitutional law problems rather than constitution problems, as they arose in the process of routinization of people's exercising constituent power. These problems were manifestations of the two fundamental questions regarding people's constituent power and revolutionary state building, namely, when the ROC was announced, in what way did the Chinese people exert their influence, and to what degree were they true source of state power, or master of the state. Such is the gist of the Xinhai Revolution constitutional question.

Obviously, the representation system doesn't mean that all people assembled together and have a "one person one vote" election, which, given the circumstances, was impossible; still, it is important that some democratic procedures were followed, to enable the people to participate by sending their own delegates to exercise constituent power on their behalf. But how can such a representation systems be carried out? We should not assume that a "one man one vote" system was the only answer. We see that neither Britain nor the U.S. adopted such a representation systems during their own constitutional moments, instead, they adopted an elitist system; the lack of a general suffrage in the constitution making in the end didn't diminish the legitimacy of their constitutions, for the representatives who exercised the constituent power on their behalf performed the duty competently, and the objective of building a modern state was achieved. When we look at the formulation of the *Provisional Constitution* and its successors, incidental factors such as the unexpected success of Xinhai Revolution and the political situation that prevented election of parliament should not be attached with too much significance. Neither should we blame too much the lack of modern citizen awareness of the public, nor the immaturity of the democratic election procedure. The question that we should keep in mind is the constitution makers, namely senators and later, the National Congress members whether and to what degree were they representative of the people.

The most essential form of political participation in the early years of ROC era was the election of the parliament. There were four central level parliament elections and three provincial level ones. The first central level parliament election was held

Quanxi's *Five Arguments on Modern Political Institutions*, China Legal Institution Press, 2008; Gao's *From Constitutional Politics to Normal Politics–Politics, Law and Other Things of Our Times*, China Legal Institution Press, 2009. Chen Duanhong: *Constituent Right and Fundamental Law,* China Legal Institution Press, 2010.

to reorganize the Provisional Parliament in Beijing. The second election took place during a period of time starting from May 1918 and ended in July. Vote buying and backroom deals were commonplace. In October, 1920, Xu Shichang, a Beiyang warlord ordered to hold a third parliament election, but his order was opposed by the warlords from Zhi faction, which led to postponement of election in most provinces. It is beyond the scope of this book to explore such a political evolutions in depth, we will focus on the constitution making in light of people's constituent power.[7] Here I take a positive view that in spite of all the shortcomings, the formulation of the *Provisional Constitution* as well as the election of parliament members reflected certain public will, thus should be regarded as a remarkable progress in China's political history: for the first time it is the people's representatives rather than the monarchs who have the power to design the national institutions.

Given that ROC was installed by a revolution, a new citizenry must be cultivated to make the republic a true commonwealth of the people; such a goal can't be accomplished until a modern citizenry is formed. Since this citizen cultivation task can't be accomplished quickly, the people's representatives, i.e. the senators and later the National Congress members, must have the consciousness to protect and nurture the burgeoning "people's spirit". Unfortunately, the people's representatives failed to live up to the task. This is especially true during the Beiyang era, when constitution making was ridden with corruption rendering the constitution impossible to reflect people's will, neither was any representation principle adhered to. Such a constitution couldn't a true people's constitution; it also betrayed the ROC's founding principles: "people are the foundation of the country; only when the foundation is stable can the country have peace".

Now we have identified two shortcomings of the *Provisional Constitution*, one concerning revolutionary state building and one people's constituent power, we will go further to explore the third problem, namely, sovereignty. According to *Provisional Constitution*'s Act 4: "Republic of China exercises its sovereignty through parliament, Provisional President and Prime Minister, and court of law." In the following three chapters, this power allocations among the parliament, President, legislation, executive and judicial departments were further specified, and a set of modern state institutions under the trias politica principle was formed. A new dispute arose as a result of the contradiction between the *Provisional Constitution* and the *Constitution* formulated under Yuan Shikai's instruction regarding the power of the Provisional President. This dispute is known as Presidentialism vs. Parliamentarianism Debate.

Enough ink has been spilled on the dispute. However, while most of scholars focus on the debates over the difference between the Presidential system and the

[7] To read more about ROC Parliament, see Zhang Yufa's *Early ROC Political Parties*, Central Research Institute Near-modern Department, 1984; Zhang Pengyuan's *China's Democratic Political Dilemma 1909–1949, Liang Qichao and ROC politics, Constitutionalism and Xinhai Revolution*, Jilin Publishing Group 2008; Zou Dang's *Chinese Revolution Reinterpretation*, Hong Kong Oxford University Press, 2002; Yan Quan: *Failed Legacy – China's First Parliamentary Constitution* 1913–1923, Guangxi Normal University Press, 2007.

Parliamentary system, power allocation between the South and the North, party struggle over interest and individual ambitions, often overlooked is a more fundamental problem, namely, a lack of constitutional stipulation regarding who should be let to govern the country and how. Personal ambition for power is not necessarily a bad thing, provided that it is under scrutiny and checked, but a precondition needs to be met, that is the realization of people's constituent power. "Government by consent" as a principle needs to be upheld and people must become a real constitution makers before the constitution can become as a real checking and balance tool. Because this condition was not met, the state was usurped by warlords, and the constitution was victimized by power struggle and individual ambitions, leading to the constant postponements and eventual failure.

2.2 Yuan Shikai's Seizure of the Throne

During the period leading up to Xinhai Revolution and afterwards, the "constitutional moment", three political forces made their distinct marks. What differentiates them from each other is whether they recognize ROC. One is the revolutionary force, who established the Nanjing Provisionary Government, and elected Sun Yat-sen as the Provincial President; the second is Yuan Shikai, who represented Beiyang military clique, who succeeded Sun Yat-sen after the armistice, and formed Beijing Provisional Government; the third is the Manchu regime, represented by Yulong Empress, Xuantong Emperor and the rest of the Qing royal family. These three, especially Yuan Shikai and his Beiyang fraction, would to a great extent decide the direction of China's future.

The hostilities between the revolutionary-controlled South and the Qing-controlled North ended with the abdication of the Qing emperor, and later, Yuan Shikai succession of Sun Yat-sen as the Provisional President. Sun represented the Revolutionary force, whereas Yuan Shikai represented the Constitutionalists and the other non-revolutionary forces, therefore, the reconciliation between the two should be regarded as the reconciliation between the revolutionary force and non-revolutionary forces in their common effort to build a new state. Although this arrangement was not perfect, it was nonetheless a milestone on China's road towards modern state building. However, once Yuan Shikai took power, he rescinded his oath of obedience to and revoked the *Provisional Constitution*, a grave breach of the agreement between him and the revolutionaries. Such an act not only antagonized Sun's revolutionary force but also caused a division among Yuan's Beiyang subordinates. Once he tore up the *Provisional Constitution,* Yuan undertook to implement an authoritarian rule and eventually declared himself emperor. His crowning led to a short-lived Hongxian Reign, which collapsed as soon as his death. Yet such an ending is nothing to be celebrated for the revolutionaries; instead, it is tragedy for ROC and heralded anarchism and chaos that would soon follow.

There has been a contentious debate over how should Yuan Shikai and his "reign" be viewed. Most participants of the debate took some sorts of historical-political views. To a good measure due to Yuan's failure to restore monarchy, he is often portrayed as a traitor of the revolution; sometimes accused of having forced the Qing emperor to issue the abdication decree in order to advance himself[8]; according to some theories, Yuan's greed for power was manifest way before his crowning. According to some highly ideologically biased narratives, by manipulating the royal family, Yuan made himself the deputy of the Qing emperor to parley with the revolutionaries, a position that would afford him great political leverage after the agreement was reached. After the abdication, Yuan immediately set about to repel the revolution. For what he did to sabotage the revolution, Yuan seems to deserve his posthumous notoriety. However, these accounts were often incomplete, lacking in both historical objectivity and theoretical depth.

Fact is that Yuan Shikai was not an enemy of the revolution from the beginning. His degeneration went through stages. Between Yuan took up post as Provisional President and later crowned himself, there were three stages. The first almost coincided with the Second Revolution. The second was between the conclusion of Second Revolution and the disbandment of the Nationalist Party and abolishment of the parliament, which marked the end of the Republican constitution making. The final stage began with Yuan's revision of the constitution and ended by his crowning.

The hostility between Yuan Shikai's force and Sun Yat-sen's revolutionaries built up and led to the eruption of Second Revolution. A common view is that the military clash was caused by some incidental events, among them three figured prominently: the assassination of Song Jiaoren, a comrade of Sun Yat-sen, the loan treaty with Japan and the Sino-Russia Secret Pact. Notwithstanding the historical significance of the three factors, one should not overlook a fundamental cause behind the outbreak of war that is the defects of the *Provisional Constitution.* Before Yuan took up post as the Provisional President, a revision was introduced to the *Provisional Constitution*, diverting much of the Provisional President's power to the Parliament, where the revolutionaries held a majority of seats. This move led to mistrust from Yuan, and finally spiraled into a crisis. Ostensibly, the trigger of the Second Revolution was the change from presidential system to parliamentary system, yet more fundamentally, the root is the *Provisional Constitution's* failure to address the problem of revolutionary state building.

After the Second Revolution, Yuan Shikai first tried to revise the *Provisional Constitution* according to legal procedure. However, such attempt was blocked by the revolutionary senators who held a majority of seats at the Parliament. Their disregard of Yuan's demand eventually led Yuan to denounce Sun Yat-sen's revolutionary party and sack all the parliament members. At this junction Song Jiaoren's assassination further precipitated the deterioration and the two sides were tittering on the edge of military showdown.

After Yuan's initial effort to participate in constitution formulation was frustrated, now he undertook to produce a constitution that suits him. In response to the

[8] See Tang Degang's *Yuan Shi-kai's reign*, Guangxi Normal University Press, 2004; also of note are the memoirs, historical fictions widely circulating among the public.

Nationalists Party' Tiantan Constitution draft, Yuan promulgated his *Constitution of Republic of China*, which is in many ways the exact opposite of the former and gave almost unchecked power to the President. Yet despite this Super Presidential System in the new constitution, the principle of separation of powers remained upheld, thus it remained a modern constitution, until later when Yuan tried to revise the constitution, with the aim to legitimize his crowning.

It is hard to tell when did Yuan Shikai begin to contemplate becoming an emperor, but there were signs indicated his hesitation. For example his conversation with Feng Guozhang, a subordinate general. Yuan also consulted American law scholar Frank Johnson Goodnow, who assisted him in justifying the restoration effort; Yuan organized Chou An Hui to stir up public sentiment. Despite all these, Yuan remained unconvinced that the public was ready for another emperor. But he was unaware that at home and abroad, the condition for restoring monarchism was nonexistent. Domestically, aside from his heir apparent, elder son Yuan Keding and his cronies, Yuan didn't have any allies. Even his subordinates, the Beiyang generals lacked interest in the idea. On the other side, the revolutionaries were preparing for a new campaign against him. Most members of the former conservative Constitutionalist Movement, following the Qing emperor's abdication, turned against monarchism. Internationally, Japan, Russia and the other powers, especially Japan, saw endorsing Yuan merely as a way to advance their interest in China. Finally Yuan received the coveted crown, yet it only stayed on his head for a short period for he was facing an opposition that was never that strong. It seems that with no real friends, Yuan's doom was sealed.

In the following paragraphs, we will give you a review of Yuan's political trajectory in order to identify the implications of the restoration of monarchism to the subsequent China's constitutionalism construction. We will begin with the first event that launched Yuan onto the political stage, namely, the *Qing Emperor Abdication Decree*.

Since Xinhai Revolution, the fast developing situation had created a condition that made Yuan the only legitimate candidate for the presidency. Aside from Yuan's political prowess, it also has much to do with *Qing Emperor's Abdication Decree*. In fact, without the *Decree*, it would be difficult to explain Yuan's historical significance.

The *Decree* mentioned Yuan Shikai's name three times, all in the body section. In one place, the Qing emperor ordered Yuan Shikai to "dispatch envoys to open peace talks with civilian and military deputies of the Revolution." It also provided the rationale of Yuan's appointment: "Yuan Shikai was previously elected to be the Prime Minister by the Political Council. In this critical moment of the new replacing the old, in order to unite the South and the North, the Emperor authorizes Yuan Shikai to be in charge of the organization of the Provisional Government". There has been conspiracy theories surrounding the circumstances under which the decree was compiled. According to some Yuan secretly revised the decree. Regardless of the rumors, the three references of his name are connotatively consistent: It recognizes Yuan's political capacity and that at a critical moment, he was authorized by Qing government to form a separate republican government and parley with the representatives from the South – the ROC provisional government to discuss unification and new state building.

From the perspective of jurisprudence, the Qing emperor didn't pass the sovereignty to the Southern revolutionary government. Instead, he appointed Yuan Shikai to parley on his behalf with the South. In addition, Yuan was authorized to form a republican government, convene parliament, and construct a "republican and constitutional state". Therefore, the constitutional significance of Yuan hinges on the fact he was appointed by the emperor to be responsible for establishing a republic that would be approved by both the emperor and the revolutionaries. Here we see another revolutionary state building initiative separate from the effort of the revolutionaries, and it was from the Qing government. The Decree stated in no uncertain terms that Yuan's duty is to oversee the transformation from monarchist legitimacy to the republican legitimacy going smoothly, that has double implications: On one hand, it granted Yuan considerable political leeway to ensure that he would have sufficient authority to do what he was asked to do, on the other, it also put restraints on Yuan's political ambition by stating that Yuan's legitimacy of power hinges on his compliance to the *Decree*. Had Yuan strayed away from the "republican constitutionalist state" objective described by the *Decree*, that would be treasonous. In the immediate aftermath of the issuance of the *Qing Emperor Abdication Decree*, Sun Yat-sen resigned and passed the Provisionary President position to Yuan Shikai. If the revolutionaries were responsible for unilaterally revising the constitution to funnel power from the president to the parliament before the presidency handover, leading to a series of undesirable consequences, then Yuan Shikai's self-crowning was a blatant breach of *Decree*, which constituted the legitimacy of his power. It would be fair to say that while the revolutionaries acted generally in accordance with the spirit of the *Provisional Constitution* as well as *Qing Emperor Abdication Decree*, and made some minor mistakes in the process, Yuan had no justification for his betrayal of the *Decree*, which was his sold source of legitimacy. It is in this sense that we think the uprisings against Yuan are justified.

From the perspective of the political constitution theory, Yuan Shikai's crowning is a violation of the "republican constitutionalist" contract in the form of *Qing Emperor Abdication Decree*. The *Decree* can be seen as a contract among four parties: the Qing Emperor, the governments from both sides and Yuan Shikai. All of them recognized that a "republican constitutionalist state", instead of monarchy, or constitutional monarchy, was the future of the country. It is under such a contract, the emperor agreed to abdicate peacefully and forsake his sovereignty. Once the *Decree* was publicized, according to the contract, Qing Emperor abdicated and the Republic of China commenced, while the document took legal effect jurisprudentially, and were binding to all parties involved.

Once the *Decree* was enacted, none of the signing parties, the North, the South, the President of the Republic of China, and the abdicated Qing Emperor, had the right to revoke it unilaterally and resume monarchism, for it would be against the provision about a "republican constitutionalist state". When it comes to constitutional implication, the "Yuan Shikai clauses" afforded Yuan the power to lead the country in the construction of a "republican" and "constitutionalist" country, but never afforded him the power to restore monarchism, either the Qing monarchy or declaring himself an emperor. Yuan's crowning therefore can only be regarded as a violation of the provision of building China as a "republican constitutionalist state", in this sense, Yuan deserved his name as the "thief of state". It may also worth mentioning aside from Yuan's attempt, there was another restoration attempt led by general Zhang Xun, who tried to restore the reign of the abdicated Xuantong Emperor. Like Yuan's act, the abdicated Qing emperor's attempt was also unconstitutional, since the *Decree* had already transferred the sovereignty to ROC, in doing so, having completed the transformation of China from a traditional monarchist state to a modern republic. In this sense, the abdicated Xuantong Emperor that Zhang Xu tried to bring back to the throne was no longer an emperor per se for the sovereignty transfer was considered done; as an individual citizen, the former emperor might be slightly special, for he remained to receive certain privileges according to the abdication deal, but nothing more. The "emperor" title that he had was titular therefore entailed no power of monarchy. The moment the *Decree* was promulgated, the classical Chinese dynastic monarchism was pronounced dead; all attempts to restore it can only be regarded as unconstitutional.

The debate between monarchists and republicans began prior to the abdication of the Qing emperor and reached a fevered pitch when Yuan Shikai proclaimed himself emperor. Kang Youwei, the constitutional monarchist leader who formed Loyalist Party abroad prior to Xinhai Revolution, was a main figure of the monarchist camp. He debated the republicans over whether removing the emperor should be a goal of the revolution. Kang believed that the emperor was more than the emperor of the Manchus, but the emperor of the fifty hundred million of Chinese people, thus viewing the Manchu emperor as an enemy is viewing the entire Chinese people as enemies. Kang also contended that one's claim to Chineseness has nothing to do with genes, but depending on one condition, namely whether the person recognizes the Chinese civilization. After over two centuries ruling China, Kang argued, the Manchu ruling group had become so enmeshed in the Chinese civilization that they had became a part of it, therefore anti-Manchu is no other than anti-China. However, after the abdication, Kang attitude undertook a change. He abandoned his former constitutional monarchism and became enamored by republicanism. He drafted a "Constitution of the Republic of China", though it was never recognized by neither the South nor the North. However, his proposition of "sovereignty belongs to the state" rather than "sovereignty belongs to the people" seems to indicate that he remained a British-style constitutional monarchist in heart.

Although revolution and republic constitutionalism gained mainstream recognition among the people, a considerable number of intellectuals and landed gentry remained in favor of constitutional monarchism. Their leader Kang Youwei disliked Yuan Shikai personally, but many believe that Confucius Religion Commission delivered assistance to Yuan's crowning. At that time, Yuan had secured the support of Chinese scholars such as Yang Du, Liu Shipei, and other four collectively called the "Six Masters of Chou An Hui" and foreign constitution scholars such as American Frank Johnson Goodnow and Japanese Aruga Nagao. Ynag Du and Goodnow's thoughts were typical among the monarchists. They agreed that in light of China's size and history, as well as the crisis that it faced at home and abroad, to implement reform, promulgate constitution and build a modern state was the only solution. However, they maintained that constitutionalism shouldn't be rushed and needed to wait until education, cultural development and political-social condition catch up, thus constitutional monarchism, given the circumstances, is a better solution. Goodnow's *Republic and Monarchism* ostensibly compares the shortcomings of the two systems; although refraining from passing a judgment, carries a strong suggestion in favor of constitutionalist monarchism. Yang Du developed Goodwill's point further in his *Constitutional Monarchism Save the Country*. He argued that in view of China's political tradition and the Western experience, China should follow the model of Japan and Germany and implement constitutional monarchism rather than republicanism. Only by ensuring the traditional monarchy's authority, he argued, could the Chinese nation achieve true unification.

Such efforts that sought to justify monarchism are undoubtedly reactionary. The reason why monarchism is not a legitimate form of conservatism is to a good measure due to the fact that the seven decades prior shows clearly that a thorough reform can't be implemented under a monarchist system. Although incremental improvement was achieved, and some members of the Qing royal family did show what seemed to be genuine interest in reform, in general, the Qing empire failed to renew its own institutions; in this sense, the revolutionaries' uprisings against it is justified. Although in Britain and Japan, constitutionalist monarchism was successful, in China, the "racial" policy that the Manchu ruling group implemented made it extremely difficult to reconcile with the Han Chinese. Finally under the assault of the revolution, the Manchu emperor was forced to abdicate; passing the sovereignty down to a constitutional republican China that would be formed through a negotiation (as opposed to the one announced by the revolutionaries) under the guidance of the Qing Emperor Abdication Decree. Here I would conjecture that the *Decree* is the embodiment of true conservative constitutionalism, for it sought to soften revolutionary radicalism in a fashion similar to the Glorious Revolution did successfully in Britain. In this way, both the *Decree* and *Provisional Constitution* should both be regarded as constitutional documents; together they formed the foundation of ROC.

After the two documents were enacted, monarchism met its end in China. It was fortunate for China that the demise of Manchu monarchy didn't lead to total collapse of order, regicides, massive bloodshed, which were not uncommon in history. Thanks to the peacefulness of the abdication, the legal system was largely preserved, that is to say the formalistic fall of the monarchy didn't affect the substantive functioning of the old legal system, which played a vital role in maintaining social order; in fact, it provided a basis of legitimacy for ROC. China was successfully transformed from an "emperor's country" to a "people's country", from monarchism to constitutionalism. Also, as we said, once the *Decree* was enacted, all attempts to restore monarchism would be unconstitutional; therefore the monarchism, which bedeviled Chinese politics for thousands of years, was solved once for all. In addition, the *Decree* enunciated that Manchus, the Han Chinese, Tibetans, Mongols and Huis would all be included in the new republican platform; together they would form the new "Chinese people". Such a deal for the royal family was not bad either.

For his voluntary giving up power, the emperor won much good will. In a way, he would have been immortalized and his name written into the constitution where he would retain a symbolic position. On the other hand, the abdication benefited the constitution for giving it an element of British-style "glory".

The *Ratio Status*[9] that constitutional monarchist Kang Youwei, Yang Du and Yuan Shikai sought after could be found in the republican political structure. They overlooked the nature of the irreversible transformation set forth by the *Decree*; therefore their efforts to revive dead carcasses and antiquated institutions was bound to be in vain. In comparison, people like Liang Qichao, Cai E, and Zhang Jian demonstrated greater historical insights and political acumen. They had the wisdom of seeing the bigger picture and saw what was coming. Once they too were advocates of constitutional monarchism, now they saw the inevitability of the revolution and abandoned the hopeless cause. While they strongly opposed the revolutionary radicalism, they also stood firmly against restoration attempts. When Yuan Shikai crowned himself, these people immediately withdrew their allegiance to the former President. In this sense, they should be regarded as the true guardians of the Republican constitutionalism.

That Yuan Shikai and Zhang Xu's attempts to restore monarchism failed is of no concern to the question that we try to answer – what are their implications to the revolutionary constitutionalist state-building and its relationship with less radical route of increment improvements. Hence what requires of us is more than simplistically accusing the two men as "traitors" or "harboring evil ambitions".

To recap, during the early days of the Republic era, a great transformation was undertaken and a consensus took shape Manchu monarchy should be replaced by a constitutional republic. In the Qing Emperor Abdication Decree, it was stipulated that the sovereignty should be transferred to the succeeding Republic. By actively facilitating the transformation, the emperor made himself a part of the new republic. Any attempt to reverse this process would be backpedaling, a form of betrayal to the Republic as well as betrayal of the will of the abdicated emperor. While the empire was dismantled and ceased to exist politically, its culture, civilization, tradition, customs, moral philosophies and literature, would survive and be inherited by the Republic. Even people's reverence for the monarch could have been preserved in certain ways.[10]

In fact, the constitution had some very favorable terms regarding the treatment of the abdicated Qing emperor and the former royal family. However, the two restoration attempts not only diminished the good will of the public, but also hampered the process of incorporating the cultural bequeath to the republican infrastructure. As much as we criticize Yuan Shikai and Zhang Xu's restoration attempts, for their

[9] See Xu Zhangrun's *Ratio Status*, Historical jurisprudence Vol 4, China Law Press, 2010.

[10] See Lin Zhihong's *"Minguo is Our Enemy": Qing Loyalists and Near-modern Political Transformation*; Taiwan University Phd. thesis, 2005 – the writer conducted comprehensive research and cited large numbers of materials; one can have a good impression of the social-cultural conditions and the complexity of the Chinese people's value and conceptions reading the article.

betrayals of the ROC constitutional laws, we should see that the Republic of China revolutionary radicalism was hardly more constructive. In their fight against the two schools of monarchists, the revolutionaries also showed little cool-headed rationality, and the principle of peace and justice was not always adhered, neither did they see the preservation of the Chinese traditional civilization as in their interest. Those so-called radical ROC defenders instigated a spirit of rebellion that proved to be hard to reverse, and created a condition making the abdicated emperor impossible to maintain his dignity. For instance, warlord Feng Yuxiang once ordered his troops to hold the royal family members at gunpoint to evict them out of the Forbidden City. Such a move not only violated the *Decree* as a constitutional law, but also severed all umbilical cord between ROC and the traditional monarchism. The impudence demonstrated by the revolutionary radicals in destroying the traditional civilization and the glory would lead to outcome that was nothing short of tragic.

2.3 Warlord Politics, May 4 Movement and Civil Revolution

The political situation momentarily stabilized following Yuan's death. For a brief moment, things seemed to have taken a turn for better and the country was again on track towards democracy and republicanism. *Provisionary Constitution* was restored, Parliament reconvened, and the South joined the North. However, underneath the serenity, crisis was brewing. Not long after Yuan's death, conflict broke out between his successor President Li Yuanhong and Prime Minister Duan Qirui. Taking advantage of the situation, a general named Zhang Xun restored the abdicated Manchu Emperor Puyi to the throne, though such an effort was soon thwarted. War soon erupted between warlords of Zhi faction and Wan faction, and the South and North split up again. Compounding to the situation was the presidential election corruption scandal, which further weakened the foundation of the republic.

This period of history is of great interest for historians and constitution scholars. At that time the constitution-making work at the Beijing-based Parliament, despite intermittences, continued. Their work had offered some hope for the contemporaries and also intrigued many later day scholars. Here, I would like to try to address two questions in the following paragraphs, namely, how did the military secessionism prevail, and what consequences did it cause to China's legal system reform.

It was not the first time that China splintered into small warring states controlled by warlords, but in the Chinese history, such periods of military secessionism had been exceptions rather than the norm. Prior to late Qing anarchy, such a situation occurred in late Tang Dynasty. During the subsequent millennium, especially after Song Emperor took the military power into his own hands by sacking his military generals, China had stayed a unified centralized empire. How did the military secessionism reemerge? Here we will not be bogged down into details, for a brief overview of history will suffice. In the mid nineteenth century, Taiping Rebellion erupted. Because the incompetency of the Manchu regular army, the Qing government turned to rely on militias trained by Han Chinese officials. During the process of repelling the Taiping rebellion, Han Chinese officials attained power that was previously impossible for them. As a result, they were allowed to raise fund to finance and maintain regular troops, at the expense of the diminishing central government's ability to intervene into local matters. Many military leaders cultivated strong personal loyalty among subordinates; as a result, officers now vow allegiance to their direct superiors, instead of the emperor. Some of the leaders such as Zeng Guofan, Zuo Zengtang, Li Hongzhang, and later, Yuan Shikai, became powerful political forces yet continued to be on good terms with the central government, but once they fell out with the central government, or died, their subordinate were prone to split. This is exactly what happened following Yuan Shikai's death.

A more important question is about the effect of the military secessionism on the progression of China's constitutionalism. I would conjecture that the effect of this phase of political development to the later-day development is twofold. One is the intellectual development in the form of May 4 Movement; the other is the practice of Civil Revolution. The two events were direct response to military secessionism and were interwoven with each other, sharing the same spirit of revolutionary radicalism. It is fair to say that the military secessionism shoved China onto an even more radical political route. This route is prepared intellectually by the May 4 Movement, and was put into execution by the Civil Revolution. It is also evident that both May 4 Movement and Civil Revolution drew their legitimacy from the consequence of the military secessionism. However, their radical revolutionary appeals, especially when the radical ideas and practice finally converged, had generated an effect that is devastating. Although throughout the modernization process, revolution was a necessary driving force behind constitutionalism; however, over a decade following Xinhai Revolution, progress stalled. As we mentioned previously, the constitutionalism requires a revolutionary counter-revolutionary stop. As another wave of movements rising on the horizon, one might have hope that these would finally bring China's constitutionalism to success. However, as history tells us, they again fell short of such objective, proven to be inadequate in addressing the question of modern constitutionalism.

May 4 Movement, a student-led anti-imperialist movement, marks the start of the broader New Culture Movement. How did the New Culture Movement come to be and acquired its "patriotic and anti-imperialist" theme? Although it purported to focus on "culture", it can only be regarded as a response to the political development in the post-Xinhai Revolution era. As contemporary writer Lu Xun observed: "(For someone who) witnessed Xinhai Revolution, Second Revolution, Yuan Shikai's Coronation, Zhang Xun's Restoration, it is hard not to become skeptical, disillusioned, and pessimistic."[11] Such a view is typical among the contemporaries. Since the Opium War, a series of movements, including Westernization Movement, Hundred Day Reform, and Xinhai Reform, had been undertaken to realize the goal of modern state building. During the process, the Chinese elites' understanding of modern state building increased with more and more having been convinced that constitutionalism and other modern political modern institutions are vital to China's

[11] See Lu Xun's *Lu Xun Complete Works* (Vol 4), People's Literature Press, 1989, p. 455.

modernization. The success of Xinhai Revolution might be incidental, but it rekindled people's hope and gave them something to expect for.

The political instability of Republic hampered the legitimacy of the new political form, especially after Yuan Shikai and Zhang Xun's attempts to restore monarchism; such an tendency became even more evident. The regimes established by warlords on the ruins of Qing Empire had no legitimacy at all. This misfortunate state of affairs led many to arrive at a pessimistic conclusion: "The republic is worse than Qing Empire" with many asking: "Why couldn't China, after so many years of experimenting and exploration, with its increasing understanding of modernization, still couldn't walk out of its own crisis and only led things to become worse?" For that question, the banner holders of the May 4 Movement, Chen Duxiu, provided a representative view. Chen believed that the reason that neither reform nor revolution could save China was because the Chinese society was infested and corrupted by backward traditional culture; Chen maintained that China's problem was neither a technological one or a political one, but a cultural one. Only a complete departure from the traditional culture, represented by Confucianism, and a full introduction of Western culture, especially the ideals of "Democracy and Science", could a bright future be brought about. Such uncompromising stance noted for its hostility towards tradition would set the tone for the New Culture Movement. Evidently, it was not the first time that China's traditional culture came under severe criticism. Prior to Xinhai Revolution, people like Tan Sitong, Yan Fu and Liang Qichao were all critical of the Confucian tradition; in a way, the New Culture Movement is an extension of this line of thinking. However, none of the predecessors matched New Culture Movement for its radicalness, which can only be explained by the dire political reality in the wake of the Xinhai Revolution. The slogan "Shut down the Confucius shop", for example, resonate with the people because the Confucianism was used by Yuan Shikai and Zhang Xun as an instrument to justify their attempts to restore monarchism, which irreversibly damaged the image of the Chinese tradition.

A greater negative outcome that the anti-traditionalism of the May 4 Movement was the complete abandonment of the conservative incremental improvement route that had contributed to China's modernization and constitutionalism. Revolution obviously is one of the strongest driving forces of the Republican sovereign legitimacy, but a modern China and constitution can't be accomplished by revolution alone. After Xinhai Revolution, not only had the constitutionalists dedicated to the cause of Chinese constitutionalism, even the Qing royal family made their contribution, mostly in the form of the Abdication Decree, whose significance to the birth of the Chinese constitution was immense. That is to say that aside from the revolutionary forces, the non-revolutionary ones, who tried to keep the old bottle yet fill it with new wine, were also a contributing force of the modern Chinese constitution building. Had the tradition and reform made peace, the transformation would have been much more smooth. However the strong antagonism towards the tradition ruled out the possibility of positive powers and wisdom from participating in the construction of modern constitution. While such stance to some degree served to relieve the historical burden, its benefit was outweighed for the cost of alienating the other political forces, and increased uncertainty for the future development.

In addition, although the New Culture Movement's onslaught on tradition mostly took place on the cultural sphere, it should be kept in mind that the social-political conditions played a vital role in its origin. Hence the political dimension of moment, instead of the cultural one, needs to be paid more attention. Although New Culture Movement initially assorted to cultural criticism as its main weapon, the limit would later be much murkier, as the movement began to exert influence onto the political sphere and sought to remedy the Chinese political and social problems. Tradition, which could have been the resources to contribute to China modernization, was renounced and forsaken. Without tradition, on what ground can the grand vision be built on? The answer, according to New Culture Movement, is "Democracy" and "Science". But the tricky part is that with the outbreak of the World War I, not only the West was forced to face the shortcomings of their own civilization, even China was forced to reexamine the Western ideals that so far it tried to imitate, resultant in diminishing authority of the West. Compounding to the skepticism, the Treaty of Versailles' transfer of German concessions in Shandong to Japan, despite China's demand to have it returned, led to outburst of nationalistic sentiment among the Chinese public. As a result, the New Culture Movement converged with the nationalist movement over the territorial dispute. A coalition was formed between the students-led May 4 intellectuals and the broader patriotic movement. Such coalition finally pushed the intellectual radicalism onto a route of self-realization through excerpting influence to the practice.

The gap left by China's increasing skepticism of the West and the renouncement of its own tradition was filled by Russia's October Revolution. Marxism and Leninism, especially the later, turned out to be highly popular among the young, jolting many who were of bewildered and pessimistic into action. These new ideas also transformed the May 4 Movement from one of anti-tradition "destruction" movement to a Marx-Leninist "construction" movement. This is corroborated by the attitude change among the intellectual leaders such as Chen Duxiu. Once a scholar who saw it his duty to criticize politics, now Cheng was turned into a vocal champion of social-political upheaval, arguing that "the primary task of a modern society is to construct a proletariat state through revolutionary means, as well as create a political and judicial system that end all exploitations of people or foreign countries." After experiencing such a transformation, China was unwaveringly on route towards what later-day historian Lin Yusheng called a "Chinese Utopia".

The anti-tradition and pro-communist New Culture Movement's prepared the country ideologically and intellectually for its battle against the "warlords". This battle is the Civil Revolution, which sought to restore the Nationalist Party's rule through military campaign. The campaign was planned and commanded by Sun Yat-sen. Sun, in preparation for the campaign, restructured the Nationalist Party according to the principle of "alliance with the Soviets, admission of the communists, assisting the proletariats and peasants". After Sun's death, the communists took over the leadership of the revolution. Under the new command, the revolution expanded into the so-called "Great Revolution". Overall, the Civil Revolution reshaped China's social-political, military and cultural conditions, and created a second "constitutional moment".

The revolutionary state building ideal upheld by Xinhai Revolution is an important element of the Chinese nation's constitutional state building spirit, yet 12 years on, not only all the effort fell short of achieving the objective, even this sprit became obscured. Although in 1923, Constitution of Republic of China, a procedurally legitimate constitutional text, was promulgated by the Parliament, but the constitution turned out just another piece of window dressing, never a functioning one that is capable of safeguarding a free and democratic republican China. The task of producing a modern Chinese constitution would be passed onto the shoulders of new generations of revolutionaries.

There were two competing narratives that offer different, sometimes contradictory accounts of the Civil Revolution. One was formulated by the Nationalist Party, the other by the CPC. The two differed in aspects ranging from the starting points, timeframe and specific events that constitute the Civil Revolution, as well as who was its real leader. The Nationalist view claims that the Civil Revolution started in 1924, when Sun Yat-sen restructured the Nationalist Party and adopted the Three Principles, also in the same year, cooperation with the Communist Party began and the Northern Expedition commenced; victory was achieved and the rule of Beiyang warlords was annihilated. In 1927, Chiang Kai-shek and Wang Jinwei launched Party Cleansing Movement and turned the spearhead against communists, extreme measure were taken in the process to persecute the "reds". When Zhang Xueliang, the last major warlord who controlled three Northeast provinces ceded power to the revolutionary government, China was unified for the first time since 1917. Thus the Civil Revolution concluded and its objective, namely, unifying the country in territory and people, was achieved.

The CPC offered a different account. One bone of contention is that the Communist Party believes that they be regarded as the real leading party of the Civil Revolution. Instead of starting in 1924, when the Nationalist Party announced its restructuring plan, CPC believes the beginning point should be 1922, when the Second CPC National Congress was convened; at the Congress, the idea of a Civil Revolution was discussed and decision was made that the Communist Party members would join the Nationalist Party to assist the later in its reform and later, conducting the Northern Expedition against the Beiyang warlords. Another point of dispute is that CPC contended that Chiang Kai-shek and Wang Jinwei should be regarded as traitors of the Revolution, and their persecution of the Communists should be regarded a blatant betrayal of Sun Yat-sen's will.

The communist's narrative also contested the Nationalists' conclusion as to the ending of the revolution, contending that the Civil Revolution concluded after the failure of the Guangzhou Uprising in December 1927 (Note: to be distinguished from the first one led by the Nationalists against Qing government).

The two sides also named the revolution differently. Before 1927, "Civil Revolution" was the standard reference in the documents of the Communist Party and among the party leaders. Later, it would be changed to "Great Revolution", the "Chinese Great Revolution", or "the First Great Revolution". These names indicate that starting the second half of 1927, the CPC had been increasingly independent of the Nationalist cause, and carried out the revolution on its own, creating a separate route different from the Nationalists'.

Through such a narrative, the CPC formed its legitimacy based on its role in the Civil Revolution, which it regarded as an extension of the 1911 Xinhai Revolution. According to the CPC's view, the Civil Revolution is a legitimate continuation of Sun Yat-sen's Xinhai revolution, and it was the Communist Party, rather than the Nationalist Party who was the leader of the movement and accomplished the task left unfinished by Xinhai revolutionaries.[12]

Such view is expressed in the Preamble to the Constitution of People's Republic of China, which stated: "The Revolution of 1911, led by Dr. Sun Yat-sen, abolished the feudal monarchy and gave birth to the Republic of China. But the historic mission of the Chinese people to overthrow imperialism and feudalism remained unaccomplished. After waging protracted and arduous struggles, armed and otherwise, along a zigzag course, the Chinese people of all ethnic groups led by the Communist Party of China with Chairman Mao Zedong as its leader ultimately, in 1949, overthrew the rule of imperialism, feudalism and bureaucrat-capitalism, won the great victory of the New-Democratic Revolution and founded the People's Republic of China. Since then the Chinese people have taken control of state power and become masters of the country."

To recap, the Civil Revolution as a revolutionary struggle against the Beiyang warlords, is the direct outcome of the intellectual radicalism spawn by the May 4 Movement, especially after the movement imbued with Marxism and Leninism, especially the later. This movement is justified for it is a response to the social-political conditions, but it also strengthened the radicalism. While it is justifiable that radicalism took precedence in the revolution, however, when the revolution achieved its objectives, it is vital that the genie be put back into the bottle to facilitate the transformation of the political system – this is a question that we need to think deeply about. Sun Yat-sen, the spiritual leader of the Civil Revolution had formulated some ideas on the transformation from revolution to revolutionary counterrevolution; these ideas were crystalized into three-phase revolution theory, which enunciated that the utmost goal of the revolution was constitutionalism and the true mission of revolution was to return sovereignty to the people. However, driven by the radical revolutionary ideologies, the revolutionaries didn't take the initiative to pull the brake. Hence, whether the revolutionary counter-revolution spirit could be implemented is a test for the revolutionary parties.

Worldwide, various forms of popular rebellions or uprisings were staged throughout the human history. Britain, France, Russia and other modern states all had their fair shares. The problem is that revolution, a form of political violence, once out of the bottle, would be very difficult to put back, hence it would be of primary importance that in the post-revolution society, the revolution spirit should be handled with great care. To phrase it in another way, the form of political order established by

[12] See Yin Tai's *Construction of Imperialism in China – Case Study of Civil Revolution in 1920s*, International Relationship Academy Journal, issue 3, 2007; Wang Qisheng's Revolution and Anti-revolution, Social Sciences Documentation Publishing House, 2010; Jin Chongji's *Brief History of China in the 20th Century*, Social Sciences Documentation Publishing House, 2009.

revolution determines the nature of the revolution. The British Revolution and French Revolution were different types of revolution because they created different social orders in their wake. The first cured the old ailments and reshaped the political order; the later led to protracted violence. The American Revolution represented a third road. It has no tradition to rely on, hence was what Mao Zedong described a "picture on a blank piece of paper" – in a sense, it was similar to the French revolution, which demanded "newness" for its own sake, however, spiritually, it has more in common with the British Revolution, for it inherited the British conservationist political tradition. Moreover, the Constitution of the United States clearly embodied a de-revolutionary or counter-revolutionary spirit. Hence we say that its nature is twofold. First, it is revolutionary. Without revolution, there wouldn't be the constitution, to which the revolution is an efficient cause. However, revolution itself is not the end. The end of the revolution is independence and state-building. Constitution hence is the formal cause of the revolution. Revolution stops the moment constitution takes effect. The implementation of constitution signifies the completion of revolution. The second fold is its counter-revolution or de-revolution nature. Through the authorization of the constitution-making conferences and people from different states, the constitution put the genie back in the bottle and established concepts such as "we the people" and "United States of America", henceforth, a state was created, and constitution was implemented, and the revolution concluded. This counter-revolution is the essence of the American constitutions ranging from Declaration of Independence to the Constitution of the United States. It is also the secret of the American politics.

Modern revolution is always accompanied by war and violence, which poses a question that the revolutionaries needs to answer – how to build a state through violence. We see that the modern polities, to certain extent, had all been bedeviled by the post-revolutionary curse. The French Revolution, Russian Revolution and the Chinese Revolution fell into the trap. In comparison, the British Revolution and the American Revolution conquered their inclination towards tyranny and bloodthirst, and achieved its aim of building a modern state. Underlying these revolutions, there is the question of legitimacy. It is worth pointing out that revolution itself is not liberty. Revolution is a destructive power. Constitution, on the other hand, rein in this power by keeping revolutionary violence at bay. In this sense, all real constitutions are counter-revolutionary, though there is a difference between the counter-revolution that comes from revolution itself, and counter-revolution imposed from without. The Divine Alliance that tired to purge the French War, or the royalists in the Independence War of America don't count as revolutionary counterrevolutions, whereas the Tories and American anti-Federalists fit the description.

Hence our examination of the Civil Revolution is not to deny its legitimacy or diminish its historical significance. In fact, facing the militarily powerful yet politically illegitimate warlords, armed revolution was both justified and righteous. However, revolution can't accomplish constitutionalism by itself. It can only achieve such an end through executing a counter-revolutionary transformation. Civil Revolution, as a logical extension of the revolutionary radicalism following the military radicalism, lacked such a mechanism that enables it to make the transformation happen, hence carried great risk for the future of the Civil Revolution. In a way, the split of Nationalists and Communists in the revolution and the experience of the Nationalist Party domination in politics foretold the long and bumpy journey of China's legal system modernization.

Chapter 3
Rule by the Party: Party Rule, Tutelage and Transformation Towards Constitutionalism

With the success of Wuchang Uprising and Qing Emperor's abdication, Sun Yat-sen and his comrades made true on their promise of expelling "the barbarians". Yet they had failed to deliver on the other one, namely, "create a people's republic". In fact, soon after the establishment of ROC, the power fell into the hands of Yuan Shikai, who betrayed revolutionary ideals by proclaiming himself an emperor. Yuan's short-lived reign ended shortly after his death, leaving behind a country in disarray. Constitutionalism and state building had hitherto all but halted; moreover, with divergence amongst different political forces deepened, war erupted, plunging the country back into chaos.

To regain the power from the warlords, the revolutionaries launched "Second Revolution". Their ultimate goal was to implement Sun Yat-sen ideal of building a republic "owned by the people, governed by the people, and benefit the people". However, neither this campaign, in which Sun himself participated, nor the subsequent State-Protecting Movement, Constitution-Protecting Movement, accomplished the desired objective. These failures prompted Sun to seek a new route. This route, outlined in Sun's "three phase state building" blueprint, is noted for entailing a stage of "tutelage". Inspired by the success of the Russian Bolshevik Revolution, Sun was convinced that a strong leadership was critical to the success of revolution and constitutionalism.

Sun couldn't envisage that his "tutelage" design would lead to "party rule" – the revolutionary party singlehandedly formed the government, which directly answered to the party; the party had so much power that it could almost revise and interpret laws at will. Although initially conceived in compliance with the ideal of "Three People's Principles" and "Five Powers", finally this design evolved into a de facto one-party monopoly of state power. Following the outbreak of Civil Revolution, "rule of party" and "rule of law" became increasingly at odds with each other. Although rule of party was designed to clear the obstacles to implement "rule of law", in practice, this process was hindered by several factors, including fights with the warlords, Japanese invasion, later, political conflict with the CPC leading to the

Q. Gao et al., *The Road to the Rule of Law in Modern China*,
Research Series on the Chinese Dream and China's Development Path,
DOI 10.1007/978-3-662-45637-8_3

outbreak of Civil War. Up until KMT retreated to Taiwan, constitutionalism failed to take hold in the country; however despite its frustrations in the Mainland, its implementation in Taiwan achieved success – after decades of KMT's authoritarian rule, democratic constitutionalism was installed in Taiwan, which provided a valuable lesson to the entire Chinese community.

3.1 The Origin of Party Rule

The lack of political legitimacy of Beiyang warlords' rule spurred China to find a new strategy. On the other hand, Xinhai Revolution failed to deliver on its promise of building a people's republic and realizing constitutionalism. Both drove China further down the road of radicalism, which gave rise to the May 4 Movement and Civil Revolution during this period. Of course, when compared with the warlords' secessionism, revolutionary uprisings were politically justified. However, Civil Revolution is different from previous revolutionary movements due to the greater level of control that the revolutionary party processed. As a result, the state of party rule, which is contradictory to the revolutionary ideal, took over, leaving us the question – how did the party rule concept, which remains influential to this day, took place?

The realization of party rule had two preconditions that need to be met. On the theoretical front, after Sun Yat-sen founded ROC, he developed a three-phase state building blueprint; his described the revolutionary party's role as instructing and educating the public on constitutionalism. On the organizational front, impressed by the success of the Russian October Revolution, Sun undertook to restructure KMT based on the experience of Bolsheviks. The two conditions are mutually reinforcing: theoretical preparations provided guidance to its action, while organizational preparation boosted the party's confidence to carry theories into execution.

Xinhai Revolution is often regarded as the start of modern China. However, for Sun Yat-sen, it was only one of his brainchildren.[1] Generally speaking, Sun's state building theory went through four stages. The first stage is noted for his preference for a moderate, incremental improvement-style reform; then he was persuaded by the idea of armed revolution, which resulted in Xinhai Revolution; the third stage is characterized by his revolutionary theory of Three People's Principles; the final stage is marked for his three phase revolutionary state building blueprint.[2]

The origin of Sun Yat-sen's revolutionary blueprint can be traced to the Revive China Society era, when members of the organization took oaths of "expel the barbarians, revive China, and establish republican government". Later, a new objective was added to the list, when Revive China Society went through a reform and

[1] See Tang Degang's *On Different Phases of Sun Yat-sen's Thoughts*, part of Late Qing 70 year Vol 5, Yuan-Liou Publishing Co., Ltd., 2004, p. 127; Jin Chongji's *Different Stages of Sun Yat-sen's Thoughts on People's Livlihood over Half an Century*, Central Party Literature Press, 2004.

[2] See Jin Zhiren's *History of China Constitutions*, Linking Books, 1984, p. 359.

changed its name to Chinese United League: "distribute land equally among the people" – these guidelines would be summarized as Three People's Principles, which was first publicized on the first issue of *Mingpao* published in the 1906. Since then, these principles had stayed largely unchanged, though the Three-phased Revolution blueprint was later introduced as specific measures to realize the Principles. Realizing that these revolutionary objectives were unlikely to be achieved shortly, Sun reasoned it would be a better to divide the task up and to tackle them one each time. According to Sun's design, the Chinese people needed to be held by hands by the revolutionaries to learn how to govern themselves so the foundation of constitutionalism would be formed – this design would later evolve into "tutelage".

The first expression of "three phases" and "tutelage" can be traced to the *Chinese United League Military Government Declaration*, which summarized KMT's plan as "four guidelines and three phases". Although Sun Yat-sen assigned specific objectives to each of the three phases, such as rule of martial law, rule of provisional constitution, and finally, constitutionalism, the lines between the three phrases were not clearly drawn, which caused certain confusion in the execution and led to some disputes among the academia. Some scholars treated "rule of provisional constitution" as the prototype of the tutelage design and overlooked the different right basis of the two concepts. The legitimacy of "rule of provisional constitution" is grounded in the "sacredness of human rights", while the tutelage is based on the "revolutionary civil rights". Although they are both interim phases, purportedly necessary steps leading up to the realization of constitutionalism, their content and implications are different. This difference would lead to different outcomes – the first is pro-universal democratic constitutionalism, the later carried a veiled element of authoritarianism.

Scholar Zhang Taiyan's famous prediction about a strong revolutionary army can hamper the revolutionary cause was vindicated – in spite of the success of the Wuchang Revolt, the Chinese United League's revolutionary guidelines failed to be implemented. Around this time, Sun Yat-sen warned several times the danger of the monopoly of power by one party, saying that one party politics "must be avoided and is as bad as monarchism". Sun's three-phase blueprint had yet completed by this point. Had Yuan Shikai who succeeded Sun and his non-revolutionary forces upheld the republican ideals and committed to the constitutionalist cause, then China would have developed along the direction of democratic constitutionalism, then the three-phase blueprint would be unnecessary. However, Yuan's abandonment of republicanism, as well as the anarchy that ensued his death convinced Sun that the three phase development was the only way to save China from collapse of order; he also suggested that "rule of provisional constitution" should be replaced by "tutelage" and "party rule". So we can say that both "tutelage" and "party rule" were responses to the frustrations of constitutionalism.

Soon after the Second Revolution, Sun Yat-sen reorganized KMT and renamed it as Chung-kuo Kuomintang. In the 1914 *General Charter of Chung-kuo Kuomintang* the three-phase blueprint was enshrined as the party's top guideline. According to the Article Four of the General Principles of the charter: "During the stage of tutelage, the Party will lead the people to achieve local self-governance" In the Article Five, "Revolutionary Period" was introduced and defined as starting from "the revolutionary army's uprising" and ending with "when constitution was implemented". During this period, the revolutionary party took control of all military and political matters. Regarding the revolutionary party, Act Six says: "all Chinese people have the right and obligation to join the Party". This is the first time that Sun formally put forward the idea of "tutelage" and "party rule". Yet up until June 1916, the year when the Chung-kuo Kuomintang was dissolved after State Protection Movement ended, these ideas were not implemented. Much evidence suggests that at this stage, although Sun was convinced of the importance of "tutelage" and "party rule", he had yet systemize his thoughts on the subject.

What prompted Sun Yat-sen to systematize his theory was his increasing disenchantment with his erstwhile allies, the "Southern Warlords". Although these military leaders attached themselves to the revolutionary cause, they did that in order to advance their self-interests. In 1919, when Sun lived in Shanghai, he systematically reviewed his revolution and state building strategy and became even more convinced that a three-phase blueprint must be implemented. Such thought was expressed both in his *Sun Wen Anthology* published in 1919, and *Kuomindang Party General Charter* published in 1920, as well as the *Chinese Revolution History* published in 1923, where Sun reiterated the necessity of tutelage as a condition to realize constitutionalism. He also explained in detail what role the revolutionary party should play during the tutelage phase, thereby formed a fairly systematical political design revolving around the tutelage concept.

Sun Yat-sen attributed the failure of the revolution to the revolutionaries' lack of faith in the ideals and strategy, resulting in insufficient willingness to carry them out. He argued that to lift the Chinese revolution out of its low ebb, the three-phase blueprint must be rigorously followed and the revolutionary party must take the lead. Here Sun compared the party's role as a tutor, reasoning that the Chinese people had lived under despotism for too long that their facility to exercise their rights had been impaired; thus they needed to be guided by a political force with superior awareness and advanced experience. Sun believed that only when the Chinese people acquired the necessarily political experience and knowledge, the transition to constitutionalism could be carried out successfully.

Sun Yat-sen wrote "We should not underestimate that the Chinese people's ignorance. Thousands of years of despotism had been such a poison that their understanding of modern politics is even inferior to that of the black slaves and other immigrants. China's republican politics is like a child who just started schooling. He must have a good teacher and be surrounded by good friends. By the same token, the Chinese people, new to the republican politics, must be educated properly. The revolutionary government should be the people's tutor to impart advanced awareness and experience… Hence the tutelage is a measure designed to facilitate the transition. Without it, anarchy would be the only outcome… The people, the masters of the Republic, is like a toddler, while the revolutionaries are the mother whose duty is to take good care of the baby and educate him. Only by doing this, when the baby grows up, he would be ready to participate in politics."[3] In a speech given at the KMT headquarters in Shanghai on November 9, 1920, Sun further elaborated: "I need to explain more about tutelage. Some asked that sovereign power is already in the hands of the people; are we trying to take it back? I would say yes. Our revolution is to take the sovereignty back into the hands of revolutionaries. We deem this as necessary based on the following reasons: The Republic had been brought about for 9 years, yet few common Chinese people know what a republic means. This led us to carry out a string of revolutions. But time is different now. We are not going to have another destructive revolution, but to build through revolutionary means – this is what tutelage is about. The term may be reminiscent of the times of emperors. In our republic, the people are the emperor. For 5,000 years, they were taught to be subjects. Now they are put on the throne, they are still not used to the power. So what we revolutionaries need to do is to teach them how to use the power, like Yi Yin taught Tai Jia. The Chinese people had been enslaved for thousands of years. Although the republic was established 9 years ago, the people still don't think they are the masters. We have no choice but to force them to learn to how to be, to teach them to exercise their rights. This is what I mean by tutelage."[4]

If Sun Yat-sen originally arrived at his conclusion of tutelage and party rule due to his frustrations in the process of realizing constitutionalism, then the success of the Russian October Revolution reinforced his convictions. This coincided with a series of events, including the coup d'état led by general Chen Jiongming in 1922, which further convinced Sun that the KMT should be reformed based on the Soviet Russian model. To this change, later-day historian Li Jiannong wrote "Yat-sen began to be convinced that during the revolution, one party dictatorship is necessary. Moreover, the revolutionary party needs to be well organized; a strong leadership principle needs to be enforced. This is the reason why Sun proposed that the revolution should be divided up into three phases, the martial law, tutelage, and constitutionalism. In practice, this sent the party's control of power and allegiance to party leaders to a new height. The Russian Bolshevik's success further convinced him that these designs are sound."[5] At the first KMT National Conference in 1924, a Party-restructure plan based on the Communist Party of the Soviet Union was announced. According to the KMT's manifesto: "the party should maintain a firm grasp on the state power while the formulation of the government is still ongoing, with a view to deter domestic counterrevolutionaries and imperialist powers' sabotage, and remove other threats that can potentially affect the party rule."[6] The reform

[3] See Sun Yat-sen's *State building strategy*, annotated by Liu Ming, Shen Qian, Zhongzhou Old Books Publishing House, 1998.

[4] Sun Yat-sen's Interpretation on tutelage, part of *Complete collection of founding father's work*, Vol 2, edited by Nationalist Party Central Party History Committee, 1984, p. 398.

[5] See Li Jiannong's *China's Political History in the Recent Century*, Fudan University Press, 2002, p. 546.

[6] See Wang Taisheng's *KMT's Party Rule Experience in China – Impetus and Impediment of Democratic Constitutionalism*, Academia Sinica Jurisprudent Journal, issue 5, 2009, Pp. 92–93.

marked the completion of organizational preparations for KMT's one party state building and party rule.

The party rule policy was in many ways a logical development of the Chinese revolution, and exerted great influence over the Chinese legal system development. Due to the difficulty to justify such a policy, the idea has been subject to contentious debate even back in the day. Later-day scholar Li Jiannong commented: "Before 1924, the debate over the Chinese politics was all about laws. Ever since the so-called "legal system restoration", the public grew increasingly fed up with the laws and the lords in the parliament who made them. As a result, nobody cared about legislation any more." The KMT'S reform based on the Russian changed the situation,[7] because "from that point on, law problems gradually gave way to party problems. Before, the constitution was something of supreme authority, now its significance was superseded by the party; people stopped debating about jurisprudential issues, party discipline was all that mattered; Law Protection Movement would be replaced Party Protection Movement; No longer there is such a thing called law legitimacy, in the future, there could only be party legitimacy."[8]

Although Sun Yat-sen conceived the idea of tutelage, he never saw it as the end of the revolution; for him, the real end was constitutionalism. According to his plan, the revolutionary party would return the sovereignty to the people tutelage achieved its desired target. Shortly after the KMT completed its sovietization reform, Sun publicized his *State-building Guidelines*, summarized as Three People's Principles and Five Rights. The *State-building Guidelines Manifesto*, promulgated around the same time, enunciated that "the goal of the revolution is to implement Three People's Principles." Well aware of the shortcomings of "party rule", Sun warned that: "by the so-called party rule, I don't mean that party members should all be officials. What I mean is that the party's principles should be implemented and upheld, so China can achieve sound governance. To put it simply. party rule is not rule of the party members, but rule of the party's principles. Everyone should be aware of it."[9]

Among other effects, tutelage theory intensified the contrast between the reality of one party's monopoly of state power and the ideal of democracy and constitutionalism. In practice, it proved to be impossible to hold a powerful incumbent party to its promise of returning the power to the people. This is corroborated by a string of delays of announcing the end of tutelage under various pretexts. In addition, the theory created a condition that justified certain practices, which became standard, such as party representatives exercising state power, party forming government, government only responsible to party, party monopolizing legislation and legal

[7] See Li Jiannong's *China's Political History in the Recent Century*, Fudan University Press 2002, p. 537.

[8] See Li Jiannong's *China's Political History in the Recent Three Decades,* Pacific Bookstore, 1930, p. 531, p. 196.

[9] Sun Yat – sen's "Party members shouldn't think themselves as overlords", quoted from Wang Taisheng's *KMT's Party Rule Experience in China – Impetus and Impediment of Democratic Constitutionalism,* Academia Sinica Jurisprudent Journal, issue 5, 2009, p. 85.

interpretation, party as the ultimate source of state power. Such a situation spelled uncertainty for China's modernization.

3.2 Degeneration of Tutelage and Setbacks of Constitutionalism Cause

Although tutelage and party rule began when Sun Yat-sen was still alive, its full implementation started after his death. At the Fifth Plenary Session of the First KMT Congress, *People's Government Organization Bill* was promulgated; the *Bill* stipulates that a KMT-dominated government was to be set up as the foundation to implement Sun's state building plan. However, implementation was slowed down due to a number of factors, this includes KMT government's limited influence, its policy to ally with Feng Faction warlords to counter Zhi Faction, mutinies led by Yang Xiwen in Yunnan and Liu Zhenhuan in Guangxi, lack of a solid political base, Western powers' mistrust, lack of military muscle, and finally Sun's failure to unify China by parleying with the North.[10] With Sun's demise, his legacies, especially party rule and sovietization reform were temporarily suspended.

Soon after the new KMT government was established in Guangdong in 1925, work was undertaken to install party rule. In the new government, KMT was given total control over political and military matters. According to the *Organic Law of the Republic of China*, Article 1: "KMT is responsible for guiding and supervising the government." This is echoed in the *Organic Law of the Republic of China Kuomin Government Military Commission*: "The military Commission, which operates under the auspices of KMT, is the top governing body of the government's military forces and military institutions." Thus, the first step towards full implementation of the party rule was made.

Soon after its establishment, in 1926, the KMT government launched Northern Expedition. The Soviet-style commissar system the revolutionary army adopted contributed to the swift victory. In 1928, the campaign ended with Zhang Xueliang, the last warlord who controlled the Northeastern region, forsook independence and pledged allegiance to the KMT government. The military victory and territorial unification seemed to have vindicated Sun's one party design.

With success of Northern Expedition, KMT set about to implement tutelage. Yet in practice, KMT didn't adhere to Sun Yat-sen's emphasis on cultivation of regional self-governance; on the contrary, much effort was devoted to strengthening the party rule, to ensure that its ideology's dominance and potential competitors were eliminated.

Shortly after the expeditionary force captured Beijing and Tianjin, two prominent KMT members Hu Hanmin and Sun Ke submitted a letter to the KMT government

[10] For more about Wang Zhenghua's analysis on KMT's postponement of forming a government, see Wang Taisheng's *KMT's Party Rule Experience in China – Impetus and Impediment of Democratic Constitutionalism,* Academia Sinica Jurisprudent Journal, issue 5, 2009, p. 95.

urging that the martial law period should conclude and tutelage to commence. Despite Hu and Sun Ke's laborious effort trying to differentiate party rule from one-party dictatorship, their interpretation of Sun Yat-sen's party rule evidently strayed away from its original meaning and morphed into a de facto one-party monopoly of state power. In addition, the two also demanded that before the final phase of constitutionalism, important posts in the government should be held by KMT members to further concentrate power to the KMT Party, strengthen its control of the government and facilitate the tutelage.[11]

In July, 1929, KMT Central Committee passed a resolution at the 16th Meeting of the Third KMT Party Congress. This new resolution further confirmed that the tutelage's principle has been changed from the decentralized self-governance to a centralized party rule.

The resolution stipulates:

1. In compliance with the principle of party rule, KMT will henceforth be the only legitimate political party in China. Political parties are forbidden to be politically active in the country; actions will be taken to terminate such organizations immediately after they are discovered.
2. The central government and lower governments should perform their duty in compliance with the Party's policies; the central and lower supervisory committee retain the power to impeach any officials who violated this principle.
3. All organization and implementation of political military, economic, educational and cultural institutions and policies must follow the *Guidelines* in order to create a solid social base to carry out the Three People's Principle. … any party members who are involved in other political parties should be sacked.

Moreover, according to the Tutelage Law, which was promulgated in this period, further legalized KMT's role as the government supervisor. Such legalization indicates that the KMT government's practice has betrayed Sun Yat-sen's ideal, and degenerated into a one-party dictatorship contradictory to constitutionalism. Under the party rule policy, the KMT exercised absolute power not only in the sphere of political life – for instance, people were required to take oaths to swear their allegiance to the Party; it also extended into everyday life, where the party line had to be toed, to the detriment of the liberty. The government was theoretically where the policies were made, yet in reality the Central Politburo, the KMT's central organ, reigned supreme and the government could do little more than executing decisions made by the Central Politburo. Although the party and the state remained two separate entities in theory, in practice, the government was subordinate to the party. For instance, KMT had the right to appoint senior government employees, and showed a strong preference for KMT cadres in these appointments.[12]

However, we must admit that even during the period when KMT government undertook to strengthen its authoritarian rule, Three People's Principles remained

[11] See Wang Taisheng's *KMT's Party Rule Experience in China – Impetus and Impediment of Democratic Constitutionalism,* Academia Sinica Jurisprudent Journal, issue 5, 2009, p. 112.

[12] Ibid., Pp. 118–119.

recognized as the top party principle. Despite the stalemates and setbacks, Sun Yat-sen's three-phase blueprint was largely followed. Some critics argue that these were just appearances to help the KMT secure its authoritarian rule as proved by that for over two decades, KMT failed to fulfill its promise of implementing constitutionalism. They overlooked the other factors that prevented a speedy realization of constitutionalism, among them three factors figured prominently.

First, military secessionism. As we said, the Civil Revolution was a response to the Beiyang warlords' reactionary rule and a continuation of Xinhai Revolution. Yet the warlords continue to hamper the constitutionalism after the Beiyang warlords were liquidated in the Northern Expedition.

The Expedition vanquished the warlord forces of Zhi and Wan factions, and ended the Beiyang warlords' control of much of northern China since Yuang Shikai's demise. In 1928, when the last major warlord Zhang Xueliang renounced pledged allegiance to KMT government, China was unified in territory. At the first glance, the objective of the expedition seems to have been achieved. However, the reality is that the victory of the expedition was only a partial one. Within the expeditionary forces, aside from the KMT troops, there were also the southern warlords. Some joined because of their identification with Sun Yat-sen's vision and their admiration of Sun Yat-sen, such as Li Zongren, who controlled Yun'nan province; but most were opportunists who joined after situation became clear; among them Yan Xishan, Feng Yuxiang, Liu Xiang, Liu Wenhui from Sichuan, Long Yun from Yunnan, Chen Jitang from Guangdong, Sheng Shicai from Xinjiang, Yang Hucheng from Shaanxi. Overall, the warlords that joined the expedition were not very different from the northern peers. After the expedition, the conflict between KMT and the southern warlords was intensified, especially after KMT government undertook to cut back on military spending and reduce the size of regular army, threatening the interests of the warlords. As a result they withdrew their allegiance to KMT government, sending the country on the brink of a new war.

Some say that Chiang Kai-shek, the force behind the military spending cut, had ulterior motive, yet such view overlooks military nationalization was fully justified back in the day – to maintain a regular army of the that size during peacetime was unsustainable – By the end of the expedition, the revolutionary forces had swollen into a massive army of 84 corps, 300 divisions and over 2.2 million servicemen, and this number didn't include the regional forces in Northeastern China, Sichuan and Yunnan. To keep such a gigantic force, 80 % of the national tax income, about 450 million silver dollars per annum, would be earmarked. Given the rising tension between KMT and the southern warlords, encouraging regional self-governance was impossible. Although Zhang Xueliang's renunciation of independence marked the end of the Civil Revolution, it would take the KMT government many years to repel the warlords' rebellions before state building resumed.

Then there came the Japanese invasion. Japan and China are in many ways similar: Both faced similar circumstances that spurred them to modernize; both encountered the West about the same time; both had henceforth undertaken reforms. But due to their different development routes, their modernization processes finally became so different from each other's. While China demonstrated greater hesitance, Japan's commitment was more resolute. Japan state capacity grew greatly, which enabled it to join the ranks of the Western powers in their quests to dominate China, and proved to be the greediest. For China, the humiliating defeat in the first Sino-Japanese War spurred it to redouble its modernization effort – this is why some historians are arguing that the First Sino-Japanese War should be regarded as the starting point of China's modern history. Moreover, Hundred Days Reform, China's first effort to bring about constitutionalism is also a response to China's defeat to Japan. Losing the war to a "tiny island country" forced the Chinese ruling elites to reevaluate the situation, setting off a new wave of reform leading to strengthening coastal defense, introduction of Western books, and Westernization Movement. The subsequent Constitutionalist Movement might be directly triggered by the foreign invasion in the wake of the Boxers' Rebellion, but also had much to do with Japan's victory in the Russo-Japanese War, which convinced the Qing dynasty that an constitutionalist reform would bolster the nation's capacity as it did to Japan. After Yuan Shikai took power, Japan proposed to him the Twenty-One Demands, which, if accepted, could jeopardize China's sovereignty. The Twenty-One Demands, in conjunction with the international community's disregard of China's appeals to take back Germany's interests in Shandong, contributed greatly to the rise of domestic nationalist sentiment.

To recap, throughout the 1920s, the KMT government regained political control from Beiyang warlords and started implementation of Sun Yat-sen's three phase blueprint, however, this was interrupted with the deterioration of the relationship with Japan, and the eruption of Anti-Japanese War.

With mounting public angst and foreign invasion looming large, KMT hastened its constitutionalism effort to placate the public discontent. A more definitive plan concerning constitutionalism was released. After Mukden Incident and Shanghai Incident, the KMT government convened a National Crisis Conference in Luoyang, where several resolutions were passed. According to them, government would take steps to promote regional self-governance and phase out tutelage policies and convene Citizen Politics Participation Conference by October 10, 1932 in preparation for implementation of constitutionalism. Later, at the Fourth KMT Party Congress Third Plenary Session, more resolutions were passed, including (1) Consolidate resources and concentrate on war effort to fend off foreign aggressors; take measures to promote regional self-governance and carry on with constitutionalism preparations; (2) Convene national conference in March, 1935; finalize constitution draft and determine the release date; (3) Release final draft constitution for public review. After *May 5 Constitution Draft* was released in 1936, a resolution was passed at the KMT First Plenary Session of KMT First Committee, which decided the National Congress's deputies should be elected by November 12. This was however delayed when Marco Polo Bridge Incident broke up and Japan began their attack on Beiping. In 1939, at the KMT Fifth Committee 6th Plenary Session, another resolution was passed, deciding to convene National Congress on November 12, 1940. This was delayed due to the protraction of war – with half of the Chinese territory having fallen in the enemy hands, getting deputies transported from across the country to attend the congress was impossible. The situation stayed unchanged until the end of the Anti-Japanese War.

It is evident that KMT's party rule delayed the progress of constitutionalism, which in turn exacerbated domestic politics. The political disarray led to a ripple effect that spread into other sectors. Later, with the war becoming protracted, honoring its commitment to constitutionalism as planned became impossible for the KMT government. Thus we can see that the Japanese invasion was the main challenge for implementation of constitutionalism during the period.

Yet the biggest challenge came in the form of the conflict between KMT and CPC. Before the Northern Expedition, facing a common foe, the two parties joined hands in their military campaign. This alliance was further strengthened by the success Sun's positive view of the Soviet Union, and popularization of Marxism, which provided the ideological foundation on which Civil Revolution was carried out.

Around the time when CPC was established, Sun Yat-sen, inspired by communist ideology, thought it could be a new direction to carry on with China's state building. This, in conjunction with the success of the Russian Revolution, led to the two political parties' cooperation in the 1920s, and marked the first turn of direction since Xinhai Revolution. However, the basis of the alliance between the two was weak. With the KMT becoming increasingly aggressive in seeking dominance, CPC was forced to pursue a route of open confrontation and building military bases.

Due to ideological difference and mutual demonization, CPC and KMT's relationship soon deteriorated beyond reconciliation. Although both recognized the revolution, both claimed to be revolutionary parities, and the other the traitor. The fact is that their conceptions of revolution were distinctly different. For COC, revolution is more than regime change; it also entails social and cultural reform – a complete proletariat revolution. For KMT, revolution is limited to political sphere. Their goal was to defeat Beiyang warlords, install democracy and constitutionalism. Thus KMT pursued a limited revolution, whereas the communists believed in a complete revolution. Military conflict ensued. Such a conflict for political legitimacy not only deepened ideological animosity, but also shaped a new revolutionary culture – since both sides regarded their difference as a fundamental one, reconciliation was ruled out with neither side willing to giving ground.

However, up until Xi'an Incident, due to the imbalance of power, an equal dialogue between the two parities were impossible, not to mention for CPC to participate in the formulation of KMT-dominated constitution. Xi'an Incident again brought the two parties together to settle their dispute. This incident tipped the balance in favor of CPC. However the frequent skirmishes between the two during the Anti-Japanese War indicated the level of mutual trust remained weak, which presaged the final breakup. After Xi'an incident, especially during the Anti-Japanese War, CPC's military and political strength grew rapidly. Finally, it was confident enough to turn the table and force the later to acknowledge its status, thereby bringing an end to the party rule, turning the relationship from one-party domination to a bipartisan contestation.

After the Anti-Japanese War, the suspended constitution making resumed. It is possible that the KMT, after realizing CPC's increased strength, and shift of public sentiment, played with the thought of including CPC in its state building effort. This is corroborated by the resolution passed at the KMT Fifty Committee 11th Plenary

Session where postwar constitution making was discussed; the resolution enunciated that the government would seek to negotiate with CPC, which was confirmed by Chiang Kai-shek's invitation of Mao Zedong to visit Chongqing. It was rather unlikely that all these gestures were just political smokescreens.

As we said, the political trust between the two parties was weak. Despite previous cooperation, the relationship was plagued by lack of good will from both sides. While the KMT was wary of CPC's rapid growth, the communist also held bitter memory of KMT's persecution. Such relationship contributed to KMT government's final decision to cut out the CPC from its constitution making process and pursue a course of unilateralism. In retaliation, CPC pursued its "national liberation." Ostensibly, with the final announcement of the new constitution, KMT fulfilled its promise; it was widely regarded as a victory of democracy and rule of the law back in the day. But with the eruption of civil war, and KMT's fast defeat, the legal system and constitution lost its chance to make a lasting effect. In fact, the civil war is an outcome of the unique political pattern and inner contradictions of ROC era. As later-day historian Deng Ye commented: "A salient trait about Republic of China politics is the high level of unity of political and military power. As a result, a political party is also a military organization. During the period, it is common that political disputes were caused and settled by military means, which constrained political development during the era." "Underlying the bipartisan conflict, this shortcoming of military – political binity is evident. Military conflict was seen back then the only way to settle the dispute, however, as we shall see, military victory alone can't bring about democracy and order."[13]

The most negative outcome is discontinuation of constitutionalism. After the victory of the Anti-Japanese War, the public demand for political order reconstruction increased considerably. With solidarity greatly boosted, China was having a great opportunity to democratize its political system. However, neither CPC nor KMT seized the opportunity and as military conflict resumed, the best opportunity to install constitutionalism since Xinhai Revolution passed by.

3.3 Transformation of the Authoritarian Politics

In 1946, the new constitution was promulgated by People's Congress. Public announcement was scheduled on January 1, while the formal enactment was scheduled on December 25. Shortly afterwards, at the KMT Party Sixth Committee and Third Plenary Sessions, Constitution Implementation Preparation Bill was passed. On the same day the constitution took effect, the KMT government promulgated a law stipulating the tutelage would conclude the next year after the newly elected President take office. This marks the formal announcement of party rule and the tutelage. While the KMT was phasing out tutelage policies and prepared for

[13] See Deng Ye's *Coalition Government and One Party Tutelage*, Social Sciences Academy Press, 2003, Pp. 458–470.

constitutionalism, CPC, excluded from the constitution making process, escalated military effort with the aim being overthrowing KMT government. Under such circumstances, KMT government released the Mobilization for the Suppression of Communist Rebellion Provisional Act (MSCRPA) in April 1948. Martial law was instituted nationwide. As a result, some provisions of the new constitution were suspended, while the government expanded its power, to the detriment of individual liberty. Thus, instead of sending the country into constitutionalism, the conclusion of tutelage was ensued by "martial law" period, during which reform to implement liberty, democracy and constitutionalism was halted.

Immediately after KMT government's retreat to Taiwan, martial law was also instituted on the island, the only place the KMT legal system was preserved. As it turned out, authoritarianism ruled the island for decades, during which military tension and repressive policies often led to popular outcries demanding liberty and democracy. Finally, in 1980s, under the directive of Chiang Ching-kuo, heir of Chiang Kai-shek, martial law was lifted, sending Taiwan back on track to pursue democracy and constitutionalism. Since Chiang the junior's demise, Taiwan has already experienced two peaceful power transfers between incumbent and oppositional parties. Samuel Phillips Huntington once remarked that one of the greatest accomplishments in the mid-twentieth century world politics was the emergence of a government with proved capacity of managing China. Obviously, Mr. Huntington referred to the CPC government. However, one should not underestimate the significance of the successful transformation from authoritarianism to democratic constitutionalism in Taiwan. In fact, its significance reached far beyond the island province, for it served as an inspiration for the Chinese community worldwide. Such an outcome marked that the KMT had finally forsaken party rule and fully committed to democracy and constitutionalism.

How should we, the Mainland Chinese, view Taiwan's transformation from its party rule authoritarianism and martial law to constitutionalism in the late 1980s?[14] Traditionally it was disparaged as a hypocritical bourgeois democracy. Such a dismissive view is being replaced by a more positive one that see it as a transformation leading to true liberty and democracy, and it is beyond dispute that Taiwan's transformation led to implementation of certain respects of constitutionalism such as restricted government power and adherence to human rights. Such progress of political civilization shouldn't be dismissed as bourgeois hypocrisy and it is a pity that there are still large numbers of people on this side of the strait like to trivialize the constitutionalist value of Taiwanese transformation. These people couldn't see the positive political implications of Taiwan's democratization transformation because their ultra-leftist thinking, one of the legacies of the Cultural Revolution.

Another question that we need to ask ourselves is why could such a transformation be accomplished in Taiwan? Many scholars attributed its success to Taiwanese people's unyielding struggles. While we acknowledge its value, it is also worthwhile to review the historical background. During the martial law period, Taiwan

[14] Read more about Taiwan's transformation to democracy, see Zhu Yunhan's *Taiwan Democracy Transformation: Revelation and Experience*, Social Sciences Academic Press, 2012.

was a political pressure cooker, where arbitrary violations of liberty and human rights abounded. Many horrendous events, such as the Free China Incident, Kaohsiung Incident, and Jiang Nan Incident, occurred during this period. Under the Martial Law, people's liberty and basic human rights, such as right to assembly, the right to form community, the right to speech, and publication, were stamped upon; freedom of speech was suppressed in general; the government leveraged the laws to justify its arbitrary arrests; political dissidents were trialed by military courts, imprisoned and even executed, among them the Leftists and those who were not even politically active. During the period between 1950 and 1987 when the martial law was announced, an estimated 29,000 political cases were reported, involving a total of 140,000 individuals, among them 3,000 to 4,000 were executed. The high political pressure maintained social order in short term, was impossible to sustainable over long term. For KMT, if it didn't seek self-redemption actively, its rule might be toppled in a new round of revolution. Its negative consequences notwithstanding, the martial law owed its legitimacy to the MSCRPA, is on solid legal ground; moreover, it was justified by the long-standing military confrontation. Under such circumstances, the only option to facilitate social development would be to revise the MSCRPA. Although some regarded that Chiang Kai-shek's revision of MSCRPA as a ruse that aimed to maintain his dictatorial power, such a move had provided a breather for the suppressed Taiwan democracy cause.

Also worth noting is that even though during the martial law period, Taiwan was under MSCRPA since 1949, the framework of constitutionalism remained functional in certain respects. For example, congress elections continued. "During a space of 31 years starting from 1950 and ending in 1981, from election of congressmen, county mayor, to National Congress membership election, from Legislation Committee membership election to General Election, a total of 43 elections were conducted, averaging 1.4 per year."[15] "In 1966 and later in 1972, amendments were introduced into the Provisional Clauses allowing certain offices at the Supervision and Legislation branch of the National Congress to be directly elected in Taiwan. Although freedom of speech, freedom of the press, freedom of publishing, freedom of association and assembly are still restricted, and the government implemented a rigorous ban on all other political parties, some non-KMT candidates, even some critical of KMT, got elected through the elections."[16] In addition, regional self-governance, a key part of the tutelage, was exercised in Taiwan, largely free from the Provisionary Clauses and Martial Law Order. Through the practice of election and regional self-governance, the public received necessary training to participate in democratic politics.[17]

[15] See Cao Siyuan's *Taiwan Constitutionalism Transformation and Revelation*, Changcheng Monthly Journal, issue 3, 2010.

[16] See Chen Hongyi's *Taiwan and Hong Kong Constitutionalism Development*, Academia Sinica Jurisprudence Journal inaugural issue.

[17] See Cao Siyuan's *Taiwan Constitutionalism Transformation and Revelation*, Changcheng Monthly Journal, issue 3, 2010.

It is beyond dispute that Chiang Ching-kuo's political decision at a critical moment was pivotal to the transformation. While KMT remained indecisive regarding democratization, Chiang singlehanded undid the shackles of Martial Law and lifted the ban on freedom of association and press, which demonstrated great political courage and vision. Such a move is vital for the return of freedom to the people. When commenting on Chang the junior's decision on revoking the martial law, the new Taiwan leader Ma Ying-jeou said: "Why did Mr. Ching-kuo make such a great decision in his late age? He spent his younger years in the Soviet Union and Western democracy was not on the curriculum. After his return, Chiang devoted himself to a military career during the Anti-Japanese War and Civil War. After the retreat to Taiwan, he was in charge of intelligence and political warfare departments. One would assume that with such an experiences, he would have a worldview of simplistic black and white and unable to accept the new trend. There are ample examples that when such a man was put in power, the country and society would have suffered. Yet what is truly remarkable about Mr. Ching-kuo is that he could always break away from boundaries imposed by circumstances, be them family background, upbringing, education and intellectual development, and make sound and pragmatic decisions."[18]

Today, over two decades had passed since the lift of the martial law in 1987. During the time, although the constitutionalism was not without defects, nobody should deny that since 1987, and especially the abolishment of the MSCRPA in 1991, the first General Election in 1996, and two power transfers among incumbent and oppositional parties respectively in 2000 and 2008, a democratic, free constitutionalist system had took hold in Taiwan. Of course, the political identification with a new Taiwan and Independence Movement could potentially led things to go astray, and cause disturbance to the cross-strait relationship and risk the future prospect. However, these were more than a challenge to the Taiwanese constitutionalist institutions, but rather a test of maturity and wisdom of politicians on both sides. The success of Taiwan's transformation also poses a question to us: In what way should we turn China into a mature, modern and civilized country where rule of law is upheld?

---

[18] Ma Ying-jeou's Remember Mr. Chiang Jingkuo, 21ccom.net: http://new.21ccom.net/plus/view.php?aid=16479 September 3, 2010.

Chapter 4
Revolutionary Legal System: From Common Program to 1975 Constitution

The success of the Anti-Japanese War opened a new window of opportunity for China to undertake peaceful state building. However, the long bitter strife between CPC and KMT greatly diminished any hope of reconciliation between the two parties. Following a 3-year civil war, CPC emerged victorious. With the end of war nearing, CPC set about to implement its state-building plans. The CPC revolutionaries took a different view about the country's future than KMT's Three People Principles; they believed the ROC (Republic of China) legal system was a symbol of the old, something that must be smashed, and replaced by a brand new communist one.

There is a clear fault line in the six decades of history following New China's establishment in 1949. Revolution remained to be the theme in the first three decades prior to the conclusion of the Cultural Revolution; in the second three decades following the conclusion of the Cultural Revolution, however, reform would replace revolution to be the new theme.

We will review the two periods in detail in the following paragraphs.

Three constitutional documents were announced during the first three decades of New China – the *Common Program*, the *54 Constitution* and the *75 Constitution*. Although the three documents reflected different states of politics, their characters and spirits different from one another, all of them followed the same inner logic. The *Common Program*, the first of the three, laid down the premise; its successor, *54 constitution* is an development of the premise, which culminated in the form of *75 Constitution* and was brought to its conclusion as well. While the revolutionary legal-political theory reached one after another "peaks", tragedies befell many families.

Q. Gao et al., *The Road to the Rule of Law in Modern China*,
Research Series on the Chinese Dream and China's Development Path,
DOI 10.1007/978-3-662-45637-8_4

4.1 "Abolish Old Codes" Movement and Onset of New China

4.1.1 Two Addresses in 1949: Extend the Legal Coherence and "Carry the Revolution Through to the End"

The revolutionary slogan – "only when the old is removed, the new can be installed" may sound commonsensical today. Yet such is the intrinsic nature of the Chinese revolution and to a great extent determined the fate of New China's legal system reform. The *Six Codes* a comprehensive body of laws, the highest achievement of legislation during the ROC era. It includes the constitution, civil law, commercial law, criminal law, civil procedure law and criminal procedure law. Yet this system was disparaged by CPC as evidence of KMT's betrayal of the revolution and a tool to maintain its reactionary dictatorship. Such repudiation was made more from a political perspective, rather than a jurisprudential one. The only KMT legislation that CPC recognized at that time was the *Resolution of Political Consultation Conference* (1946), and those regarding the Coalition Government, which to CPC was the "expression of Chinese people's constituent will". Although the KMT's 1947 Constitution mainly based upon the Resolution would be suspended by MSCRPA at the outbreak of the Civil War, it's authority remained to be recognized by KMT.

In 1949, in his New Year Address, KMT leader Chiang Kai-shek's assured the public that his government was willing to parley with CPC on the condition that ROC state form and legal system to be retained in the new government. Given KMT's breach of *October 10th Agreement* and the *Resolution of Political Consultation Conference* (1946), it is unlikely that CPC would accept the terms. For CPC, Civil War was justified both by its communist doctrines, as well as its rightful demand to put those responsible for the war to justice. If the agreement between the parties can be seen as a political contract, then KMT faced liability in both legal and political sense. Therefore it is clear that the ROC institutions hinged on KMT's political survival. In Chiang's New Year Address, he offered to "take personal responsibility" for the war, which was duly turned down by CPC, who viewed Chiang as merely one of the war criminals, and insisted the entire KMT political and legal system, rather than individuals, should be held responsible for the war.

Soon after Chiang Kai-shek's address, Mao Zedong also made his address. In it, Mao urged the revolution be "complete". He described the ultimate goal of the revolution as building a republic of "people's democratic dictatorship": "The question facing the entire Chinese people and people's organizations is whether should we carry the revolution through to its end or give up halfway. If we carry the revolution through, then all reactionary forces must be destroyed. We should be resolute in our fight against imperialism, feudalism and bureaucratic capitalism, and ultimately, overthrow the reactionary rule of the kuomintang nationwide and establish a republic of people's democratic dictatorship. In the new republic, the proletariat will be the leading class, and the worker-peasant alliance will be the power base." This people's democratic dictatorship, its proletarian leadership, and worker-peasant alliance power base, was poles apart from the ROC political and legal form that Chiang tried to preserve; moreover, it is also different from the New Democracy state form that Mao himself delineated in his *On Coalition Government*. That Mao changed his goal to building a socialist country people's democratic dictatorship seems to suggest that the New Democracy coalition government is merely an expedient. By referencing a fable about a farmer saved a snake and got killed by it, Mao Zedong made it abundantly clear that CPC was not to compromise.

On April 22, 1949, Nanjing was captured. Mao wrote a poem *The PLA Captures Nanjing* around this time. The poem echoed the point he made previously that the revolution must be "carried through to the end". Literary value aside, the poem gives us some inklings about Mao's mindset: "With power and to spare we must pursue the tottering foe. Not ape Xiang Yu the conqueror seeking idle fame." Such relentlessness is characteristic of radical revolution, which is contrasted by constitutionalism's conciliatoriness. The later is closer to the ideal of Confucianism: to educate and enlighten rather than to expel and exclude. Such Chinese wisdom would find an similar expression in the west in the form of Baron Acton's adage "compromise is the soul of politics". Compromise, as we shall see, is indeed the essence of the modern constitutionalism.

The addresses from both leaders showed two types of personalities; it also revealed the unreachable gap between their political philosophies and revolutionary ideals. More importantly, they offer us a window from which we can see where the new China legal system modernization was going.

4.1.2 The Essential Logic of Revolution: Innovation and Breakaway

To understand China's legal system modernization, one has to understand its revolution. Mao Zedong's expression of "carrying the revolution through to the end" in the 1949 New Year address as well as his purported goal of establishing "people's democratic dictatorship" suggest that in the revolutionaries' minds, revolution was synonymous to modernity. For CPC, the word *ge ming* or revolution, here has little to do with its Chinese traditional usage, such as *Tang Wu Ge Ming*. Neither was it related to the British conservative revolution. Its lineage can be traced back to French Revolution, with whom, both are class revolutions characterized for their "breakaway" from tradition. This "breakaway" is the essence of the Chinese revolution as of 1949: its objective, rather than establishing a new government, was to form a new society, therefore Chiang Kai-shek's hope that the state form and legal system of Republic of China could be preserved was bound to be in vain. The KMT leader displayed little understanding of the "breakaway" aspect of the communist revolution.

If breakaway is CPC revolution's answer to tradition, then innovation is its attitude towards the future. The communist revolutionaries saw the new state they were to build not another dynastic cycle, but the beginning of a completely new time. Today, debates linger regarding the qualification of the Hundred Days Reform as a "revolution". The three movements that occurred in its wake were less controversial – Xinhai Revolution put an end to monarchism; New Culture Movement renounced the tradition and sought cultural rebirth; the 1949 Communist Revolution brought about a "proletarian dictatorship". Once we understand this logic of the revolution, it is not surprising that the old institutions would be abandoned.

4.1.3 Revolution's Breakaway Logic Applied in Legal System: Abolishment of the Six Codes

In February 1949, shortly after the capture of Beiping, the CPC Central Committee issued a directive titled *On Abolishing the Nationalist's Six Codes and Establishing Judicial Principles in the Liberated Regions*.[1] The directive, drafted by Wang Ming, a CPC leader who studied law in Soviet Union, announced the abolishment of the *Six Codes*. The directive was also a resounding rejection of Chiang Kai-shek's proposal expressed in his New Year address. By this time, Nanjing was still controlled by KMT and the new Political Consultancy Conference had not been convened. As a result, this directive was only applicable in the CPC-controlled "liberated regions".

The *Directive* has six provisions; the first four are a recital of the negative consequences of the *Six Codes* and justification for the abolishment. The fifth provision described the legal and legislation system in the liberated regions, as well as CPC's policy towards law professionals who had served in the KMT judicial system. The final item requested CPC party cadres to study the directive.

The abolishment of the *Six Codes* sounded the trumpets for a broader Anti-Old Law Movement. In adherence to the spirit of "destroy the old to introduce the new", reeducation programs were set up to "reeducate" the ROC law professionals; constitution making was given top priority, leading to the promulgation of the *Common Program* by the Chinese People's Political Consultative Conference; and later the promulgation of the *54 Constitution* in 1954. The *Common Program*'s origin can be traced to Mao Zedong's elaboration on New Democracy constitution and Coalition Government. Mao believed that the new China should be a New Democracy Republic where "all revolutionary classes have a joint dictatorship". In *Constitutionalism and the Foundation of State*, scholar Ji Pomin took an positive view on the New Democracy concept: "the New Democracy is both the guiding political theory of the Chinese revolution and the guiding constitutionalist theory for China's new government."

[1] See the full text of the Directive on People Online: http://cpc.people.com.cn/GB/64184/64186/66650/4491574.html

Ji Pomin also argues New Democracy and *Common Program* held the answer to why China chose this particular development route.[2] This opinion was echoed by Professor Chen Duanhong, who believed that *Common Program* put forward a third road other than the route of a KMT-dominated government and a CPC-dominated government one. When compared with the KMT constitution, the ideas behind *Common Program* and the formulation were noted for their indigeneity. In comparison, later, when the entire country increasingly looked up to the Soviet Union, the creation of *54 Constitution* was greatly influenced by the 1936 Soviet Union Constitution. However, aside from the most basic political principles, most of the provisions and especially those concerning citizens' rights in the *Common Program* failed to be carried into execution in everyday practice. When it came to the normal laws, directives and movements reigned supreme whereas regular legislation was constantly delayed. As a result, for decades, the New China didn't have civil law, criminal law or procedure law. Such a legislation stalemate lasted throughout the Mao era. It was until later when the Reform and Opening-up policy was adopted, legislation began to normalize. A number of factors, including lack of common laws, lack of sufficient legal training and education, hindered China's legal system modernization; legal development was impaired due to excessive "politicization" and "democratization". Overall, New China legal system modernization during the Mao era is noted for its tendency of "politicization" and "democratization" which had much to do with the chaos that was seen during this period of time. Such characteristics can be traced back to the legal practice in CPC-controlled liberated regions during the Civil War. Also noteworthy is that while "democracy" is upheld in both constitutions, a check and balance system was absent in both, which led to serious consequences on the New China legal institutions.[3]

4.1.4 Mao Zedong's Three Theories on Democracy Constitution: New Democracy, New Democracy Constitutionalism and Coalition Government

Mao Zedong began his theorization over China's state building in the middle stage of the Anti-Japanese War. His thoughts during this time were crystalized into his "three theories" – the New Democracy theory (Jan, 1940), New Democracy constitutionalism (Feb, 1940), Coalition Government theory (Apr, 1945). These theories would exert great influence over the formulation of new China's first constitution, thereby should be regarded as highly significant when it comes to study of China's constitutionalism.

[2] See Ji Pomin's *Constitutionalism and the Essence of State – reflection and review on New Democracy and Common Program*, Hong Kong Strong Wind Publishing House, 2007.

[3] The Federalists were mainly concerned with separation of powers and check and balance instead of democracy, as well as how to tame democracy by institute a sound legal structure to tame democracy, which differs greatly from CPC leaders' conception of constitutionalism circa 1949.

4.1.4.1 New Democracy: A New and Comprehensive State-Building Theory

On New Democracy was published in the January issue of *Chinese Culture* magazine in 1940. In the article, Mao Zedong systemically delineated his New Democracy theory. At that time, the Anti-Japanese War had entered the phase of attrition. KMT leader Wang Jingwei's collaboration led to a new wave of defeatism among the public. In a time when China seemed to be tittering on the brink of defeat, Mao's article came as a beacon light that guided the public regarding Chinese political and cultural development. In the article Mao argued that China's new revolution demanded a new culture; this new culture would not only have to transcend the traditional one, but also needed to be more progressive than the one that proposed by Sun Yat-sen in his Three People's Principles. Given that the May 4 Movement had already established a solid foundation of cultural radicalism, such an argument was not surprising. What is more controversial is the bit regarding Sun Yat-sen's Three People's Principles, for the Principles was not only the foundation of the first cooperation of KMT and CPC, but also the basis of the Anti-Japanese National United Front.

Describing CPC's target in the cultural construction, Mao wrote: "We the communists… want to build a new China, build a new Chinese culture – this is our goal in the cultural realm."[4] In the article, Mao coined the phase of "Chinese National New Culture". In order to prove Chinese revolutionary legitimacy, this form of culture combined elements of both nationalism and revolutionariness, hence foretold the direction of cultural development – sinolization of Marxism. As for the scope, Mao believed that it should be more than a political-economic revolution, but a cultural one as well – such idea would be corroborated by the Cultural Revolution. In the article, Mao applied the old-new dichotomy quite frequently, a manifestation of the "breakaway" spirit of Marxist historical view and the May 4 Cultural Radicalism.

The new Chinese culture that CPC tried to install was meant to be a revolutionary culture that would facilitate the Chinese revolutionary task. This is the rationale behind Mao's Two Phase theory, which divided the revolution up into the Democracy Revolution phase and Socialist Revolution phase.

The concept of New Democracy contained three components – the economic, the cultural and the political. The economic target largely repeats Sun Yat-sen's vision of "restrain capital", "equal rights to the use of land"; at the cultural level, it demanded a "national culture" that is both scientific and popular. As for the political, the New Democracy is a mixed bag of Three People's Principles, sinofied Marxism, and Mao's state-building theory.

Mao's New Democracy theory is deeply rooted in the Chinese revolutionary tradition and sinofication of Marxism, hence to understand New Democracy theory, one has to have a proper grasp of its relationship with Sun Yat-sen's Three People's Principles and the Marxist ideology. As for the relationship between the two, Mao

[4] Ibid., P. 624.

commented that: "the Three People's Principle and communism have much in common, but they are also different in some respects:

1. Commonality: Both served as most fundamental guidelines in the stage of bourgeois democracy revolution.
2. Differences:

   (a) Some divergence concerning specifics
   (b) Whether there should be a socialist revolution
   (c) Different worldviews
   (d) Degree of completeness"[5]

Mao Zedong then compared the old version of Three People's Principles with the new one, which was first announced at KMT's First National Congress in 1924. According to Mao, the Three People's Principles that New Democracy revolution acknowledges and adheres to is the new version, which differs from its predecessor in that the later added some pro-Soviet, pro-communist content. This new version of Principles was recognized by the Left Wing of KMT, but rejected by the anti-CPC Right Wing, who insisted that the older version was the only legitimate. Thus Mao's theory not only systematically explained CPC's revolutionary vision, but also served to isolate the Right Wing KMT.

Mao Zedong's democratic state-building theory previously put forward the Coalition Government theory, which outlined the state form and the political form. The state form concerns the status of different social classes in the new state while the political form addresses the question of how the new regime should be constructed, or that "the state apparatus enabling the ruling class to protect itself and defend against its enemies."

Mao Zedong defines the New China's state form as "united dictatorship of all revolutionary classes". According to him, "the country will be a democratic republic ruled by a joint dictatorship formed by all the Chinese people who stand against imperialism and feudalism. These parities would be united under the leadership of the proletariat. This is the New Democracy Republic, a republic that upholds the New Three People's Principles and implements the Three Policies." He also posited that "All countries in the world fall into three groups depending on their ruling classes: (1) republic of bourgeois and capitalist dictatorship; (2) republic of proletarian dictatorship; (3) republic of joint dictatorship of multiple revolutionary classes."[6] Mao's coalition government theory as a state building solution shines political wisdom. It is neither Euro-American parliamentary democracy, nor a Soviet Union style proletarian dictatorship, but a government where different classes are united by a sense of common mission, a pan-democracy in the broader sense of the word. This topic would be further elaborated in his other two articles – the *New Democracy Constitutionalism* and *On Coalition Government.*

[5] Ibid., Pp. 648–649.
[6] Ibid., Pp. 635–637.

Here Mao Zedong also put forward the "democratic centralism" concept: "Election will be held at the National People's Congress (NPC), provincial-level congresses, county-level congresses and township-level congresses. Government would be elected by people's deputies. Voters will not be discriminated for sex, religion, wealth, and educational background. Only through such truly equal elections, revolutionary classes' status could be secured, true public opinion be expressed and revolutionary struggles in accordance with the spirit of New Democracy could be conducted and directed effectively. That is what I call a system of democratic centralism." This "democratic centralism" would be the basic principle of the NPC system. Because *On New Democracy* was published during the Anti-Japanese War, Mao drew on his experience of building the Anti-Japanese National United Front. During the war, in CPC controlled regions, a Three-Three system was adopted – this system is widely accepted as an embodiment of Mao's conception of democratic constitutionalism.

4.1.4.2 New Democracy Constitutionalism: Mao Zedong's "Democratic Constitutionalism"

Shortly after *On New Democracy* was published, Mao Zedong made a speech at the Constitutionalism Promotion Conference[7] in Yan'an, CPC's wartime base. In his speech, Mao elaborated on his Democracy Constitutionalism and addressed a number of related questions. The conference was held shortly after KMT launched a new propaganda campaign publicizing its effort to implement constitutionalism. The KMT's propaganda led to confusion among some CPC members. Under such circumstances, Mao placed a strong emphasis in his speech on the democratic dimension of constitutionalism.

Mao Zedong began the speech by identifying two factors that had prevented successful implementation of constitutionalism in China: Lack of independence and lack of democracy. These two conditions corresponded roughly with the two overarching themes of Chinese modern revolution, namely, anti-imperialism and anti-feudalism; they also defined the external and internal borders of China's modern state sovereignty. Mao elaborated: "The answer (to true constitutionalism) is democratic politics. What kind of democratic politics are we striving for? The answer is New Democracy Politics and New Democracy Constitutionalism. It is not the old obsolete European and American-style democracy, which is democracy of bourgeois and capitalist dictatorship. Neither is it the Soviet-style, proletarian dictatorship democracy. … In the future, when conditions are met, we will implement a Soviet-style socialist democracy. But in view of the current conditions, the democratic politics that China truly needs is neither bourgeois democracy nor socialist

[7] See Mao Zedong's *New Democracy constitutionalism, Selected Works of Mao Zedong,* People's Publishing House, 1964.

democracy, but the New Democracy and the constitutionalism that we are striving for is New Democratic Constitutionalism."[8]

Here Mao Zedong used an "equation" to summarize his understanding of constitutionalism: "constitutionalism = democratic politics". Orthodox normativist constitutional scholars probably would disagree; for them, such an equation would better be "constitutionalism = limited government" or "constitutionalism = judicial review". In this legalist understanding of constitution, constitution is the higher law, a law that restrained democracy, thereby functions as an institutional safeguard to procedural democracy. Yet Mao's understanding focused more on the political and functional respects of constitutionalism, thus for him, implementation of democracy is a critical part of constitutionalism. How did Mao arrive at such a view, instead of adopting the law scholars' formalist and legalist one? This has much to do with Mao's unique perception and understanding of history, especially China's unsuccessful attempts at constitutionalism.

When describing the nature of constitution, Mao Zedong said "all forms of constitutionalism, no matter the British model, the French model, the American model, or Soviet Union model, took the form of a set of fundamental laws being enacted after democracy was established through revolution. (Only after such conditions were met,) the laws can be called constitution."[9] However, China's experience was different from that of Britain, France or America. Mao noted: "It is very easy to make a constitution, or to elect a President. But what about the democracy and liberty? We saw neither having been delivered. China had several constitutions already. Even Cao Kun (Note: a President of ROC who notorious for corruption) made a constitution. As for Presidents, there are even more. But where is democracy and liberty?"[10]

Based on his understanding of world experience of constitutionalism, Mao Zedong divided the task of realizing constitutionalism into three stages: "revolution", "realization of democracy" and "recognition". He pointed out the most critical of the three is the second– "realization of democracy". To accomplish constitutionalism, Mao contended, the revolutionary classes must seize state power; once this is achieved, the rest would fall into place naturally, as the constitution is little more than an official confirmation of the status quo. Obviously, Mao's understanding of the constitutionalism is pragmatist and history-based rather than jurisprudential; neither did he go into detail explaining the specific implementation measures and safeguarding measures. Such an understanding is clearly substantialist. Mao focuses on the systematic support that democracy would provide to the cause of constitutionalism as well as realization and maintenance of democracy rather than individual equality and liberty. Such an understanding of democracy appears to have much in common with the British "political constitution" theories, though the latter is

[8] Ibid., Pp. 690–691.
[9] Ibid., p. 693.
[10] Ibid., p. 694.

primarily concerned with everyday scenarios and procedures,[11] while Mao's theory and practice evidently reached beyond the purview of Western "democratic constitutionalism".

Mao Zedong contended that China was in the middle of the second stage, namely the stage of realization of democracy: "China is different. Its revolution hasn't succeeded yet. Although democratic politics has been achieved in the liberated regions, national implementation has not been accomplished. China remains a half-colonized, half-feudalistic state. In view of this situation, even a sound constitution would have limited effect and it would be diminished by the feudalist and traditional forces. Therefore it is impossible to truly implement a constitution right now. The task of our constitutionalist movement is to realize democracy first, rather than to make a constitution to recognize that democracy has been established. This will be a hard battle. It is not something that can be done at one stroke." [12] Mao believed that to achieve New Democracy Constitutionalism, democracy must be established prior to implementation of constitution as European countries and American did. He then surmised that without a sound democracy, constitution is meaningless. Worth noting is that by democracy, Mao meant more than universal suffrage and political liberty in the general sense, but a revolutionary classes' "dictatorial democracy", a condition that can only be achieved through class struggle. He also used the example of Latin American pseudo-democracies to support his substantialist view of constitutionalism.

In keeping with the logic in *On New Democracy,* Mao Zedong defined New Democracy constitutionalism as "a coalition dictatorship formed by multiple revolutionary classes". If previously the "revolutionary class" concept is only loosely defined, here provided a clearer definition.

Mao Zedong's view on New Democracy constitutionalism, constructed on historical and political basis, would prove to have long-lasting effect on China's constitutionalism and legal system modernization. It ushered in a new era when the concept of "democracy" dominated the Chinese socialist practices and theory, and to certain extent led to law scholars supporting "judicialization of constitution" being sidelined. Such a view was so influential that even today we still haven't walked out its shadow – one example is the contentious debate over "democracy take precedence" versus "rule of law take precedence" and lingering dispute regarding the nature and direction of the Chinese constitutionalism. However, one shouldn't be too critical of Mao; his New Democracy Constitutionalism theory is a politician's view grounded in historical facts; his great insights let him to be aware of the problems that hindered constitutionalism back in his own time. Thereby for today's law theorists, if they want to critique Mao, they must address the problems that Mao identified some 70 years ago, which is still highly pertinent in today's world.

[11] See Tian Feilong, *Coexistent and Prior: A Theory of Political Constitution within Normal Politics*, Journal of Beihang University (Social Sciences Edition), Vol. 27, No. 3, 2014.

[12] See Mao Zedong's New Democracy constitutionalism, Selected Works of Mao Zedong, People's Publishing House, 1964, p. 693.

4.1.4.3 *On Coalition Government*

The topic of post-war state building, which *On New Democracy* and *New Democracy Constitutionalism* refrained from touching on, was elaborated by *On Coalition Government*. In the report, first publicized at CPC's 7th Party Congress, Mao delineated his state-building theory, which is a fairly realistic plan to bring about democracy in China and by all accounts, coherent with the articles that came before it theoretically and politically.

As the war approaching its end, Mao foresaw the priority would soon be switched from military campaign to meeting people's postwar political demands, including "convening the National People's Congress on a democratic basis; form a formal coalition democratic government participated by all political parties and personalities without party affiliation." Mao envisaged that the new "government will lead the Chinese people in the postwar construction to turn China into an independent, free, democratic, unified and prosperous state" .[13] If Mao's plan was carried out, the state power can be transferred from one ruling party to a coalition of different parties; with a representation system in place, factional conflicts among the parties would be softened and ideals such as "independence", "liberty", "democracy", "unification", "prosperity" would be upheld. With victory of the war already in sight, the coalition government idea gained great public support. Neither KMT nor CPC wanted to be perceived as obstructive to the cause. Thanks to their effort, political consultation conference was convened soon.

In *On Coalition Government* Mao reviewed KMT and CPC's performances during the war, as well as their relationship and political positions. In describing CPC's political guidelines, Mao repeated his points already expressed in his *On New Democracy* and *New Democratic Constitutionalism*. In terms of the relationship between CPC Leadership and Coalition Government / Joint Dictatorship as well as the party-politics relationship and cross-party relationship, Mao wrote: "A New Democracy state based on coalition of multiple classes is fundamentally different from a socialist state of proletariat class dictatorship. Although it is without doubt that New Democracy institutions would be constructed under the leadership of the proletariat and the communist party, as long as China was still in the stage of New Democracy period, we can't and shouldn't seek to build a single class dictatorship, or a one party government. As long as the other parties are willing to cooperate with us, then there should be no reason that we do not work with them. In Soviet Union, although the government was formed by one party – the Bolshevik, it still pursues a policy of "alliance of workers, farmers and intellectuals", rather than building a one party system or a system of an alliance of parties; such a design enabled people other than workers or Bolsheviks to work in the government agencies too."[14]

Mao also stressed that the proletariat and CPC should assume overall leadership in the construction of the new state; such leadership should also be reflected in the

[13] See Mao Zedong's On Coalition Government, Selected works of Mao Zedong, People's publishing house, 1964, Pp. 930–931.

[14] Ibid., Pp. 962–963.

constitution making once the new state was established. Yet he also suggested that a New Democracy government should not be controlled by neither a single class nor a single party, went so far as hinting at possibility of including KMT in the new government, though how sincere Mao was is anyone's guess. If this description of CPC leadership is just a way to emphasize CPC's contribution to the revolution, while the constitution-making right remain to be placed in the hands of the people's representatives, then such an arrangement would remain congruent with modern democratic constitutionalism ideal; however, if the leadership means monopoly of constituent right, then, it would devoid the coalition government theory of modern progressive element. Who will be eligible to join the government is of little constitutional relevance, given that it is more an organic law problem, rather than constitutional problem. In addition, if the coalition government stopped at achieving a class or political parties representation system, rather than an individual citizens' representation system, it would still fall short of the standard of modern democratic constitutionalism. In spite of the elaboration, questions remained who would represent the people and who will exercise the power of making political decisions.

In his speech addressing to an audience of CPC cadres and members of minority democratic parties, Mao Zedong proposed a two-step plan to implement democracy: "First, we should form a provisional government approved by representatives of parties and non-party affiliation personalities. Second, convene People's Congress which will be attended by people's representatives elected through a free and fair election; then form a coalition government open to all classes and parties willing to join. Under a common program, we will strive to win the Anti-Japanese War and build a new state."[15]

Worth noting is that Mao's conception of Democratic Constitutionalism is built grounded in his unique representation theory and constituent power theory. A central premise of the representation theory is CPC is the only true representative of proletariat, representative of the vast majority of the public. Such an idea derived its legitimacy from Marxist doctrines, and, to a lesser degree, CPC's contribution to the Chinese revolution. In Mao's theory, the smallest units eligible to exercise constituent power are classes, as opposed to individual citizens; constitution making was participated by parties representing their own classes, whereas individual citizens held no place. The democracy theory that Mao proposed has two components: an election-based constitution-making system and "cooperation-style political participation" system. The minority parties' eligibility to participate in constitution making hinged on whether they recognize CPC as the sole legitimate representative of proletariat and whether they approve CPC's political guidelines. This is a rather simplistic criteria to decide whether a party is revolutionary – as long as a party recognizes CPC, it is regarded as revolutionary and democratic, otherwise, it would be reactionary, undemocratic, and should be subject to the "dictatorship". This dichotomy sows the seed that would give rise to tension between Mao's representation theory and the conventional democracy procedure theories. This origin of such tension can be traced to Mao's coalition government theory, yet would take a long

[15] Ibid., Pp. 969–970.

time to manifest itself. At that time CPC's top concern was pressurizing KMT to uphold democracy and winning over minority political parties to its side. Given the circumstances, the democratic constitutionalism theories were designed to rally support from minority parties. Later with KMT removed from the scene, such pressure was no longer existent. Overall, *On Coalition Government* is representative of Mao's thoughts on liberty, unification, land reform and industry development of that time; it also outlined CPC's political agenda and constitution making plan.

4.1.4.4 History Cycles and Democracy: Mao's Talk with Huang Yanpei in Yan'an

Shortly after the CPC's Seventh Congress, Mao Zedong met with Huang Yanpei, a renowned progressive political activist who visited Yan'an. Prior to the meeting, Huang knew little about CPC. All his knowledge was from Edgar Snow's 1938 book *Red Star Over China*. In 1945, upon his return, Huang, to the chagrin of KMT, published a book titled Return from Yan'an in which he recounted his visit. Huang's visit to Yan'an opened a dialogue between CPC and other progressive political forces in the KMT controlled regions. Especially worth noting about Huang's trip is his meeting with Mao about the historical vicious cycle.

On July 4, 1945, Mao Zedong invited Huang Yanpei to visit him at home. Following an exchange of pleasantry, Mao asked Huang about his impressions of Yan'an. Huang said emotively: "I have lived over 60 years and have bore witness to, not to mention heard about, rises and falls of several regimes. A man, a family, an organization, a region, or a country, it appears that none of them could break free the law of historical cycle. Once a regime was established, everyone was enthusiastic and great efforts were pulled to improve it despite the high odds against it. When the environment improved, people began to slacken in their effort. As time passes, this slackening became widespread and became so strong that even the most powerful leader couldn't reverse it. The expanded territory drained administrative capacity. When situation worsened, the rulers would often be caught ill-prepared. As the old sayings goes: "Lazy emperor led to powerful eunuchs". "When the emperors die, they take their dynasties with them". All in all, nobody seem to have got away with this cycle. I have learned a little about the CPC, and I hope you can find a new way to break free from it." Pondered a moment, Mao said confidently: "We have found the new path. It is called democracy. As long as the public maintains their oversight of the government, the government will not slacken in its efforts. When everyone takes responsibility there will be no danger that things will return to how they were even if the leader has gone." Huang expressed agreement: "Only by involving the public in decision making, can the power lust of politicians be curtailed; only by disclosing state affairs to the public, can people commit to apply themselves to make their country a prosperous place. Using democracy to break free the law of vicious cycle, this is perhaps the most effective way."[16]

The historical cycle seems to be a curse that had beset Chinese politics. As much as Huang was impressed by the vigor and spirit demonstrated by the CPC, he was aware that many new dynasties were also very vigorous at the beginning. As a rule, the first generations of rulers were often the most diligent, capable, but such qualities were hard to sustain. Eventually a line was crossed and the dynasties embarked on a road towards destruction with no return. Mao's reply might come off as a bit grandiose and short on details. He mentioned "people's oversight" and "individual responsibility", but didn't explain how such concepts could be realizaed. In comparison, Huang's reply was more technical-oriented, as he talked about a democratic decision making system and regional self-governance in the form of a federal state form allowing local political matters to be decided locally.

Although both invoked the concept of democracy in their speeches, it was evident that they meant different things. Mao is more inclined towards a "pan-democracy", which is in many ways different of Huang's normativist understanding of democracy. However, such engagement of thoughts took place more at a philosophical level, hence both sides were general rather than specific, which prevented their divergence from being revealed. However, following the establishment of new China, with development of political and legal system, these fundamental differences would soon manifest.

4.1.4.5 Summary: A Pan-democratic Constitutionalist View

To recap, Mao Zedong's *On Coalition Government,* published at the final stage of Anti-Japanese War, expressed CPC's outlook over the post-war state; it is logically coherent with Mao's views, especially his New Democracy theory and New Democracy constitutionalism theory. It was also meant to be a rebuttal to Chang Kai-shek's *China's Destiny*.[17] The article laid bare the differences between CPC and KMT in ideology and methodology as to how to carry on with China's revolution. Overall, it is an expression of CPC's view regarding the future revolution, especially that democracy should be the direction and fundamental method of China's state building and constitutionalism.

New democracy theory, new democracy constitutionalism theory and coalition government theory formed the bulk of Mao Zedong's thoughts on democracy and constitutionalism. As a statesman and party leader, the pan-democratic constitutionalism view that Mao took set a new trend in terms of democratic constitutionalism thinking; this way of thinking would become the new doctrine in the post-1949 China that would exert great influence over the Chinese legal system development

[16] The passage is quoted from Huang Yanpei's *The Recent 80 years,* China Literature and History Press, p. 158; Also see Zhu Guang's *Mao Zedong and Huang Yanpei on Historical Cycle*, Bright Daily, January 20, 1993.

[17] See Chiang Kai-shek's *China's Destiny*, Zhongzheng Books, 1943.

for many years to come. Yet as the modernization continued, it became increasingly clear that democracy alone would not be sufficient to meet requirement of constitutionalism construction. As much as this emphasis on democracy facilitate CPC's effort to establish political legitimacy in its struggle against KMT and facilitated political mobilization and state building in the early stage of New China, it failed to be routinized and institutionalized to incorporate the regular legal system.

4.1.5 Common Program: The Onset of Revolutionary Legal System Reform

At CPC's Seventh Congress Second Plenary, Mao Zedong, certain of imminent victory of the civil war, envisaged a shift of focus from military campaign to postwar construction: "We will prove that we are not only good at destroying an old world, we are also good at building a new world."[18] By the "old world" Mao unmistakably suggested ROC under the rule of the KMT. The message he tried to convey is that destruction of the old is a necessary start of new construction. Such statement is corroborated by the fact that a few days prior to the plenary session, the Communist central government issued a directive demanding the abolishment of KMT's Six Codes, putting an end to the KMT constitutional and legal system.

Questions remained to be answered as to why the ROC legal was abolished, and what sort of picture would be painted on "the blank canvas". When we review the history of People's Republic of China, very often we traced its start to Mao's declaration to the public at the top of the Tian'anmen Gate. In fact, it is that New China was born the moment when the constitution was created. This "constitution moment" took place during the political consultation conference when the *Common Program* was reviewed and enacted by parties including both CPC and minority political parties. This conference is extremely significant for the *Common Program* that it passed outlined the principles of the ensuing People's Republic of China in all meaningful respects. Thus, the promulgation of *Common Program* should be regarded as the start of the CPC as well as its new legal system.

The political design prescribed by the *Common Program* is a complete departure from all predecessors. Not only were the KMT's Five-Powers Constitution discarded; the constitutionalism ideals that had been preserved since late Qing dynasty were also abandoned. The new system was groundbreaking – it opened the door for full implementation of CPC's state building plan, thus concluded a historical period. In consideration of the historical background, *Common Program* is rather an effort for CPC to legitimize its political position, thus a review the evolution of CPC's political positions is advisable for anyone who want to have a solid grasp of the significance of *Common Program*.

---

[18] See *Mao Zedong's Selected Works* Vol 4, People's Publishing House 1991, Pp. 1438–1439.

If *Common Program* is an expression of CPC state building plan, then this plan was conceived before the formal promulgation of *Common Program*. The prototype, as we can see now is Mao Zedong's new democracy state building theory, expressed in the three articles that we already introduced. Given the communist ideology and the centralization of power that it advocated, the National People's Congress (NPC) was the only solution to realize democracy. As a political institution, NPC system is noted for combining both legislation and executive powers; the origin of such a design can be traced to Karl Marx's *The Civil War In France* and his other comments on the Paris Commune.

The *Common Program* is also noted for its lack of a clear definition of the relationship between the central government and lower ones, which is to a good measure due to strong emphasis on power centralization. According to Article 16: "Central People's Government and local People's Government's responsibilities should be defined by the Central People's Government Commission in the form of directives, with a view to maintain national unification while allowing certain level of flexibility in handling local maters."

At the first plenary session of the Chinese People's Political Consultative Conference, Deng Biwu (vice Chairman and president of the Supreme People's Court of the People's Republic of China) made a speech that explains the democratic concentration system and combination of legislative and executive powers: "The purpose of democratic concentration system is our answer to the separation of powers principle in the Old Three People's Principle. The European bourgeois ruling class deliberately divides up their dictatorial government into three departments – legislation, administration, and legislation. Ostensibly they check each other, but in reality, the only help the ruling class to strengthen their grip on power. The Old Democracy parliament is a place where oppositional parties are allowed to give speeches. They are allowed to talk because they are no threat to the power at all. Such political ploy could barely conceal their true intension, which is manipulating the public opinion and profit from it. In this sense, legal system is only an intricate ruling tool. It doesn't serve the people, but the ruling class. We don't want to play the bourgeois trickery; our combination of legislative and executive powers is one that concentrate all power in the hands of the People's Congress and its government."

It is hard to give a fair judgment of the CPC's democratic concentration system if one is to apply the classical Western constitutionalism standards. Unlike the Western systems, which stress separation of powers, the *Common Program* placed its emphasis on concentration of powers. This concentration of powers, however, demonstrated the revolutionary logic underlying *Common Program*. According to this logic, the legitimacy of revolutionary constitution is derived from class struggle, which by necessity requires centralized power structure.

4.2 Debate Over Formalism of the Revolutionary Legal System

With an emphasis placed on revolution and democracy, the early stage of post-1949 legal system modernization showed great disregard for regular legal institutions such as court system and professional judiciary. That law is a product of class repression is elevated to be a doctrine, whose effect would last for decades. However, it was not free from criticism. Many critics were ROC era legal professionals, who grew to be skeptical of the new system. Among them, law scholar Yang Zhaolong was perhaps the most prominent. Yang's Legal Inheritability Theory tacitly criticized the abolishment of the *Six Codes* as well as other prevailing legal theories of the day. New China's jurisprudence framework suffered certain birth defects, thus Yang's "legal inheritability theory" is in a way an effort to amend the defects, such as an over-emphasis on revolution and complete departure from the past. Yang's intent is to prove that some old components were still of value and could be incorporated into the new legal system.

To fully appreciate the value of this debate, we need understand complexity of China's legal reform back in the day and the integrity of the Chinese law scholar.

Yang Zhaolong's Legal Study Anthology[19] has a brief bio of the law scholar: "Yang Zhaolong, also named Yifei, lived between 1904 and 1979. After he graduated from Department of Philosophy, Yenching University, Yang went on to study at Law School of Soochow University where he received his Master's. He obtained Phd in law at Harvard University and went to at Berlin University as a research fellow. Well versed in eight languages, including English, French, German, Spanish, Russian, Czech, Polish, Yang was a scholar par excellence in the field of Continental Law and Anglo-American Law. During the period between 1928 and 1952, Yang taught over ten subjects at Shanghai Chizhi University, Shanghai Politics and Law University, Sun Yat-sen University, Zhejiang University, Chaoyang, Northwestern United University Commercial Law School, Fudan University, Soochow University Law School. He worked as magistrate, lawyer, member of (KMT's) Constitution Drafting Commission, Resources Commission, director of Criminal Law Department of Justice Administration Ministry, and Deputy Procurator-General of the Supreme People's Procuratorate. He was elected by Hague Academy of International Law as one of 50 outstanding law scholars, among them two were from China. Up until 1949, Yang had three million characters of work published.

Such impressive professional credentials may have given Yang the courage to stand up against the establishment and voice his skepticism in a time such an act required great courage. We can also see that despite the abolishment of the *Six Codes* and waves of political movements, Yang's faith in law was never shaken. That, in combination with erudite and integrity, demonstrated the finest quality of a ROC era law scholar.

---

[19] See Ai Yongming, Lu Jinbi (ed)'s *Yang Zhaolong Law Writing Anthology*, China Law Press, 2004.

The December issue of Journal of East China University of Political Science and Law carried an article written by Yang Zhaolong, titled *Class-ness and Inheritability of Law*. In the article, Yang took on a prevailing doctrine of the day, according which class is by and large the primary attribute of law.

Yang began by a recital of misconceptions regarding law's "class-based characteristics" and went on to answer whether the old laws can be utilized in a new society, or in his words – "law's inheritability": "That law has its class-based characteristics is widely accepted, while its inheritability was often dismissed. Among the arguments refuting law's inheritability, the most common one is grounded in the "class-based characteristics". For instance, we often hear people say that the ROC era law reflects the reactionary nature of KMT, thereby can't be used in New China, because the social classes are different. Hence there is nothing we can do about the old laws, according to that theory, but to abolish them …Given the prevalent belief that law's inheritability is determined by its class-based characteristics, hence to solve this inheritability problem, one must first study the "class-based characteristics".[20]

Such an acknowledgement of law's class-based characteristics is not only a tactical expedient, but also shows Yang's grasp of the Marxist class struggle theory and CPC's class-based jurisprudence system. Rather than directly repudiate law's class-based characteristics, Yang strategically focused on proving the validity of law's inheritability from the point of view of a social scientist. Given that the *Six Codes* directive was labeled as a product of class repression back in the day, Yang was taking on a conception widely accepted as a doctrine.

4.2.1 Law Class-Based Characteristics Argument: Criticism and Judgment

In Yang Zhaolong's class-based characteristics analysis, domestic law and international law were treated separately. Here we will focus on the part dealing with domestic laws. Yang's approach is to recount the five influential points of views and rebutted them one by one.

The first view, named "law's origin argument", contends that a law's nature is determined by its class origin. In rebuttal, Yang argued that such a view is guilty of having exaggerated the effect of origin. "If that is true, then any law that originated in a class-based society must carry a indelible mark indicating which class that it belongs to. Such an argument is false because it regards the origin as the only determinant of the law's nature, while refusing to acknowledge other factors such as social-economic conditions as well as political and cultural ones."[21] Yang then tries to demonstrate the social and historical dimensions of a law by citing two

[20] Ibid., p. 577.

[21] Ibid., p. 578.

examples – he argued that both murder and theft were two of the most ancient crimes, yet these crimes remained punishable under the Soviet Union law, despite fundamental change happened in terms of the class structure.

The second view contends that the class-based characteristics are fixed and unchangeable. In rebuttal, Yang called such a view mechanical and isolated: "It assumes that all laws produced by a class-based society will continue to serve the same class that they originally meant to or that its class-based characteristics can't be removed even this law is adopted by a different class … Such mechanical and isolated view didn't account for the fact that law when applied in the newer society, where economic and political cultural conditions have changed, can generate a completely different effect"[22] Yang went on and argue that such a view wrongly chained an abstract law to a specific class, while neglecting that the law is essentially a tool. Yang further exposed the fallacy by citing the Soviet law scholar M. Рейс Нер, who contended that the Soviet law fell into three categories, namely, the working class's socialist law, the farmers' land law and the bourgeois class' civil law – which proves that as advanced as the Soviet Union's socialist legal system, not all the laws are all socialist.

A third view contends that the form of a law determines its nature. Yang rebutted by pointing out that if this claim is true, then all laws that share the same form will of necessity have the same nature, while fact is that laws of identical forms can led to different effect. When applied in different social-economical and cultural conditions, laws that share the same forms can caused different outcomes and serve different classes, thus demonstrate different nature.[23] In addition, if one form of law can only serve one class, then it is impossible to explain why in socialist countries, the criminal laws often share the same forms with those of the capitalist countries.

A fourth view contends that all legal norms in a given legal system reflect their classes the same way and always to the same degree, to which Yang responded: "Such a view convenes reality… fact is that all legal norms in any society can be divided into two categories: the primary norms and the secondary or subordinate ones. While the primary norms are often general guidelines and principles, the secondary ones have specialized applications. While primary norms are often attached to certain classes, the secondary ones often do not, in fact, they can be used by any society regardless their class structures."[24]

Worth noting is that in his rebuttal, Yang applied taxonomy as his main weapon; by dividing laws into primary norms and secondary ones, he convincingly demonstrated that laws is more than their class-ness – while some reflect the will of ruling classes, some are just tools that can be used by anyone. Thus Yang suggested that while the primary norms of the old society should be ditched, it would be a good thing to retain secondary ones and put to use after adaption. Yang was tactful enough not to categorically deny class-based characteristics, but drew a line between the scientific and the ideological. He conceived the concept of "secondary norms"

[22] Ibid., p. 578.

[23] Ibid., p. 578.

[24] Ibid., p. 579.

which provided a refuge for the salvageable components of the old legal system. The primary legal norms that Yang referred to are often those highly politicalized ones, those that evidently contravened the new China's political principles. Meanwhile, the secondary ones are procedural and value-neutral. Although such insights were vindicated by China's legal system development in the reform era, back in the day, despite his strenuous effort, little was achieved to change the situation; many ROC era legal theories and institutions were ditched simply because they were made by the wrong class.

Finally, there is a view that contends that any given society can only generate laws with uniform class-based characteristics. Such a argument, according to Yang, overlooked the complexity of exploitive societies, where it is not always true one single class have total control of power. Although in modern capitalist countries, the capitalist class dominated politics, but with rising political awareness among the proletariat, their dominance is not total… This is even confirmed by the 20th Presidium of the Communist Party of the Soviet Union, which passed an resolution indicating that in some countries, possibility exist to accomplish transformation from capitalism to socialist through parliamentary struggle.[25] With a recital of history, Yang showed that worldwide it is common that a law demonstrated characteristics attributable to different classes, and these characteristics also constantly evolve and change leading to the increasing level of democracy. Such a view, back in the day, is unorthodox and could easily be branded as "revisionism".

Yang final concluded: "the shortcoming of above-mentioned five incorrect views is that they are mechanical, isolated, simplistic, formalistic, and unanalyzed. The right approach should be a specific analysis that takes into account of legal norms' individuality, viewing them in connection with specific economic and social-political conditions, then determine what class-based characteristics these laws possess."[26]

Although Yang's article is a potent rebuttal to the prevalent doctrine of the day, the methodology he employed was in line with the popular Marxist dialectical materialism and historical materialism, which reduced the risk of being dismissed on the ground of unorthodox methodology. Overall, Yang championed a more delicate and balanced view in handling the subject, rather than passing a simplistic judgment, which is undisputedly the attitude that all legal science workers should acquire.

Based on his rebuttal, Yang suggested that all legal norms, depending on their characteristics, fall into four groups:

1. Reactionary legal norms. This category demonstrated inherent hostility towards certain classes; they can be anti-human, anti-justice and anti-humanitarianism. Drawing on his own extensive knowledge and experience in judicial practice, Yang drew a long list of these norms, including property laws, racial discrimination laws, laws repressive of fundamental human rights, laws against legitimate procedures. He acknowledged that these laws were "backward" and carries attributes of reactionary classes; abolishment is the only right thing to do. Of note is

[25] Ibid., Pp. 578–579.

[26] Ibid., p. 580.

that here the criteria that Yan employed in deciding whether a law is progressive is whether it facilitates human civilization progress.

2. Progressive legal norms: Defined as "legal norms that are intrinsically just and reflective of people's demands." Yang likewise provided a recital of examples, such as laws protecting fundamental human rights, equality, legitimate procedural legislation, principles such as "no crime without a law", etc. These norms were widely adopted in bourgeois legal systems. Although under the rule of bourgeois class, there laws were often abused and used for purposes different from the ostensible ones, they were at least normatively progressive; in a proletariat society, their potential can be fuller tapped.
3. Resistant legal norms: Defined as "legal norms that constrained the power of ruling class". One example is the law that protects people the right to strike. This legal norm is advantageous to working class in exploitive societies, giving them the means to resist the ruling class; however, in a proletarian state, where working class has become the ruling class, whether such a law is necessary is a mater of debate. Here Yang conferred to the communist doctrine, namely that the right to strike is not necessary in socialist China, though his real intension of using the example is to convey the complexity of the class-related characteristics: Even in exploitive societies, laws don't always side with the ruling class.
4. Secondary legal norms: This category refers to "legal norms that don't have distinct class-related characteristics, and played secondary and supportive roles in societies." These norms, such as procedures governing social relationships, are often historical heritages that are derived from long time practices. The rationale of treating this category separately is that these norms are fruits of human legal civilization, thus shouldn't be dismissed merely because they are created by certain classes. This category is further divided into two subsets: legal relationship regulatory norms and legal procedural norms.

One application of such a categorization is to conduct class analyses over any specific legal system of any given country, to decide whether they are worth of being kept. The unique significance of Yang's work is that it provides a scientific basis to define laws class-based characteristics, and expanded inheritable norms from secondary ones to include progressive and resistant ones. Through such a specific analysis, Yang suggested a new possibility beyond the dogmatic class-determinism that is based on sound logical reasoning. However, at that time class-determinism was enshrined as a sacred cow and Yang's theory was bound to have little effect to change the situation.

4.2.2 Legal Inheritability: Formal Exposition

In his article, Yang wrote, "Some people believe that acknowledging law's inheritability is a form of revivalism. The fact is that nothing new can be conjured up from nothing; it has to be made from something, something that has already been in existence. To make something new, we always need something old, ether raw material, or experience. Law is not exception in this regard."[27] By pointing out that the commonness of inheriting in other legal traditions, such as Roman one, French one and British one as well as the other modern democratic states, Yang suggests that inheriting is universally accepted way to maintain coherence of legal systems. Such a discovery is grounded not only in legal theories, but also philosophical reasoning and history study. For instance, "nothing new can be conjured up from nothing; it has be made from something" is a basic philosophical principle has been proved by modern science, the same principle behind the law of energy conservation of modern physics. Those who subscribe to Christian creationism and other religious faiths may take a different view, but they were unverifiable. However, Yang's emphasis on continuation of the old and new seemingly contradicted revolutionaries' view that the new has to be a complete departure from the old, hence was regarded as a threat to the prevailing revolutionary narrative of the day. In his argumentation, Yang reiterated that his legal inheritability theory should be a living and developing thing that constantly adapt itself to the changing social-economical and political-cultural conditions, must be understood, and utilized with consideration to the specific conditions – such a view shouldn't be regarded as a form of revivalism, but rather a form of pragmatist rationalism.

Yang ended the article by expounding on the importance of legal inheritances: "The phenomenon is not incidental. There is a clear inner logic. Once a state is established, it can't create a whole set of legal institutions that are new both in form and substance. This is not only true for an inchoate state, but also true for fairly established ones. When a new state is founded, it can only formulate some new primary legal norms, but even these can't be conjured up from nothing, instead much has to be borrowed from past or learned from other countries' experience. As for the secondary norms, which are much larger in scope, they are rather the fruits of human civilization and wisdom accumulated over a long course of time, thus dismissing them on the ground that they were created by the older generations or other countries, is narrow-minded and counterproductive … As these examples indicate, legal inheritance is a critical to development of legal systems and creating of successful governance models for all ruling classes."[28]

Yang's view should be regarded as a response to New China legal system development. Yet with the Abolishing Old Law Movement reached frenzy, few heeded such a rational voice. The popular slogan of the day is everything had to be built anew. However, in reality, systematic legislation was almost halted, and it was impossible to create brand new legal system given the conditions. The abolishment of the old laws, and disregard of the universal rules led to stalemate of development. As a result, there weren't enough laws for judicial system to function normally, contributing to judicial arbitrariness. It was until after the Reform and Opening-up, which set forth three decades of legislation, these problems began to be solved. In a recent statement, Wu Bangguo, Chairman of the Standing Committee of NPC

[27] Ibid., Pp. 585–586.

[28] Ibid., Pp. 587–588.

declared that China's socialist legal system with Chinese characteristics had been completed. But strictly speaking, some important department laws such as compulsory administrative enforcement law, administrative procedural laws, information freedom laws are still in the making, hence this completion is only a preliminary one; the judicial system still has much to be desired.

Yang's theory caught some academic attention back in the day. For example, the Shanghai Jurisprudence Study Society organized a symposium to discuss Yang's class-based characteristics and inheritability theory. Within the academia, Yang's theory received certain understanding and resonance. Some questions raised by Yang in the article was responded by peers.[29] However, such activities were only possible when the "letting a hundred flowers bloom" movement ushered in a brief period of freedom; it was to be followed by great political austerity when expression of opinions were made much harder. Overall, Yang's theory demonstrated the ROC law scholars' serious theoretical reflection on New China's legal system modernization. Had their thinking been recognized and adopted, then the development of New China's legal construction would have been a different story. Yet, what has happened can't be revised. In another article Yang tried to identify some impediments that hampered China legal system modernization: "overemphasis on political correctness while disregard of law's nature as a specialized discipline and a form of science; legal professionals of the old system being sidelined, deemed unfit for the new society; distrust of non-CPC members and reluctant to use them."[30]

To recap, in the early stage of New China China's legal system modernization suffered some major setbacks. The abolishment of *Six Codes* marked the start of the wide adoption of law – class paradigm; the reeducation program diminished respect and trust between the older law professionals and the revolutionaries. In a time of when politics reigned supreme, party allegiance was valued more than professional expertise and specialized training. That law is and should be a form of science was disregarded. Yang Zhaolong's experience should serve as a reminder for us not to commit the same mistake today.

4.2.2.1 54 Constitution – The Emperor's New Clothes That Never Got Worn

In his three articles, Mao Zedong enunciated that Chinese revolution would have two stages – the New Democracy revolution and socialist revolution. He also predicted that first stage – the New Democracy revolution would take a long time.

In *On New Democracy*, Mao wrote: "The historical characteristic of the Chinese revolution decided that it should be divided into the two stages, democracy and socialism." Repudiating the path of capitalist dictatorship, Mao wrote: "Without a

[29] For more details, see Shanghai Law Society on Law's class-ness and inedibility symposium, included in Yang Zhaolong's law anthology, China Law Publishing House, 2005, Pp. 599–591.

[30] See Yang Zhaolong's *Distinction between Party and non-Party in the law profession*, Wenhuibao, May 8, 1957.

doubt, the present revolution is the first step, which will develop into the second step, that of socialism, at a later date. And China will attain true happiness only when she enters the socialist era. But today is not yet the time to introduce socialism. The present task of the revolution in China is to fight imperialism and feudalism, and socialism is out of the question until this task is completed. The Chinese revolution cannot avoid taking the two steps, first of New Democracy and then of socialism. Moreover, the first step will need quite a long time and cannot be accomplished overnight."[31]

In his *On Coalition Government*, Mao Zedong wrote: "We Communists do not conceal our political views. Definitely and beyond all doubt, our future or maximum programme is to carry China forward to socialism and communism." Then, he emphasized: "It is a law of Marxism that socialism can be attained only via the stage of democracy. And in China the fight for democracy is a protracted one. It would be a sheer illusion to try to build a socialist society on the ruins of the colonial, semi-colonial and semi-feudal order without a united new-democratic state, without the development of the state sector of the new-democratic economy, of the private capitalist and the co-operative sectors, and of a national, scientific and mass culture, i.e., a new-democratic culture, and without the liberation and the development of the individuality of hundreds of millions of people-in short, without a thoroughgoing bourgeois-democratic revolution of a new type led by the Communist Party."

However, Mao changed his mind soon afterwards. Only 3 years after *Common Program* was enacted, establishing the New Democracy political form, now it was decided that the New Democracy constitutionalism should be changed to socialism. Such a change is often attributed by the later-day scholars often try to the provisional nature of *Common Program*, and the rapid economic growth in the early days of the New China.

On December 24, 1952, at the first Chinese People's Political Consultative Conference 43th enlarged meeting, Premier Zhou Enlai, on behalf of the Political Consultative Committee, submitted a proposal to the Central People's Government requesting to convene National People's Congress and Local-level People's Congresses: "According to *Common Program*, our country's political form is National People's Congress system. When the republic was established, in consideration of that the Liberation War was still in progress, national political social reform had yet been completed, economy needed recovery, hence we decided to postpone the convening of NPC. According to *Common Program*, before NPC is convened, the Chinese People's Political Consultative Conference (CPPCC) would function as the highest organ of state power, responsible for organizing election to form the Central People's Government Committee, who will represent the people to exercise the state power. Before the local-level NPC are convened, the local-level people's representatives' conference will exercise the power of the local-level people's congresses. Now the interim period has passed, our country has entered a period of large-scale economy development. To facilitate this objective, it is necessary to convene NPC and local-level people's congresses according to the require-

[31] See Mao Zedong's *On New Democracy*.

ments of Common Program, to further expand people's democracy, and fully utilize people's enthusiasm and energy. Therefore, the Party proposed that CPPCC Standing Committee to advise the Central People's Government Committee to exercise its power granted by the Central People's Government Organization Law and convene NPC and local-level people's congresses, and to undertake preparations for the drafting of the election law and constitution."[32]

On January 13, 1953, at a Central People's Government Committee meeting, Mao delivered a report. In his evaluation of the situation, Mao said that combat mission on the Mainland was at its final stage, Land Reform was nearing completion, and organization of people had been accomplished, condition was ripe for convening the national as well as local-level people's congresses. Mao also listed the benefits of convening NPC: it would strengthen the democracy, facilitate economy development and gave a morale boost to the army engaged in anti-American military campaign in Korea. Mao then promised that the government would continue to be a coalition government where all ethnic groups, democratic classes, democratic parties and people's organizations would be fully represented, a government that would auger the wellbeing of all the people.[33] Professor Xu Chongde echoed Mao's assessment: "New China was established, Mainland China was unified under the leadership of CPC and its government, military actions largely ceased, land ownership reform had completed, extensive and thorough crackdown on reactionary forces and all sorts of democratic reform moments had been undertaken, and the economy was recovering. In 1953, the first Five Year Plan was initiated. The *Common Program*'s successful implementation indicates that conditions are ripe to implement universal suffrage, convening NPC and launch constitution making."[34]

With military and political victory already in sight, CPC might be in a better position than ever to begin constitution making. Yet, few have noticed that the direct cause that led to the constitution making is a "kind" prompting from Soviet Union leader Joseph Stalin.

All began with the visit of Liu Shaoqi, China's vice Chairman, to Soviet Union in 1952.

In October 1952, prior to Liu's visit to Soviet Union, in a letter to Stalin, Liu intimated CPC's thoughts on NPC and constitution making – this letter was also sent to Mao Zedong for review before it was sent to Stalin.

In the letter, Liu wrote: "Three years has passed since the first Chinese People's Political Consultative Conference (CPPCC) was convened in 1949. Now the second CPPCC will be due soon. If it has to be postponed, then the first NPC shall be convened either next year or the year after. Because CPPCC was highly popular among the democratic parties, they showed eagerness in participating, whereas the enthusiasm for the CPC is not so high. The preparations work for national election is still in progress. Thereby we are considering to convene the second CPPCC ether next spring or summer and postpone NPC by 3 years. … Even inside the Party, there are

[32] See *Zhou Enlai Chronology* (1949–1976), Central Party Literature Press, p. 274.

[33] See *Mao Zedong Biography* (1949–1976) Vol 1, Central Party Literature Press, p. 310.

[34] See Xu Chongde's *History of PRC Constitutions*, Fujian People's Press, 2005, Pp. 106–107.

voices demanding constitution. But to make the constitution, we will have to convene NPC. Yet we are not confident that constitution making is something that should be given first priority at the moment. In consideration that we already have *Common Program,* which functions as a constitution. If we need to make a constitution right now, much of its content, especially the part concerning the capitalist and bourgeois class, won't be too different from the *Common Program.* There may be some cosmetic changes such as phrasing of certain articles and the names of certain provisions. Hence, we are thinking whether we should keep the Common Program as the provisional constitution for the time being, while postponing the constitution making. We can revise *Common Program* and introduce amendments through CPPCC and NPC, until the transformation of class relationship is completed, and socialism has been installed, then we will aim to make a socialist constitution."[35]

In his reply, Stalin wrote: "If you don't make the constitution or hold (NPC deputies) election, it would only give ammunition to enemy's propaganda machine to instigate rebellion among the masses. They would accuse that your government wasn't an elected one; or your country is a constitutionless state. Because the CPPCC members weren't elected by the people, the enemies may say that your government was formed at the point of bayonet. Moreover, the *Common Program* was not promulgated by NPC, which is supposedly fully representative of the people, but drafted by one party, and approved by the others, so they may say that you don't have laws. You shouldn't give the enemy such an opportunity. As for your proposal of turning the *Common Program* into Constitution, I think such a constitution will be a bit rough, but still better than nothing… I think you should start preparation and prepare to hold election in 1954 and begin the constitution making immediately afterwards." Stalin also said that, "If the CPC members won a majority of seats, then your one-party government will be justified. For those minority parties, give them something to keep them grateful, which will benefit you eventually."[36]

Professor Xiao Beisheng believes that Stalin's reply contains three suggestions: First, he wanted the CPC to strengthen its political legitimacy through a public election and a constitution; second, suspending promulgation of constitution may cause disenchantment from other minority parties and they might even divulge state secrets to hostile Western powers, since ties were still retained between the Western countries and these parties; third, through an election and constitution, a one-party government will be legitimized. According to Prof. Xiao, although the first suggestion sounds sensible, it is not what the Stalin's main concern. At that time, Soviet Union might be more adherent to procedural democracy than its Chinese ally, but only marginally so. Neither treated the election procedure-derived political legitimacy quite seriously; both follow Lenin's theory advocating seizure of power through violent means and not to be concerned about whether their governments

[35] See *Liu Shaoqi's Writings since the Establishment of PRC,* Vol 4, Central Party Literature Press, 2005, p. 530.

[36] The telegraphs describing meeting with Stalin sent to Mao Zedong and Central Committee can be seen in *Liu Shaoqi's writings since the establishment of PRC, Vol 4,* Central Party Literature Press, p. 536.

were elected or not." As for the so-called "secret divulgence", given the hostility that the two blocs towards each other during the Cold War, it seems to be a legitimate concern. However, for China at that time, such worries were rather unwarranted. Although the minority democratic parties maintained ties with the West, their loyalty to the country and CPC was sincere; but more important, these parties never had access to state secrets. Xiao hence concluded that what truly convinced Mao and CPC to commit to their constitution making process is the last suggestion, the most tempting of all, namely through a lawful election, form CPC-dominated one party government to replace the coalition government. Once this is achieved, the minority democratic parties could be squeezed out of the power structure. Such "wisdom" is refined from Soviet Union's own experience in handling the East European political matters. For CPC, a coalition government, though not entirely an expedient, can't be tolerated for too long. One has a good reason to suspect that CPC might already had plans to transform the coalition government into a one-party government, now at Stalin's urge, CPC was more than happy to oblige. Soon the preparations for election and constitution making were carried out according to the timetable suggested by Stalin.[37]

In November 1952, CPC initiated preparations for NPC and constitution drafting. On December 1, CPC formally released *Circular On Convening Party's National Congress*, approved by Mao Zedong himself, announcing that the country was ready to convene NPC and making constitution. On December 24, CPPCC's Standing Committee held the 43rd meeting, at which Zhou Enlai, on behalf of CPC Central Committee, submitted a proposal requesting CPPCC to advise Central People's Government to conduct preparations to initiate constitution drafting. On January 13, 1953, CPPCC's proposal was approved by Central People's Government Committee at the 20th meeting and announcement was made deciding that the conditions to convene NPC had been met. Based on the *Organic Law,* in 1953, representatives elected through general election on levels of township, county, province would attend congresses at local levels. The NPC would be held immediately after the first Five Year Plan Outline was deliberated and approved and the new Central People's Government members were elected. In addition, the meeting also decided that the Constitution Drafting Committee chaired by Mao Zedong and Election Law Drafting Committee chaired by Zhou Enlai would be formed.[38]

In February 1953, *Election of National People's Congress and Local-level People's Congresses Law* was promulgated. The law stipulates that direct election would be held to elect NPC deputies for each provinces; it also decided the ratios of the number of deputies to local population, which varied to reflect factors such as the region's level of urbanization, the density of ethnic minority inhabitants; The elections are to be held at levels of townships, countries, districts and cities, and

[37] See Xiao Beisheng's *Behind the Constitution-making Ritual – From Common Program to 1954 Constitution*, Contemporary China Research, issue 2, 2003.

[38] See *Selected post-1949 significant archival literature*, Vol 4, Central Party Literature Press, Pp. 16–17, 1993.

took the form of a show of hands, whereas elections at county levels and higher will be conducted through secret ballot.

From the second half of 1953, constitution formulation work, overseen by Liu Shaoqi, commenced. From the second half of 1953 to summer of 1953, in the space of less than a year, preparation work such as national census, voter registration, and local level elections, were completed. In terms of constitution drafting, on December 24, Mao Zedong and the rest of the drafting committee, including Chen Boda, Hu Qiaomu, and Tian Jiaying arrived in Hangzhou, where the drafting commenced. According to Mao's plan, the first draft would be completed on January 31, before they were sent to other central leaders for review. During the second half of the February, an committee meeting would be held to further review the draft; this meeting will be participated by Deng Xiaoping and Li Weihan in addition to the drafting committee members. The edited draft would be submitted to the Politburo and Central Government Committee members in Beijing for further review and deliberation. This step was scheduled to conclude in March. 4. In April, another round of revision would commence, followed by another review by the Politburo. The edited version would be relayed back to the drafting committee for approval. On May 1, the constitution draft would be announced to solicit feedback from the public. Revisions would be made based on feedback before they were finally submitted to NPC for final approval.

The work had been on schedule. After the third draft and the fourth draft were thoroughly studied and revised at the Politburo meetings, Mao returned to Beijing on March 23, 1954, where he convened a meeting of the drafting committee to finalize the draft that was already approved by the Party.

In June 1954, at the 30th meeting of the Central People's Government Committee, presided by Mao himself, two documents, namely the People's Republic of China Constitution (draft) and Resolution on People's Republic of China Constitution (draft) were passed. It is said that over 150 million people participated one way or another in the drafting and 1.38 million suggestions were submitted. Finally, the constitution draft, named *54 Constitution*, was passed unanimously at the first NPC on September 15, 1954. Judging by the drafting process, *54 Constitution* is not only created under the leadership of CPC, it was the brainchild of Party leaders, including Mao. Through the organization and planning, special care was taken to ensure Party leaders and CPC's control.[39] When it comes to design of political form, *54 Constitution* stuck to the "combination of legislative and executive powers" principle of *Common Program*; institutions such as NPC, multi-party cooperation under the leadership of CPC as well as ethnic regional autonomy were retained. Overall, the new constitution is more systematic and refined than its predecessor, but the difference is not substantial.

The biggest change is the status of minority democratic parties and their leaders in the new government. At the beginning of the New China, among the 56 Central Party Committee members, 26 were minority party members, accounting for 46.5 %

[39] See Wang Renbo's *The Chinese Characteristics of Constitution – the Background of 54 Constitution*, 21st Century, online edition, Issue 46, 2005.

of the total number of seats. The Politburo, aside from Premier Zhou Enlai, vice Premiers Dong Biwu, Chen Yun, Guo Moruo, Huang Yanpei, non-party affiliation personages accounted for 50 % of the total seats. Among the 15 Political Affairs Committee members, nine were non-party affiliation personages, 60 % of the total. Among the 34 ministries and ministry-level agencies, 15 leadership positions and 42 deputy positions were taken up by minority party members or non-party affiliation personages. Following the promulgation of *54 Constitution*, although CPPCC was retained, it would function more as a consultation body, whereas its role as the highest political organ was superseded by NPC. Political Affairs Committee was dismissed, replaced by the Top State Affair Conference which was made up by National Chairman, vice Chairmen, NPC chairman, State Council Premier, vice Premiers. Political Council changed its name to State Council. The non-party affiliation personages vice Premiers were relieved from their positions, replaced by CPC members. The number of ministers who were democratic personage also dropped – from 15 to 12 out of a total 36; those who remained would retire over the subsequent years. Evidently, the first NPC is a turning point in New China's political and institutional evolution. Through constitution making, the new state political form transformation was completed, and political legitimacy was consolidated. However, although NPC's role as the highest organ of state power was written into the constitution, it would exist more as a rubber stamp during this period; its role as the highest body of legislature was also mostly nominal. The only law that it produced during the early years of the People's Republic is the Marriage Law.

Many people took a highly positive view regarding the 54 Constitution.[40] When the draft was still in the review stage, it already received large number of praises from democratic parties' representatives; it was regarded as a symbolic achievement of the Chinese people demand for a constitution for over half a century, all thanks to Chairman Mao and CPC, without whom the Chinese people's dream wouldn't have come true. Back in the day, *54 Constitution* was widely recognized as China's first "people's constitution". To the significance of the constitution, Xu Chongde commented: "It has been less than a century since China had its first constitution. During such a relatively short period, quite a few had been made. When compared with its predecessors, *54 Constitution* is distinctly different. One can say that it is a true monument in the history of China's constitutionalism. Before it, the old constitutions were like small creek, often jammed by silt; the new constitution is like a great river, powerful and magnificent." Recently, scholar Xue Jianfu voiced a similarly exuberant view: "the emergence of Chinese democratic politics and its development was a bumpy journey. The promulgation *54 Constitution* is undoubtedly a symbolic event. It established socialism as the direction of the Chinese people's democratic political construction. It enshrines a wide range of rights and liberties. Despite the

[40] For more historical materials and interviews, see Han Dayuan (ed.) *1954 Constitution and China's Constitutionalism*, Wuhan University Press, edition 2, 2008.

difficulty in practice, this constitution provided valuable experience for our democratic political construction and development."[41]

Indeed, some provisions of 54 Constitution were surprisingly progressive – Article 78: "The people's courts administer justice independently and are subject only to the law." Article 85: "All citizens of the People's Republic of China are equal before the law", Article 90: "Citizens of the People's Republic of China enjoy freedom of residence and freedom to change their residence". However, in practice, we are to be disappointed to find that many provisions were not implemented. One example is during the process constitution making coincided with Hu Feng's Counter-revolutionary case and Gao Gang – Rao Shushi Anti-party Fraction. In the handling of neither of two cases, the constitution was adhered to and those involved in the cases were deprived all their rights. In fact, no matter how progressive *54 Constitution* was from other constitutions or constitutional documents since *Provisional Constitution*, their fates were not different – they lacked real power and often used to conceal something too unpleasant to meet the eyes.

4.3 75 Constitution – The "Continued Revolution" Mania

The establishment of People's Republic of China presented the best opportunity in a century for China to undertake its modernization. From the way that people participated in the CPPCC as well as the formulation of the *54 Constitution*, the public enthusiasm was high. Unfortunately, following the promulgation of the constitution replacing Common Program, and the transformation from Coalition Government to one party government, a modern China that upholds the principle of rule of law didn't emerge as hoped. On the contrary, the country would stray further from the route towards modern rule of law and grew to be its very opposite, finally completely abandoned the rule of law principle.

To this phase of historical development, Li Shenzhi, former dean of Academy of Social Sciences, gave an somehow emotive account: After Mao Zedong declared in his *On People's Democratic Dictatorship* that repudiated any forms of merciful rule, the country has seen a whirlwind of political movements: Land Reform, Repressing Counter-revolutionary, Three Evils, Five Evils, Elimination of Counter-revolutionaries were undertaken with short intervals. These, according to the Marxism-Leninism theory, may be justified for they targeted the class enemies. But in 1955, after the arrests of Pan Hannian in April and Hu Feng in May (I would refrain from mentioning the Gao-Rao case in February, for little detail has been disclosed), apparently the revolution had begun to devour its own children. In early 1956, at the 20th Congress of the Communist Party of Soviet Union, Khrushchev denounced Joseph Stalin, whereupon Berlin Incident and Poznań 1956 Uprising occurred – this had amplified the political tension in China. Later that year, "counter-

[41] See Xue Jianfu's *54 Constitution and Chinese Democratic Political Model's Construction, Northeastern Normal University Journal (Philosophy and Social Sciences Edition)* Issue 3, 2010.

revolutionary" incidents occurred in Poland and Hungary. Mao Zedong, sensing the situation developing unfavorably, decided to forestall challenges by "luring the snakes out of their holes". In early 1957, he announced that the end of "stormy class struggle", and said in the future, conflicts within the people would be of first priority. In the second half year, Anti-Rightist Movement began in earnest; this led to denouncement of around 550,000 people, who were charged with the crimes of "anti-party and anti-socialism". Taking advantage of the momentum, in 1958, Mao launched Great Leap Forward Movement and People's Commune Movement. These led to massive starvation that claimed tens of millions of lives over the course of subsequent 3 years, not to mention the massive deforestation as a result of the steel production plan. In the middle of the two campaigns, "Anti-Right Deviation Movement" was initiated as a sideshow to boost morale, leading to the imprisonment of some "state-founding generals" such as Zhang Wentian, and Peng Dehuai. These movements took a staggering toll on the society and economy, Liu Shaoqi and Zhou Enlai were sent front by Mao to divert blame away from him. Some measures were introduced to amend the mistake, and the ravaged economy was given a breather. Mao, afraid that he would be held accountable, struck preemptively by launching the Cultural Revolution in 1966. This decade-long revolution annihilated literally all cultures, with over 100 million out of a total population of 800 million having been persecuted. As the Cultural Revolution continued, Party leaders Liu Shaoqi and Lin Biao were denounced. Later, even Zhou Enlai, who was sometimes criticized as "blindly loyal" to Mao came under attack, spared only by the death of Mao and later, his own. Up until the year of 1976, the People's Republic went through two decades of bloody plight.[42]

It is doubtful that Mao Zedong and his CPC had no sincerity to install rule of law from the very beginning. On June 14, 1954, at the 30th Meeting of Central People's Government Committee, Mao gave a speech titled *On People's Republic of China Constitution*, in which he stated: "There is no question that the draft constitution is plausible, and it must be carried out. Of course, today it is only a draft; but in a few months, it will be formal once it was voted by National People's Congress, so we should begin preparation for its implementation immediately. Once it is in effect, every citizen should follow it, especially the government personnel, including you (Note: the audience he addressed to). Those who don't will be deemed as opposing the constitution."[43] In 1956, a political resolution was passed by the CPC 8th Committee: "Our Party, and the Chinese people under its leadership, have achieved complete success of the bourgeois revolution, as well as the preliminary success of socialist revolution. As a result, social conditions have changed profoundly… The main conflict within the country now is between people's demands for an advanced industrialized state and the reality of a backward agrarian one, between people's demands for fast economic growth and culture and the reality of economic and cultural development at a level that can't meet people's demands… The priority of the

[42] See Li Shenzhi's *Five Decades of Tumult*, History Monthly, March, 2000.

[43] Quoted from Xu Chongde's *History of PRC constitutions*, P. 257. Fujian People's Publishing House 2005.

Party and the people would be to concentrate resources to resolve this conflict, namely to transform our country from a backward agrarian country to an industrialized one. Such a challenging task requires us to adopt right policies, to unite all forces that can be united, at home and abroad and take advantage of all advantageous conditions." The resolution reiterated the importance of realizing democracy in the phase of socialist construction: "Now the country is in the socialist construction period, the task of bolstering our democratic life on the state level is picking up urgency for it is vital to our struggle against bureaucracy. Persistent struggle against bureaucracy, exemplified by "out of touch with the masses" and "out of touch with reality", must be carried out by bolstering supervision to the government agencies, bottom up and top down, from the Party, from people's congresses, from masses and low-level government employees."

In his article *On the Correct Handling of Contradictions Among the People,* Mao wrote: "Our state is a people's democratic dictatorship led by the working class and based on the worker-peasant alliance. What is this dictatorship for? Its first function is internal, namely, to suppress the reactionary classes and elements and those exploiters who resist the socialist revolution, to suppress those who try to wreck our socialist construction, or in other words, to resolve the contradictions between ourselves and the internal enemy. … The second function of this dictatorship is to protect our country from subversion and possible aggression by external enemies. … Dictatorship does not apply within the ranks of the people. The people cannot exercise dictatorship over themselves, nor must one section of the people oppress another. Law-breakers among the people will be punished according to law, but this is different in principle from the exercise of dictatorship to suppress enemies of the people. What applies among the people is democratic centralism. … Our dictatorship is the people's democratic dictatorship led by the working class and based on the worker-peasant alliance. That is to say, democracy operates within the ranks of the people, while the working class, uniting with all others enjoying civil rights, and in the first place with the peasantry, enforces dictatorship over the reactionary classes and elements and all those who resist socialist transformation and oppose socialist construction. By civil rights, we mean, politically, the rights of freedom and democracy."

However, between the Anti-Rightist Movement in 1957 and Mao Zedong's demise in 1976, China was, as Li Shenzhi described, a society dominated by political forces, rather than one regulated by the law. This tendency grew increasingly evident along the course. After the promulgation of 54 Constitution, under the instruction of Mao, China embarked onto a course of constant radical revolution; in this sense the 75 Constitution that replaced 54 Constitution was the finale of this rather disconcerting orchestra.

Some may regard the 75 Constitution as a counteraction to 54 Constitution. However, when held against their historical background, it is clear that such a view regarding the new constitution as a regression from its predecessor is over-simplistic. The primary goal of 75 Constitution may be to legitimatize radical revolution. But it is also an effort to stabilize political order. However, such hopes that its creators invested in the 75 Constitution were doomed to fail for they couldn't solve the inner contradiction of stabilization and radical revolution.

The new constitution's promulgation was originally scheduled to be circa 1970. Mao himself had instructed that 54 Constitution would be updated 15 years after its promulgation. Although Mao's opinion was undoubtedly a factor (maybe the only one that was explicitly expressed), another often neglected cause is that the power dynamic that had been formed during the Cultural Revolution needed to be legitimized and solidified.

Like the preparations prior to the making of the 54 Constitution, the revision was kept internal inside CPC. The project started after Mao Zedong issued an advice on convening the fourth NPC and revising the Constitution on March 8, 1970. In the immediate aftermath, CPC central committee formed a constitution working group led by vice Premier Kang Sheng. From March 17 to March 24, Premier Zhou Enlai hosted meetings attended by members of Politburo, revolution committee groups from provinces, municipalities, and autonomous regions, as well as all PLA leaders in charge of various general departments, services and arms and military area commands. The purpose of the meetings was to allocate workload regarding election prior to the 4th NPC, and solicit opinions regarding the revision. On March 16, constitution group leaders gave a presentation at the working meeting, which stated the rationale behind the revision and guidelines the revision would adhere to, measures to be taken as well as questions that need to consult with Mao.

A circular issued after the meeting provided the rationale behind the revision. It states: "In accordance with great leader Chairman Mao's instructions, the 4th NPC will be convened to revise the constitution. Chairman Mao instructed the post of State Chairman should be canceled; his decision was unanimously supported by Politburo members after discussion. Five meetings were held by the constitution committee. First, the reason why did Chairman Mao want to revise the current constitution is not because that it has any defects. Chairman Mao made clear that the constitution was provisional and would be in effect for 15 years. His great insights have been vindicated. Today, our proletariat dictatorship is stronger than ever, the Great Proletarian Cultural Revolution has achieved great success, and Chairman Mao creatively developed Marxist-Leninist State Theory to a new height. As Vince Chairman Lin Biao stated in the Ninth CPC Congress report, Chairman Mao had put forward a new theory of Continued Revolution Under Proletariat Dictatorship. To adapt to these new conditions, our constitution has to be revised. Our goal this time is to produce a socialist constitution."

As for the guidelines that would be adhered to in the revision, the circular says "We believe (the revision) should be based on Chairman Mao's great state theory and practice. O socialist revolution and socialist construction, especially the Great Proletarian Cultural Revolution, provided great theoretical and practical materials for our continued revolution under proletarian dictatorship. Our direction of socialist revolution and socialist construction were pointed out at CPC's Ninth Party Congress. Hence the revision of constitution, in practice and in theory, is grounded on a solid foundation."

On July 17, 1970, Constitution Revision Drafting Committee was formally established. Mao Zedong was the director; Lin Biao the deputy director. On July 21, CPC Central Committee issued a circular regarding the election of the 4th People's Congress deputies. On August 23, at the Second Plenary Session of CPC Ninth Committee, discussion was held about the revision. At the meeting, People's Republic of China Constitution Revision Draft was voted on and passed. According to the schedule, the opening date of the fourth NPC was set between September 15 and September 24. But during the Second Plenary Session of CPC Ninth Committee, Lin Biao and Chen Boda insisted that the post of State Chairman should be retained. Their move displeased Mao who responded by launching a campaign called "Criticize Chen Boda and Rectify The Style" immediately after the meeting. In 1971, shortly after Lin Biao died in the September 13 Incident, "Condemning Lin Bao and Confucian" movement was launched. After several postponements, 4th NPC was final suspended.

Although Lin Liao's event forced the revision to stop and prompted the CPC leadership to make some policy adjustments, yet none of these changes was significant enough to switch the direction that the country moving along. Overall Lin Biao Incident didn't have much effect on the revision which soon resumed. After some preparations done at CPC 10th Congress in 1973, in September, CPC Central Committee again proposed to convene NPC and revise the constitution. Finally on January 8, 1975, at the Second Meeting of the Tenth CPC Congress, hosted by Zhou Enlai, *People's Republic of China Constitution Revision Draft* and *Report on Constitution Revision* were voted on and passed; they would finally receive approval at the subsequent 4th NPC and became what we know as 75 Constitution.

Comparing side by side with the 1970 constitution draft, the formal version 75 Constitution has a rewritten Preamble and General Principles. Like its predecessors, it contains four chapter and 30 provisions. In adherence to Mao Zedong's request that no person's name should appear in the Party Charter made at the 10th CPC's Congress when the Party Charter undertook a revision, the names of Mao and Lin Biao were removed from the constitution – The Article 2 was originally "Chairman Mao is the great leader of all ethnic groups, the head of our country's proletarian dictatorship and is the command in chief of the national military forces, Lin Biao vice Chairman is Chairman Mao's intimate comrade, successor, as well as the vice commander in chief of the national military forces", was changed to "the Communist Party of China is the core of leadership of Chinese people. Working class lead the country through their vanguards, namely the Communist of China." Article 26 "the most basic right and obligation of a citizen is the loyalty to Chairman Mao and his intimate comrade Lin Biao vice President" was removed. The rest remained unchanged largely except language that deemed capable of inspiring cult of personality. The extreme leftist ideology remained intact. In 75 Constitution, the word "revolution" appeared twenty five times and stated in no uncertain terms that the Revolution should not only be the means but also the end. In fact, the purpose of the constitution is to help turning the country into a revolution base, transforming the society into a hotbed for revolutions, and its people into the so-called "new people". Phases such as "constant revolution", "continued revolution", "perpetual revolution" smack of such a radical revolutionary spirit. Zhang Chunqiao, vice Premier, in his *On Constitution Revision* submitted to First Plenary Session of Fourth CPC Committee wrote "Chairman Mao conceived a plan specifying China's socialist stage – this stage will be protracted. During it, social classes will continue to exist, so will be class conflict and class struggle. The struggle between socialism and capitalism will continue. The danger of capitalist restoration will persist. We should avoid underestimating the duration and complexity of the struggle and stay alert. Socialist education should be undertaken. Class conflict and class struggle should be understood correctly and handled properly. Contradictions between the enemies and ourselves and among people themselves should be separated and treated by different standards. Otherwise, a socialist country like ours may degenerate into what it stands against and restoration will occur. Therefore, from this moment onwards, we must remind us constantly of the danger, to see things in clear eyes and understand that Marxist – Leninist route is our Party's lifeline as well as our country's lifeline. This is what we learned from our experience and should be the guiding principle in the revision of the constitution."

The same revolutionary rhetoric is also manifest in 75 Constitution's Preamble: "For the last 20 years and more, the people of all nationalities in our country, continuing their triumphant advance under the leadership of the Communist Party of China, have achieved great victories both in socialist revolution and socialist construction and in the Great Proletarian Cultural Revolution, and have consolidated and strengthened the dictatorship of the proletariat. Socialist society covers a considerably long historical period. Throughout this historical period, there are classes, class contradictions and class struggle, there is the struggle between the socialist road and the capitalist road, there is the danger of capitalist restoration and there is the threat of subversion and aggression by imperialism and social-imperialism. These contradictions can be resolved only by depending on the theory of continued revolution under the dictatorship of the proletariat and on practice under its guidance."

"We must adhere to the basic line and policies of the Communist Party of China for the entire historical period of socialism and persist in continued revolution under the dictatorship of the proletariat, so that our great motherland will always advance along the road indicated by Marxism-Leninism-Mao Zedong Thought. We should consolidate the great unity of the people of all nationalities led by the working class and based on the alliance of workers and peasants, and develop the revolutionary united front. We should correctly distinguish contradictions among the people from those between ourselves and the enemy and correctly handle them. We should carry on the three great revolutionary movements of class struggle, the struggle for production and scientific experiment; we should build socialism independently and with the initiative in our own hands, through self-reliance, hard struggle, diligence and thrift t and by going all out, aiming high and achieving greater, faster, better and more economical results; and we should be prepared against war and natural disasters and do everything for the people."

Under this revolutionary political logic, revolution must the gravity center that everything else must revolve around. Hence "the state applies the principle of grasping revolution" (Article 10); "firmly put proletarian politics in command" were upheld as the guiding principle of all government personnel (Article 11); The proletariat must exercise all-round dictatorship over the bourgeoisie in the superstructure, including all spheres of culture. Culture and education, literature and art, physical education, health work and scientific research work must all serve proletarian politics, serve the workers, peasants and soldiers, and be combined with productive labor (Article 12); The state safeguards the socialist system, suppresses all treasonable and counter-revolutionary activities and punishes all traitors and counter-revolutionaries. The state deprives the landlords, rich peasants, reactionary capitalists and other bad elements of political rights for specified periods of time according to law, and at the same time provides them with the opportunity to earn a living so that they may be reformed through labor and become law-abiding citizens supporting themselves by their own labor (Article 14).

The Constitution also highlights the CPC's political status. Article 2 stipulates: "The Communist Party of China is the core of leadership of the whole Chinese people. The working class exercises leadership over the state through its vanguard, the Communist Party of China." The Article 15 stipulates: "The Chinese People's Liberation Army and the people's militia are the workers' and peasants' own armed forces led by the Communist Party of China; they are the armed forces of the people of all nationalities. The Chairman of the Central Committee of the Communist Party of China commands the country's armed forces. The Chinese People's Liberation Army is at all times a fighting force, and simultaneously a working force and a production force. The task of the armed forces of the People's Republic of China is to safeguard the achievements of the socialist revolution and socialist construction, to defend the sovereignty, territorial integrity and security of the state, and to guard against subversion and aggression by imperialism, social-imperialism and their lackeys." The Article 16: "The National People's Congress is the highest organ of state power under the leadership of the Communist Party of China." The reason to stipulate the people's basic right is also to reinforce the rule of Communist Party. Article 13 stipulates: "Speaking out freely, airing views fully, holding great debates and writing big-character posters are new forms of carrying on socialist revolution created by the masses of the people. The state shall ensure to the masses the right to use these forms to create a political situation in which there are both centralism and democracy, both discipline and freedom, both unity of will and personal ease of mind and liveliness, and so help consolidate the leadership of the Communist Party of China over the state and consolidate the dictatorship of the proletariat." Article 26 stipulates: "The fundamental rights and duties of citizens are to support the leadership of the Communist Party of China, support the socialist system and abide by the Constitution and the laws of the People's Republic of China."

In terms of political structure, the NPC political form was retained, but reformative measures were undertaken to further revolutionize it. The Article 17 stipulates: "The functions and powers of the National People's Congress are: to amend the Constitution, make laws, appoint and remove the Premier of the State Council and the members of the State Council on the proposal of the Central Committee of the Communist Party of China." Article 21 stipules: "The local people's congresses at various levels are the local organs of state power." Article 22 stipulates: "The local revolutionary committees at various levels are the permanent organs of the local people's congresses and at the same time the local people's governments at various levels. Local revolutionary committees are composed of a chairman, vice-chairmen and other members, who are elected and subject to recall by the people's congress at the corresponding level. Their election or recall shall be submitted for examination and approval to the organ of state at the next higher level. Local revolutionary committees are responsible and accountable to the people's congress at the corresponding level and to the organ of state at the next higher level."

The judicial system was reduced into a subsidiary of the government. Article 25: "The Supreme People's Court, local people's courts at various levels and special people's courts exercise judicial authority. The people's courts are responsible and accountable to the people's congresses and their permanent organs at the corresponding levels. The presidents of the people's courts are appointed and subject to removal by the permanent organs of the people's congresses at the corresponding levels. The functions and powers of procuratorial organs are exercised by the organs of public security at various levels. The mass line must be applied in procuratorial work and in trying cases. In major counter-revolutionary criminal cases the masses should be mobilized for discussion and criticism." The contradictions and confusions are evident in the constitution, but such contradictions are consistent with the revolutionary logic underlying the constitution.

From Sun Yat-sen's Chinese United League and the racial revolution to the Civil Revolution, now Communists assumed the mantle and carried on with the revolution. After two decades of struggle, CPC formed the People's Republic of China. The glorified revolutionary history has been written into the Preamble of the constitutions of New China. There is no denying that the Chinese Revolution under CPC was sincere in their state-building goal. This goal is defined by Mao Zedong in different occasions – first, a "third road" New Democracy republic under the leadership of the Communist Party according to the 1949 Common Program, then a socialist null People's Republic under the dictatorship of proletariat class described by 54 Constitution. Although changes were made in terms constituent power, constitution-making organ, constitution form, government structure and rights protection mechanism from the Common Program, however, the revolutionary state building principle remains the same in both constitutions, and revolutionary spirit was enshrined in both. This spirit was not dissolved after the 54 Constitution (which proved to be impossible); on the contrary, it would grow stronger and reach new heights.

Revolutionary constitution making is the basic feature of modern politics, as indicated by the experience of Britain, United States as well as France and Germany. China's revolutionary experience proved that it is no exception in this regard. However, the relationship between revolution and constitution is of paramount importance for it has a direct effect on the state building process. This is also how the Anglo-American constitutionalism differs from the French and German counterparts; the Soviet Union's, which endeavored to build a proletarian dictatorship, is different from all others. Constitution is made by revolution, yet it is also supposed to check and terminate revolution. For Britain and America at least, the Glorious Revolution and Independent Revolution achieved the desired revolutionary counter-revolution end. By implementing a constitution, politics and law were united; extreme politics would be moderated and transformed into everyday politics; political constitutionalism was transformed into judicial constitutionalism. Chinese revolution, which is more in common with the French and Bolshevik Revolution, failed to introduce a constitution that could terminate revolution; on the contrary, they perpetuated revolutions – in this regard, the Chinese constitution makers evidently beat their Soviet Union counterparts by launching one after another revolution. For them, constitution was the trumpet for revolution, a tool to arouse the masses into action. Revolution to their understanding is about distinguishing enemies from their own, and a revolutionary constitution is a tool to smash the enemies, be they the landlords, rich farmers, reactionaries, criminal elements, rightists, and overseas reactionaries as well as capitalist roaders within the party with ultimate ruthlessness.

75 Constitution's is often undervalued by scholars who dismiss it as a product of extreme leftist ideology. But the constitution deserves more credit for it is a constitution centered around "continued revolution under the dictatorship of the proletariat both in theory and practice", an inevitable outcome of modern China's revolutionary logic as well as a historical riddle that packed answers for some of the most contentious fundamental questions. It also shows what harm could be done by the neglect of "revolutionary counterrevolution". As a constitution 75 Constitution has nothing remarkable except that it is more radical compared with 54 Constitution and Common Program that came before it, hence its unique academic value lies in that it is an example of culmination of hundred years of Chinese revolutionary radicalism, and a summary of the Cultural Revolution that was a indelible part of our history.

Chapter 5
Transformation to Daily Routine: Reform and Governance

One may get the impression that the basic principles of governance had stayed largely unchanged during the six decades of the post-1949 era, if he only looks at the CPC Congress reports during the period. He may not realize that in the year of 1978, a great transition took place that had tremendous impact on China's rule of law development. By rule of law we means not only democratic political and legislative institutions, but also adherence to the law in enforcement as well as a modern bureaucracy system and a relatively independent judicial system to ensures this to happen.

During the first three decades prior to 1978, under the revolutionary guidelines, the legal system reform took an anti-convention, anti-establishment, and political-movement direction. With its focus entirely placed on social movement and sustaining the revolutionary mood, little importance was ascribed to legal system reform. Such situation, compounded by the insufficiency of a democratic representation system and legal norms, placed legal system at the mercy of revolutionary leaders' whims.[1] As a result, the legal system reform during the period is characterized by disregard for standardized legislation procedures, ill-functioned law enforcement department, and sackings of law professionals. For such a development, scholars like Yang Zhaolong expressed deep concerns[2] back in the day. The cause of it, at least according to economic professor Lin Yifu, has much to do with the government's overwhelming priority on developing heavy industry.[3] At that time, political

[1] This political governance model characterized by its circumventive law – professional bureaucrats strays away from Webb's formalist rationality, and should be regarded as a social revolution mobilization and expansion model.

[2] See Yang Zhaolong: *Law's class-ness and inheritability*, East China Politics and Law Journal, December 1956. For more academic criticisms of Yang's theory, see Shanghai Law Society's Law's class-ness and inheritability symposium report, *Yang Zhaolong's law anthology*, Pp. 588–591,, China Legal Institution Press, 2005.

[3] See *Lin Yifu's China miracle – Development Strategy and Economic Reform*, Shanghai People's Publishing House, edition 2, 1999.

Q. Gao et al., *The Road to the Rule of Law in Modern China*,
Research Series on the Chinese Dream and China's Development Path,
DOI 10.1007/978-3-662-45637-8_5

power centralization and central planning were two principles that were adhered to in economy construction; the Party controlled the country and regulated through top-down decrees, while remnant elements of self-governance and market economy from ROC era were all rooted out. Such a governance model is actually more than what Prof. Lin's "high priority to develop heavy industry" could explain; a more convincing explanation is that it was part of the new regime's effort to prove socialism's superiority to the Western models. However, their idealism overreached itself – it demanded too much more than the material conditions – be they industry development or population quality – could deliver; neither could the leaders envisage the internal fights among party leaders as the mass movements grew out of hand nor the outcome of the movements such as Cultural Revolution and People's Commune Movement. Among the main achievements during the period, three versions of constitutions, namely *Common Program, 54 Constitution, 57 Constitution* were enacted consecutively; in terms of the regular legislation, a new *Marriage Law* was the only thing. Due to the stalemate of legislation, the gap left by the abolishment of the KMT civil law and criminal law remained unfilled throughout the period. Overall, China's road towards rule of law suffered great setbacks; large number of law professionals were sidelined, even facing persecution. As a result, the country suffered greatly from disorder, a searing reminder of what can happen when a sound legal system is absent. Perhaps this is the reason why judicial system construction was given such high priority after the Cultural Revolution.

During Mao era, under the guideline of "continued revolution under proletarian dictatorship", a "revolutionary counter-revolution" became impossible– such task would be left to be accomplished during the subsequent Deng era, when political normalization was initiated and a gradual improvement approach was adopted. As we know, a revolutionary counter-revolution is distinctly different from a restoration effort. The former was achieved by revolutionaries highly critical of themselves, resultant in self-consciously repression of the revolutionary passion and violence, restoration of rule of law safeguarding the political principles of the revolution. This process is a healing process, as opposed to the destruction of revolution. Even during the post-1978 era, it was not all smooth, however, in the main, it is a golden age since the Opium War in terms of China's judicial construction. Those who are nostalgic about the late Qing legal reform and Republic of China's Six Codes tend to trivialize the achievement during the three decades. The author of this book, however, takes a highly positive view – Although certain progress was made in the late Qing period, with many legal texts introduced and jurisprudence study undertaken, the legal system reform of that era suffered one fatal shortcoming, namely, the absence of modern state sovereignty. This is corroborated by two facts: (1) China's sovereignty was greatly undermined by Western powers' intervention, resultant in inconsistence of China's legal system construction; (2) Domestically, since late Qing Dynasty, the central government's grasp over local matters begin to slacken; as a result, laws promulgated by the central government were often ignored at a local level, leaving the central government unable to implement and reinforce its own laws. China in Dong era was a different story. Internationally, the "sovereignty building" effort during the Mao era had borne fruit. China was not only recognized as an independent country, but also played an increasingly significant role in international affairs. This external environment conducive to China domestic legal system construction was something that can only be dreamed of in the late Qing dynasty. Moreover, CPC's central government has unchallenged authority with local "feudalist fortresses" had all but pulverized in the revolutions; as a result, strong state capacity provided a solid foundation for legal system reform, which is also facilitated by a flattened state – citizen social structure. Such is the background of the reform era legal system reform.

Rule of law is about order and liberty. Order without liberty is tyranny; liberty without order is utopia. The legal system reform in the post-1978 Reform era has two themes – stability and development. The "stability" refers to the recovering the seriously damaged social order during the Cultural Revolution; specific measures in this regard include the promulgation of Criminal Law and Criminal Procedure Law, two laws that were essential to curb riotous activities. The other theme, "development" entailed implementation of a wide range of institutions to ensure economic development, which has become a top priority in the reform era. This led to the promulgation of commerce law and construction of related litigation system, which are essential for the smooth operation of "commodity economy", or what was later called market economy. One specific measure in this regard is the promulgation of General Principles of Civil Law in 1986. The *82 Constitution* outlines what kind of new legal system that was to be built. Although the constitution was never "judicialized", which weakened its effect, it nonetheless provided a set of standards that formed the basis for resolving disputes concerning legality of government policies. Overall, *82 Constitution* was significant more for the awareness enhancing value than as a functioning fundamental law. In mid-1980s, after the political institutional reform began, common law reform showed fast progress, especially with the formulation of *Administrative Procedure Law* in 1989, China's public law development made unprecedented headway, transforming the government-public relationship from one-sided repression to equal contestation, which had huge implications in shaping people's identity in the society as legal subjects. Overall, a new governance model noted for openness took shape in the reform era, a departure from the Mao era. Meanwhile, the Party's Leadership principle was also strengthened through the implementation Four Basic Rules and was enshrined by the new constitution, though in practice, its effect had been moderated with the recovery of regular legislation and counterbalanced by new values such as social self-governance and market freedom. In adherence to the "transformation" guideline, experiments were carried out to find out alternative solutions, which spurred the party's leadership to adapt itself and actively took steps to facilitate state's normalization, social self-governance and market freedom. Such a transformation was not bottom up, but top down in the form of decrees from the central government and political decisions.

To fully appreciate the Reform-era rule of law development, one needs to steer clear of all sorts of prejudices. For example, from the perspective of pure judicial independence and constitutional judicialization, China's legal construction may not be fit the conventional Western description of rule of law; this has led to argument that although China has a constitution, it doesn't have constitutionalism or rule of law at all.

However, when we examine the fundamental aspects of China's constitutionalism, it is clear that notwithstanding lack of independence, lack of judicialization, a new form of department law self-governance had been burgeoning, and in spite of the less than ideal environment, exploration and self-perfection were undertaken, resultant in the implementation of a judicial interpretation system and legal case supervision system. Other noteworthy innovations include an "administrative adjudication white paper system",[4] "judicial proposition right" and "People's Congress's inquiry power". Despite that there was a populist tendency in legal system since 2008, it didn't reverse the course of the legal system reform as some worried; in fact, it was a stress test. One example is that even during the heyday of Chongqing's "Sing Revolutionary Songs and Crack Down Mafia Crime" movement, the Mao era movement-style model (as demonstrated by the trial of lawyer Li Zhuang) failed to be reinstalled, to a good measure due to the opposition of the normal law departments and the lawyers' community. While China's constitutionalism still has much to be desired, the role of legal system reform should not be overlooked for the support it provided to the constitutionalist progress.

Legal system reform during the post-1978 era took place on two fronts, one is constitution and the other is normal laws; progress was relatively slow in terms of constitution –"judicialized constitutionalism" as a new development, failed to achieve the desired outcome, while "politicalized constitutionalism" made some headway. In comparison, strides have been made on the front of normal laws, at the first stage, private law gained priority due to the high priority accorded to economic development, later, as the social-political reform deepened, giving rise to the task of legitimacy renewal, which, in conjunction with the government's shift of focus from economic growth to social reform, renewed attention was poured onto public law. Overall, we see that China's rule of law has approached a new critical stage of creation and generation during the post-1978 period. In the following paragraphs, we will undertake to provide an analysis of this transformation; while we will try to identify its achievements, we will not hesitate to point out the shortcomings, in order to construct a basis to allow us to better appreciate the of China's legal system development.

[4] For more on the Whitepaper, see Tian Feilong's *Administrative Adjudication White Paper System: Construct a Dialogue System between Legal Construction Rational Powers*, People's Court Journal, Jan 15, 2010.

5.1 Constitution and Mechanism of the Transitional Rule of Law

We have already briefly reviewed the Reform era's legal reform characteristics. Here we will take a bipartite approach to view the uneven development between constitutionalism and ordinary laws. To be specific, the lack of development in terms of constitution, as opposed to the fast progress in terms of normal laws.

Circa 2006, the draft of Property Law bill was publicized to solicit public opinion. Gong Xiantian, a professor at Peking University Law School, wrote a public letter addressed to the central government, in which he criticized the bill as in violation of the constitution. His view caused a stir among the Chinese law academia. Many civil law experts found fault with Gong's supposedly lack of specialized knowledge on civil law as a professor of jurisprudence. Such proprietary attitude is an evidence of the fact that over two decades, civil law academia and related civil law departments had gained great level of monotony and maintained high degree of control over China's civil law legislation. As a result, outsiders rarely got the chance to partake in civil law-related matters, and Gong's speech was seen as an intrusion.[5]

We will focus on one issue that arose in the debate, that is self-governance of normal law departments, which represented a remarkable progress in the legal system reform. However, we should also remind you that notwithstanding its significance as a strategy enabling law scholars and professionals to protect legal reform achievement, this self-governance is not what China's legal system reform all about.

One implication of the debate is that in its wake normal law theories and standards are increasingly applied in discussions about constitutional law issues. There is an increasing belief that China's law should be treated as a unified whole, indifferent of status difference between the constitution and ordinary laws.

Overall, normal law departments' self-governance is the main achievement over the three decades of legal system reform in the reform era; given the great resistance that another development – judicialization of constitution has met, it will likely to stay the main achievement for a considerable time in the future.

The common way to define the concept of "transformation" or "reform" is a descriptive evolutionary portrayal, usually taking the forms such as "from traditional agrarian society to modern industry society, or from traditional rule of men to modern rule of law, from planned economy to market economy, from state and society as one to separation of state and society", etc. Notwithstanding their sociological validity, such way of defining the subject holds little to no normative value. One outcome is that although we use terms such as transformation or reform abundantly, and admit that we have benefited from transformation or reform, we lack a

[5] For more details about the dispute, see Liu Yiqing, Zhang Deqin's *Gong Xiantian Whirwind Report – A Discussion over Property Law Bill*, China Finance and Economics Press 2007. Tian Feilong has a review of the debate in his *Property Law Bill* unconstitutionality debate main argument points and thinking, Jiangsu Police Academy Journal, issue 1, 2007.

normative theory that enables us to reflect on and interpret the reform with more depth; such a theory, had there eve been any, should be called transformology, or reformology.

The descriptive theories regarding transformation or reform often overwhelmingly focus on the outcome, whereas the author of this book proposes a bipartite analysis approach mainly due to his convictions that transformation or reform being an independent process, theories related to them should be primarily concerned with identifying the evolutionary patterns of the institutions and procedures; in the process, try to obtain normative substantiality and avoid the traps of portraying reform or transformation in an idealistically fantastic ways, but to demonstrate it as a realistic, gradualist and organic process of improvement and creation as it is.

With that in mind, we will set about to recount the three decades of reform era legal system modernization.

Due to the revolutionary counterrevolutionary course that China's undertook, its reform is characterized by conservativeness and caution. A structural change of constitution requires a stable and continuous social political environment; as a result, certain amount of authoritarianism is necessary to maintain social stability. In comparison, normal laws, as opposed to constitutional laws, have closer ties to economical activities, where reform has greater breathing space thanks to its relative independence from political intervention. Also noteworthy is that legal system reform originally took a bipartite development pattern, yet as with the independence level of normal law department increasing, this pattern is dissolving. Such a trend can be seen in China's judicial development during recent years, during which the boundary between normal laws and constitution is becoming increasingly obscured; the shift of priority from private law to public law in legislation give people hope that the boundary will finally be removed and a unified logic will apply all laws equally, and a real constitution-based rule of law will finally emerge. Had that happened, it would be a major step forward for China's legal system reform.

In the following paragraphs, we will examine the evolution of the constitution – normal laws bipartite structure during the three decades of reform era and try to identify some basic patterns in this phase of legal system reform.

5.2 Rule of Fundamental Law: From Judicial Independence to Constitutional Judicialization

The so-called "rule of the fundamental law" refers to a state where constitution functioned as the fundamental law and through its normative implementation, creating a condition where state power is exercised in adherence to the constitutional requirements. Professor Karl Loewenstein, German law scholar, divided constitutions into three types depending on their relationships with the political realities – nominal constitution, semantic constitution, normative constitution. Nominal constitution serves mainly a nominal function; it neither accurately reflect nor exert influence over political reality; semantic constitution portrays the state's political reality but retains a minimal influence in restricting political reality; normative constitution, however, both portrays as well as assert normative restraints on the state's political reality.[6] Apparently, when we talk about "rule of the fundamental law", we are mainly talking about the third type, namely, normative constitution.

When China's Reform and Opening-up started, there was little consensus as what China's constitutionalism should be. Back in the day, the two top political principles, namely, class struggle and "Two Always" were just ditched, causing a brief moment of confusion regarding how to carry on with China's socialism construction. To fill the gap, a pragmatic "crossing the river by feeling for the stones" principle was introduced.

During the 1980s, Western constitutionalism theories were introduced in large quantities. At that time, China's understanding of constitutionalism mainly came from three sources, namely, the Soviet Union socialist tradition, the French revolutionary tradition, and the American constitutionalist tradition. The Soviet influence waned after China – Soviet relationship broke and the collapse of USSR; the French tradition remained an significant source of influence, especially the *Declaration of the Rights of Man and of the Citizen* and its axiom "a society in which the observance of the law is not assured, nor the separation of powers defined, has no constitution at all"; the American tradition, at that time had yet gained the level of recognition as it did in the twenty-first century.

Based on these three traditions, the Chinese academia set about to build their own constitutional theories. Among different schools of theories emerged during this period, professor Li Buyun's *Three Factors* figured prominently. Prof. Li contended that constitutionalism contains three key elements: democracy, rule of law and human rights.[7] His view was disparaged by some as overly empirical, simplistic and lacked the logical rigor and coherence. In 1990s, constitution scholar Chen Duanhong, after studying different schools of constitutionalism theories, arrived at a somehow controversial conclusion that constitutionalism equals "limited government".[8] The French *Declaration* whose influence on China's constitutionalism construction was evident, is a classical European interpretation of constitutionalism – its separation of power concept was drawn on French philosopher Montesquieu's classification of state power, to which German philosopher Immanuel Kant provided a logical proof[9]; the concept "right" stemmed from British philosopher John Locke's liberalist view, and his thoughts regarding constraining the state power.

Since the onset of China's Reform and Opening-up era, the Chinese government, in its effort to improve governance, experimented with different models – "rule of law

---

[6] See Lin Laifan's *From Constitution Normativism to Normativist Constitution – A Preamble of Normativist Constitutionalism*, China Law Publishing House, Pp. 264–269, 2001.

[7] See Li Buyun's Towards Rule of Law, Hunan People's publishing house, 1998.

[8] See Chen Duanhong, Primary Theory on Constitutionalism, Journal of Comparative Law, 1992(4).

[9] See Harvey Mansfield's *Taming the Prince*, trans Feng Keli, Yilin Press, P. 3, 2005.

government", "accountable government", "innovative government", "service-style government", "open government" and even "people's livelihood government". However, a "limited government", an ideal upheld by the Western liberal tradition was never officially mentioned, which shows that the government's thought liberation still has much to be desired.

It is evident that China's rule of fundamental law had been hindered by lack of theoretical preparations. From 1978 to 2000, the only development to speak of in terms of constitution is government-dominated amendments and some grassroots level intellectual movements; little progress was achieved in terms of institution reform. However, this situation changed considerably since 2000 when more people began to see American judicial review system as a potential model for China to follow. Within the academia, many began to regard judicialization of constitution as the direction that China's constitutionalism should pursue, as opposed to political constitutionalism, which see political process as the ultimate solution to constitutionalism. This shift has two contributing factors: The first is the Qi Yuling case, which set off an intellectual movement supporting constitution's judicialization; the other is the Chinese law academia's interest in the American-style constitutional judicial professionalism. With constitutional judicialization gaining momentum, renewed effort was undertaken to instill elements of Western constitutionalism to China, including effort to turning the People's Supreme Court into a place to carry out constitution judicialization. Also worth noting is that the academics' voices were often enthusiastically responded by the judiciary. The academic-judicial alliance further promoted the progress of judicial self-governance, a development that converged with constitution judicialization after 2000; together they were often referred to as Judicial Constitutionalism. However, Judicial Constitutionalism also demonstrated certain shortcomings that prevented it from achieving greater effect; for instance, it contravened two fundamental political principles: Party Leadership principle and NPC Supremacy principle. Moreover, Judicial Constitutionalism's impatience and its refusal to acknowledge the reality that China's constitutionalism need time to mature caused negative effects, including the Supreme Court's 2008 revocation of the judicial review it previously issued regarding Qi Yuling Case in 2001. Due to its shortcomings, Judicial Constitutionalism gradually lost momentum to Political Constitutionalism, which advocating constitutionalism implementation through political process. This development indicates the conflict between idealism and political reality in China's legal system reform.[10]

To recap, the main developments on the front of rule of fundamental law during the post-1978 era includes: a constitution revision movement aimed to facilitate economic reform and incorporate new legal elements into the political process;

---

[10]The first advocate of political constitutionalism is Beijing University law school professor Chen Duanhong. See Chen's *On Constitution as A Fundamental Law and Advanced Law*, Zhongwai Jurisprudence, issue 4, 2008; about the academic development of political constitutionalism, see Quanxi's *Tian Feilong's Political Constitutionalism's Question, Identification and Method*, Suzhou University Journal (philosophy and social science edition), 3rd issue, 2011; more about political constitutionalism's location in the spectrum of constitutionalism, see Tian Feilong's *Political Constitutionalism in China's Constitutionalism Study*, Xuehai, issue 2, 2013.

judicial self governance and judicialization of constitution; the rise of Political Constitutionalism indicates waning idealism and a return to realism.

5.2.1 Constitution Revision: Evolution of Reform Era Constitution

Two constitutions, namely *78 Constitution* and *82 Constitution*, were born during this period within a short interval. Aside from the two constitutions, four major revisions were introduced in 1988, 1993, 1999 and 2004. The first constitution of the reform era, *78 Constitution*, is noted for its provisional nature and relatively short life; content-wise, it retained many Cultural Revolution-era relics, making it unsuitable for the reform practice. The 82 Constitution, in comparison, is widely recognized as real reform era constitution.[11]

There are two major views regarding the nature of the post-1949 Chinese constitutions and their relationship. The normativist view asserts that all constitutions should be regarded as revisions of the Common Program for they were introduced through "provisional procedures"; the substantialist view insists that judging by their contents, *54 Constitution* and *82 Constitution* are similar, both emphasizing state's normalization and construction, whereas *75 Constitution* is closer to *78 Constitution*, both having exalted proletarian dictatorship and continued revolution.

The author of this book concurs with the normativist view, regarding the constitution evolution during the post-1949 period as a concatenation of revisions, but for a different reason than the one gave above – neither the constitution-making subjects nor the state form had changed during the period – the subjects who exercise constituent power, remained "the Chinese people under the leadership of the Communist Party of China", so was "people democratic dictatorship" as the state form. Among the constitutions, *82 Constitution* is sort of special, for it alone provided foundation for legislation, leading to great success – in 2011, the government announced that China's "socialist legal system with Chinese characteristics" has been completed. In terms of the fundamental law, although the frequent revisions may have weakened the stability of constitution, they served to confirm the constitutionality of Reform and made timely introduction of new legal elements, hence helped to maintain certain flexibility, inclusiveness, expandability and a formalistic institutionalization.

Of the four constitution revisions, despite their different priorities and objectives, the inner logic was the same, that is adapt the constitution to accommodate economic reform and incorporate new legal concepts. The 1988 revision, for instance, addressed the property right issue of collectively owned land, and legalized land trade, which is demanded by China's urbanization. A side effect is that it provided

[11] There is little dispute that Common Program is a provisionary constitution, the key point of disagreement is the nature of the evolution of constitution in the post-1954 era.

unwanted incentive to local governments and encouraged their forceful evictions. The 1993 revision introduced "socialist market economy" thus enshrined free market economy as a fundamental principle. The 1999 revision confirmed "rule of law" as the goal of government reform. The 2004 revision ensures protection of human rights and personal prosperities.

However, while new provisions were constantly introduced, rarely did the old ones get removed. Among the side effects that such "additionalist" approach revision caused, there are "benign unconstitutionality" and "contradictions of principles".

Benign unconstitutionality is a problem that is typical of China's reform era constitution making. It was mainly caused by lack of judicialization and judicial interpretation system. Such a shortcoming, compounded by laggard revisions, gave rise to phenomena of government policies being temporarily "unconstitutional" until the constitutions were revised later to change the situation.

Like socialist market economy, "benign unconstitutionality" sounds oxymoronic, though a closer look reveals that "benign" is concerned with the consequence, while "unconstitutionality" is more about the procedure. There is a major debate in 1996 deliberating the issue, participated by constitution scholars, who were discontent for not being allowed a more active role in constitution making.

Professor Lin Laifan commented on the "benign unconstitutionality" debate as having "dropped a pebble into the pond of Chinese constitution circles". Thanks to this pebble, new constitution theories blossomed in the aftermath. Professor Hao Tiechuan, soon after he coined the phrase of "benign unconstitutionality", attracted critics of all stripes. Among them, Hao Tiechuan and Zhang Qianfan represent the functionalists of constitution scholars. In an article titled *On Benign Unconstitutionality*, Prof. Hao put forward two criteria, namely, those that facilitate economic development, and those that are conducive to helping the national interest.[12]

Prof. Zhang Qianfan originally opposed the idea of "benign unconstitutionality", but his stance softened considerably over time. In his *Constitutional Flexibility and Local Experiment*, Zhang contended that technically, the Chinese government doesn't need to violate the constitution if it so wished; the Chinese constitution is a "soft constitution", which means the alteration can be achieved relatively easily; he also argues that for the local governments, which didn't possess the power as the central one to alter the constitution, should be allowed more leeway when it comes to constitutionality to encourage them to be more experimental-minded.[13] Meanwhile, in his *What Should Constitution Not Do*?, Zhang argued that not all provisions in the constitution should be adhered with the same rigor, instead, he

[12] See Hao Tiechuan's *On Benign Unconstitutionality*, Jurisprudence Study, issue 4, 1996 and *Limitation of Social Reform and Written Constitution*, Legal Study, issue 4, 1996.

[13] See Zhang Qianfan's *Constitutional Flexibility and Local Experiment*, Jurisprudence Study, issue 1, 2007.

advised a certain "selectivity".[14] Zhang's most severe critic is Prof. Tong Zhiwei, who insisted constitutional norms should be literally adhered to; and all forms of unconstitutional government behaviors, benign or not, should be strictly forbidden, due to one often doesn't have the foresight to judge the consequences of a behavior, or that it is benign or not.[15]

Another view was presented by Professor Han Dayuan, who proposed that "benign unconstitutionality" issue should be resolved through constitutional interpretation. When a dispute arose, a constitutional interpretation should be issued to settle all similar disputes. This view also fall into the purview of normativism.[16] Overall, "benign unconstitutionality" theory had more detractors than supporters; the majority are of the view that conflicts between constitution and policies can be solved through either interpretation, revision or other constitutional procedures. To solve constitutional disputes through means external to constitution runs the risk of diminishing public's confidence in the fundamental law as well as politicalization of constitutional norms. Overall, normativist views dominated the academia, though some holders of the views leaned towards liberalism while other towards conservatism. A decade later, the main critics of "benign unconstitutionality", both Hao and Tong, remained adamant[17] in their opposition. This indicates the lack of a potent theory to explain and regulate the relationship between constitution norms and reform practice, which prevented a meaningful consensus from being achieved.

Given the laggardness of constitution revisions, a routinized day-to-day mechanism should be established. Many suggest that the answer is a constitution interpretation system. Following the promulgation of *Legislation Law* in 2001, the NPC Standing Committee finally approved a procedural review system for normal laws and policies. Although many expected a similar system would be applied for constitutional review, in reality, since 2001, despite the great number of applications for constitutional review s, none of such requests were accepted.

If benign unconstitutionality was a pebble that disturbed the pond of Chinese constitution study circles, then the property law constitutionality dispute was a pebble for China's civil law study circles. At the heart of it is the contradiction of new provisions in the constitution. On August 12, Beijing University constitution jurisprudence professor Gong Xiantian publicized a letter addressed to the central government criticizing the fourth draft of the *Property Law Bill* as unconstitutional; Gong received a barrage of criticisms from civil law scholars. As more civil law scholars and constitution scholars entering the fray, it soon spiraled into a major

[14] See Zhang Qianfan's *What the Constitution Should not Stipulate*, Jurisprudence Forum, issue 3, 2005.

[15] See Tong Zhiwei's *Benign Unconstitutionality Should not be Recognized*, Jurisprudence Study, issue 6, 1996; *Constitution Flexibility's Bottom, Jurisprudence Study*, issue 5, 1997.

[16] See Han Dayuan's *Social Change and Constitution's Adaptiveness– on Mr. Hao and Mr. Tong's Debate over Benign Unconstitutionality*, Jurisprudence, issue 5, 1997.

[17] See the speeches of the two professors and papers that they submitted to the national symposium over "legalization" of the relationship between central government and local governments at Beijing University' constitution and administrative law research center (2007).

dispute. Gong's main argument is that without an provision confirming the "socialist public property is sacred and inviolable" in the constitution (Article 12), the bill was in violation of the constitution in the formalist sense, while the "equal protection" provision in the bill is against the "socialist economic system of the People's Republic of China is socialist public ownership of the means of production" provision in the constitution, and constituted a violation of the constitution in the substantialist sense.[18]

In his criticism, Gong contended that the bill contravened the constitutional stipulation that "socialist public property is sacred and inviolable" as well as its socialism principle. Such a view was rebuked by the civil law scholars. Most of these criticisms are grounded in liberalism underlying the civil law, and supportive of the bill on the ground that the draft bill is pro-equality and pro-universality and its legislation should be independent.[19]

A large number of criticisms attack Gong's lack training in property law. As scholar Chen Duanhong observed, most of the criticisms presented by the civil law scholars failed to "engage Chen's argument at the same level", thus failed to disprove Gong's point that the socialism principle is violated by the bill.[20] Although many constitution scholars participated in the debates, only a small number were supportive of Gong's view; most of them lent their support to the civil law scholars,[21] hence it would be inaccurate to say that the debate is between constitution scholars and civil law scholars. Overall, this debate reveals the chasm between "fundamentalist normativism" represented by Gong and "liberalist normativism" represented by many of his critics. On this debate Prof. Tong Zhiwei made a remark: "The socialist public ownership provision and the market economy provision (in the constitution) were invoked by both sides to attack each other … due to this inherent contradiction of the constitution, violation is inevitable."[22] Finally, Tong decided that he would side with Gong in the debate.

If the benign unconstitutionality issue and additionalist-style constitution revisions are any indication, they show the need for a routinized everyday solution to

[18] See Gong Xiantian's *An Unconstitutional and Anti-socialist Property Law bill – A Public Letter Calling for Abolishment of Constitution Article 12, and 1986 Civil Law General Principle's Article 73*, Beijing Law Information Online: http://article1.chinalawinfo.com/article/user/article_display.asp?ArticleID=32266

[19] See Wang Liming's *Why the Equal Protection Provision is Completely Constitutional?* Bright Daily, January 22, 2007; *Property Law is the Foundation of the Law Edifice*, Democracy and Law, issue 1, 2007; Liang Huixing's *Property Law Bill and Multiple Problems*, China Jurisprudence, issue 1, 2007.

[20] See Chen Duanhong's On constitution as the fundamental law and advanced law, Zhongwai Prudence, issue 4, 2008.

[21] See Zhang Qianfan's *The Use and Misuse of Constitution – How to Treat the Constitutional Problem in Property Right Law*, Jurisprudence magazine, issue 3, 2006; Han Dayuan's *Multiple Constitutional Problems related to Property Law Bill*, Jurisprudence Magazine, issue 3, 2006.

[22] See Tong Zhiwei's *How Can Property Law Bill Pass the Gate of Constitution – Comment on A Constitutionality Dispute Caused by A Public Letter*, Jurisprudence Magazine, issue 3, 2006; *Second Comment on Constitutionality Problems in Property Law Bill*, Jurisprudence Study, issue 7, 2006.

better meet increasing demand for constitutional review. However, a judicial review system advocated by the Judicial Constitutionalism may not be answer; the answer can be, and perhaps should better be what Political Constitutionalism advocated – a legislation review system. This is corroborated by the fact despite the *Legislation Law* was promulgated over a decade ago, and supposedly offers judicial review, requests for constitutional review have never been accepted. This failure to meet the demand, if can't be addressed properly, can hamper China's political stability and constitutionalist progress in the long run. It takes a major political commitment to activate the review mechanism.

5.2.2 Judicial Constitutionalism: Idealist Pursuit and Institutional Challenge

Judicialization as a way to realize rule of law is rooted in the Western rationalist and aristocratic legal tradition, where law was an traditional, well-respected profession and judges were living embodiments of rationality and justice, wearing the halos of law-protector; the judiciary was a defense line to maintain social harmony and order. The natural justice principles established by the British Magna Carta, are regarded the most fundamental judicial principles. In near-modern times, under the impact of a new wave of democratization, this rationalist judicial tradition, originally sought to check tyranny of autocrats, turned its priority to tyranny of the masses. This has given rise to tension between judicial review and democracy.[23]

The method that the West adopts to ease this judicial-democracy was derived from its own tradition. After the strenuous effort of generations of law professionals and judges, what we know as judicial constitutionalism was implemented. In such a system, judges are assigned the role of constitution protectors; two fundamental principles, namely, independence of judicial process and judicialization of constitution are upheld. Judicial independence is another notion rooted in Western tradition where practicing law was traditionally seen a highly specialized craft that entailed a certain degree of autonomy from politics. Hence constitution judicialization can be seen as judicial tradition's response to the provocation posed by modern democracy. Constitution judicialization presupposes that all social-political depute should be viewed as a legal dispute that can only be solved through judicial process; it also sees rational debates as the primary way to ensure law's authority and strengthen rationalist consensus in the society. Its claimed superiority lies in two respects: first, it has greater consensus building capacity; second, it is more rational and reliable than political alternatives in resolving disputes over basic rights.[24]

[23] This is especially prominent in American jurisprudent study in the nineteenth and twentieth century.

[24] This argument is criticized by Mark Tushnet in his *Why Constitution is Important*, Tian Feilong, trans, China University of Political Science and Law Press, 2012.

As mentioned before, during the first three decades of New China, the importance of justice system was disregarded as the government assorted to a political-social movement route. This situation was only reversed after China adopted a policy of Reform and Opening-up, during which, measures were taken to restore the justice system. Such decision was made to a good measure due to the lessons learned from the Cultural Revolution when justice system was dysfunctional. Measures were implemented to rationalize state administration through law and justice and protect individual's personal rights and property rights. Throughout 1980s and 1990s, increasing demand for judicial independence, in conjunction with the promulgation of three litigation-related laws and judicial professionalization reform during Xiao Yang's tenure as the Supreme Court president, influenced judicial system's development, especially in terms of normal laws.

However, notwithstanding the progress, the road towards rule of law during the reform era was not a smooth one. In terms of judicial independence, progress was hindered by three factors, namely, collectivism, "localness" and "limitedness". Although *82 Constitution* and *Court Organic Law* both upheld independence of judicial process, this "judicial independence" was granted to the courts rather than individual judges, thereby, such "judicial independence", collective in nature, is different from the individualistic Western norm. China's courts of law are traditionally part of the government and meting out justice is regarded a governmental function. Given that, one should not be too surprised by the fact that in China, former PLA offers with no legal professional training to speak of used to be sent to courts to work as judges.

In China's collective judicial system, judges' decisions are often subject to external influences in the forms of instructions or "suggestions" from court leaders or adjudication committee leaders; the courts are likewise influenced by intervention from the government. One example is that local courts are under pressure to provide "judicial assistance" to local governments in their forced eviction programs. In addition, under the current political structure, local courts of law are often organizationally and financially reliant on local governments, which both diminished their independence, and led to failure to meet the normative requirements of the law.

China's judicial independence also has other catches. Although judicial system is by law independent of government administrative agencies, social communities, and individuals, but it remains subject to intervention from NPC and CPC. Such level of independence obviously can't meet the standards set by progressive law scholars, who demand higher degree independence from all political intervention, and court to exercise jurisdiction based only on law. But in practice, such ideals often fall short of reality. Interventions mostly come from local government, but the lack of independence to National People's Congress and the Party made the limited independence even more precarious.

In fact, NPC's "case supervision" institution has long been criticized as detrimental to judicial independence. After the promulgation of *Supervision Law* in 2006, the "case supervision" practice has largely ceased. In addition, through the Politics and Law Committee, the Party sent instructors as advisors to courts. These instructors often acted as the courts' de facto leaders who can influence the rulings.

As a result, ideals such as specialization, independence, and authority of the judges are diminished and judicial system is often treated as subsidiary to government; their function is purely instrumental. Hence, during the three decades of the reform era, great efforts have been undertaken by law professionals and academics to promote judicial independence. Not only lawyers and academia participated in such efforts, some judges, especially those who received education abroad, also joined the ranks of people demanding independence and professionalization. This is exemplified by the first and second Supreme Court five-year reform guidelines formulated under Xiao Yang's tenure.

Two factors contributed to the slowdown of judicial professionalization after 2000: First, as the development of "constitution judicialization" expanded beyond the realm of legal system reform and became increasingly vocal in demanding political institution reform, the government began to feel uneasy. Secondly, reform led to mounting political-social tension, which expressed in frequent "mass incidents". During its handling of the incidents, the government grew to rely on non-judicial means. Despite such impediments, certain progress was achieved, such as the enactment of the "Administrative Ruling White Paper" system. Meanwhile, "people's justice" movement saw rapid growth in influence, leading many law scholars to worry that it may further negatively affect the professionalization.

In comparison, greater progress was achieved in the realm of constitution judicialization. Constitution judicialization is not the logical consequence of judicial independence. Judicial independence is a classical legal phenomenon, while constitution judicialization is judicial independence's response to modern democracy. During the past three decades, great efforts has been undertaken to study and incorporating Western judicial independence theories, leading to two major outcomes: First, they enhanced public's awareness of modern judicial culture; second, they promoted normal law reform. Constitution judicialization also has profounder effect on institution reform. Professor Wang Lei at Law School of Beijing University, first put forwarded constitution judicialization theory, advocates that constitution should be treated, first and foremost, as a law. Such a view was originally known among constitution scholars, but gained broader audience after the Qi Yuling case in 2001. The person involved in the case, a woman from Shandong province named Qi Yuling. In 1990, Qi passed the entrance exam for technical secondary schools. Another student, with the assistance of the schoolmaster, stole the admission letter and studied using fake papers. The difficulty of the case is that right to education was not a statutory right under ordinary law, nonetheless, it is a constitutional right. In response to local court's request for judicial interpretation, on August 13, 2001, the Supreme Court issued a reply, which confirmed that Chen Xiaoqi and others had infringed Qi's right and they should pay corresponding damages. On the same day, a Supreme Court judge published an article on *People's Court News,* expressing support that a constitutional right should be enforced like regular legal rights.[25] The case commanded great public attention, but it is not considered a typical "judicial

[25] See Huang Songyou's *Constitution Judicializaiton and Its Implications*, People's Court News, August 13, 2001.

review" case because no abusive use of public power was involved – which many believe is the reason that the Supreme Court had the "courage" to make a decision in favor of constitution judicialization; many argued that had State Council or NPC involved in any constitutional violation, it would be very unlikely that the Supreme Court would make the same decision. But typical or not, what is special about the case is that the Supreme Court's reply enunciated that constitutional rights are guaranteed by civil law; in case of constitutional rights violation, the court of law is obliged to provide legal relief and constitution provisions can be cited to justify such rulings. Qi Yuling case is often compared with the Marbury v. Madison case in academic discussion with many hoping that it would prompt China to officially recognize judicial review. As a result, in the aftermath of the case, constitutional review and basic rights study attracted much academic interest. However, 7 years later, Supreme Court revoked its "Reply" during the height of the "people's justice" movement. While this "people's justice" movement gained momentum, judicial professionalization and constitution judicialization hit their low ebbs. Worth noting is that not all academics were supportive of constitution judicialization; some also believe that constitution as the basis of judicial rulings is not exactly constitutional review system.

Around the same time when constitution scholars were debating over the Qi Yuling case and constitution judicialization, another group of scholars, among them professor Zhang Qianfan is one of the most influential, undertook to systematically introduce American "constitution professionalism" to the Chinese academia.[26] Their effort gave a boost to the judicial professionalization, though many overlooked the fact that China doesn't have the US's common law tradition. Because this tradition, although today few Americans heard about the 1803 Marbury v. Madison case, it doesn't diminish the validity of it as a judicial precedent.

China's law as of 2001 has some distinct traits of the continental law system. For example, it doesn't give precedential authority to prior court decisions. Given that there is no clearly stated constitutional provision, the Supreme Court technically doesn't have the authority to conduct constitutional review. Moreover, different from judicial independence movement, whose influence is limited to the realm of normal laws, constitution judicialization concerns the most fundamental components of constitutionalism; moreover, it not only sought to bring about changes within the legal system but also without.

Scholars supportive of constitution judicialization didn't want Qi Yuling case's implications to be limited to level of judicial rulings; they sought to use it as a catalyst to bring about an American or German-style constitutional review system. Such demand for a radical overhaul of current political form is more than China's constitutionalist system can tolerate. Because Chinese constitution is deeply wedded to the NPC system, judicial review system, which met relatively little opposition in other "transformative" countries, faced far greater resistance in China. As a result of

[26] See Zhang Qianfan's *Western Constitution System – American Constitution* Vol 1, China University of Political Science and Law Press, 2000, *Western Constitution system – European Constitution* Vol 2, China University of Political Science and Law Press, 2001.

such resistance, none of the abovementioned efforts achieved much. This is corroborated by the fact that Supreme Court revoked its judicial reply regarding Qi Yuling case. The revocation is widely attributed to the Chinese government's toughened stance against constitution judicialization, thus a new solution must be found to give a new impetus to China's stalled constitution reform.

To recap, a rather rudimentary framework of rule of law has been instituted during the past three decades, yet problems remain. Judicial independence movement was suppressed. The quality of judicial self-governance is relatively low, yet two developments, namely judicial professionalization, implementation of Supreme Court judicial interpretation system, had expanded the space of independence for judicial system. The "Administrative Ruling White Paper" system is another example that shows the initiative of the judicial system.

On the other hand, constitution judicialization's influence waned as a result of its failure to be recognized by the establishment, mainly because its contradiction with the Party Leadership principle and NPC system. Thus the likelihood of it playing a significant role in China's future constitutional reform is rather slim. However, this doesn't diminish constitution judicialization's importance as an indicator of the maturity of a country's constitutionalism development. If constitution judicialization is not a plausible solution for China, what are? Some believe that political constitutionalism, whose influence has been on the rise in the Chinese academia, is an alternative answer. This theory proposes to identify the political elements in China's constitution through empirical analysis and normative analysis, thereby recreating a complete, authentic Chinese constitution rich in pragmatic rationality. Professor Gao Quanxi summarized the relationship between Political Constitutionalism and Judicial Constitutionalism as: "picking the judicial constitutionalism fruit using the hand of political constitutionalism",[27] such a view echoed the English constitution theorists who described the relationship of the two as "coexistent yet have different precedence levels" – both existed in the British constitutional system, but political constitutionalism has more priority and is deemed as a better alternative in safeguarding the political equality and non-dominant republican liberty.[28]

[27] See Gao Quanxi's *From Extreme Politics to Daily Routine Politics – on Modern Political-legal System and other Subjects*, p. 3,, China Legal Institution Press, 2009.

[28] See Richard Bellamy, *Political Constitutionalism: A Republican Defense of The Constitutionality of Democracy*, Cambridge University Press, 2007; For Chinese, see Tian Feilong's *A Coexistent and Precedential Regular Politics Constitutionalism – Development of Bellamy's Political Constitutionalism*, unpublished.

5.2.3 The Rise of Political Constitutionalism: Rationalization of Transitional Rule of Law

Supporters of Judicial Constitutionalism both in academia and the court system tried to establish Qi Yuling case as a precedent like the American Marbury v. Madison case. Although such an attempt has commanded great academic interest, even led to a boom of comparison study in the field of judicial reviews. However, due to the peculiarity of China's constitution, little concrete progress was achieved, suggesting there is an invisible wall between the academic idealism and the institutions. If the wall has to be torn down forcefully, then China's constitutionalist reform, so far has been moderate, may be turned into another radical revolution. It is worth mentioning that constitution study as an academic discipline that is proud of its conservativeness; it is about curtailing revolutionary radicalism through rationality and normative procedures, thus the idea of radical revolution based on pure idealism should be seen as a betrayal of the discipline. In a time when the pursuit of judicial constitutionalism stagnated, some constitution scholars draw on French-German public law tradition and English constitution philosophy resources, and put forward a political constitutionalism view, trying to find a route that is more empirically rational for China's constitutionalism. Two scholars holding this view figured prominently – Prof. Chen Duanhong and Prof. Gao Quanxi.

In August 2008, Prof. Chen Duanhong published *On Constitution Being The National Fundamental Law And Supreme Law*. In this groundbreaking article, the author put forward a view urging applying Political Constitutionalism principles in China's constitutional reform. This article, essentially an interpretation of the 1982 Constitution, shines the political constitutional rationality. It is widely regarded as a milestone in constitution by the academia. In the article, following a historical review of English political constitutionalism, the author went on to bridge the gap between political constitutionalism and republicanism by proposing a multi-layered constitutional review system based on the principle of "It is the duty of the sovereign to protect constitution", suggesting that the burden of conducting constitutional reviews should fall on the shoulders of CPC. Prof. Chen is primarily concerned with the question of how to construct the Chinese sovereignty and politics under increasing pressure of post-modern de-sovereignty and de-palatalization tendency. Chen's intellectual direction is greatly influenced by German political philosopher Carl Schmitt, yet he is also well versed in the French Enlightenment thinking, especially, those of Rousseau and Sieyes. The political constitutionalism system that he proposed contained four basic elements – democracy within the Party, parliamentary democracy, information disclosure, and public participation. Since 2004, Chen's study has been focusing on two areas – sovereignty theories and constituent power; in addition, he also set about to conduct an analysis of the structural problems of China's Constitution, and the results were expressed in two books: *Constitutional Rule and Sovereignty* and *Constituent Right and Basic Law*. Both are cool-headed reflection of academic activities in the wake of 2001 Qi Yuling Case and the later Constitution Judicialization. Critical of the normativist approaches that emphasize on norms and minute textual details, preventing one to appreciate the bigger picture, Chen provided an understanding of the constitution that is distinctly different form the mainstream constitution scholars.

Prof. Gao Quanxi, on the other hand, approached the question more from the angle of intellectual history. First, he identified the position Chinese constitutionalism in the landscape of the Chinese intellectual history. Gao's observation and judgment is that China since the onset of Opium War strived for twin goals – building a modern state and building a modern citizenry. Such the twin goals have never fully accomplished, hence China's development level resembles Western countries in their early modern ages. Gao introduced the concept of early modern, and put forward his thesis that China's problems today are structurally identical to those faced by the West early modern era, which he summarized into three pairs of themes: war-revolution, wealth-property right, religion-soul. In addition, Gao undertook to identify China's constitutionalism development level as of today by a review of history. Gao contends that since 1840, Chinese political and cultural elites took strenuous efforts to find a state building strategy, which was rather unsuccessful, and urged that the Chinese today should have the courage to acknowledge this reality and carry on with the mission, which is the only way to be historically responsible. Gao also delineated the constitutional implications of China's First Republic and Second Republic. The first refers to ROC, which was founded in 1911, the first Republic in Asia. The first Republic started the tradition of party-state in China. The Second Republic refers to CPC's New China, during which the party-state continued to cause trouble to its constitutions. Gao believes that the unification of PRC and Taiwan should be unification of two constitutions, or rather, the institutional integration of the First Republic and the Second Republic; he warned against a textualist interpretation or a purely normative view of constitutionalism, which may hinder the great unification cause of the Chinese nation.[29]

Today's constitution scholars focused overwhelmingly on the "universal value norms" and judges' interpretations, while showed inadequate intellectual depth and overall strategic thinking that a constitution maker should have. Due to their limited academic vision fields, they sometimes treated universal questions as unique to China, often overlooking the real "China problems". More specifically, we are facing the task of "depoliticizing", yet if a modern nation wasn't politically mature enough, and hasn't reached the logical "utopian state of rule of law", they are unlikely to be intellectually ready for such a task. This is clearly shown by the experience of many developing countries, which suffered from their lack of self-reflectiveness and prudence. Here I would conjecture that Chinese political constitutionalism's biggest objective should be accumulating experience, establishing procedures, and identifying patterns based on the real practice of constitution decision-making; in the process, identifying dominant principle and rational rules, and turn them into theories and institutions. In fact, China's constitution is not all about bill of rights; the real progress is often more evident in the Preamble and

[29] See Gao Quanxi, Tian Feilong's *Political Constitutionalism Questions, Identification and Methods*, Suzhou University Journal (philosophy and social sciences), issue 3, 2011.

General Principles sections. Contrary to what some constitution scholars believed, Political Constitutionalism possessed a strong normative consciousness. What led to the birth of Political Constitutionalism is not only a deep-reflection of the less-than-ideal reality, but also the urge to establish connection between the constitutional political norms and political decision-making. It is concerned with discovery of rules in existence and the rules' relationship with constitutional political principles. It regard rules identified through sociological discovery as raw materials, the principles depicted by the constitution text as a transformer, and its priority is to search, identify, and produce constitutional norms, in doing so, make the constitutional political principles more applicable and clearly defined; it seeks to make constitution's implementation and adaption an organic process that reflect the facts and stay normative. But such a task should not only be undertaken by judges, or limited to rights. To make itself stay uncorrupted, it should be limited its role to interpreting constitution rules, for once it get mixed up with political factors, it may lose its theoretical legitimacy.

When it comes to specific institutions, political constitutionalism argues that constitutional democracy should have higher priority than judicial review. We believe that during the transformation period, the public's constitutional rights to participate in politics can be better supported by democratization than an elitist approach of constitutional judicialization due to that the former is easier to be accepted politically by the current constitutionalist institutions. Although some law scholars have been arguing that judicial review system is the one of the safest and "frictionless" approach, such a view is based on overseas experience and can't be simplistically applied to China disregarding its specific conditions. China's current constitutionalist institutions pose three obstacles for the successful implementation of a constitutional review system. First, the state form, namely, the People's Democratic Dictatorship, and the Party's Leadership; secondly, the political form, namely National People's Congress system, which processed the power according to the constitution to overrule the Supreme Court – this is almost impossible to change in the short run; third, the government's "executive power" should be tamed by the court system. It is worth noting that such a tradition was never disrupted either by revolutionary radicalism or the post-1978 era "judicialization". Given the reasons provided above, if dramatic changes can't be introduced to adapt the constitution, contrary to many people believed, a judicial review route would prove to be much difficult to pursue than the more NPC-friendly "constitutional democracy" route. The difference of the two routes lies in that the judicial review is based on purely idealistic theoretical inference rather than a realistic political assessment; on the other hand, constitutionalist democracy rote is grounded in the "democracy precedence principle", and "democratic procedural rationality", hence are more compliant with the constitution's reconciliatory and pragmatically spirit. The later seeks to solve the problem from two respects, namely, democratic deliberativeness and social self-governance. By referring to democracy, we focus on substance over form, therefore it is not our concern how elections were conducted. By deliberativeness we mean that NPC as a parliamentary deliberative institution should play a central role in forming political constitutionalist institutions; to achieve that purpose, effort should be made to enhance NPC's representativeness, transparency, quality of debate, and level of public participation, in doing so, improve its efficacy and enable it to better respond people's political demands, resolve conflicts and intermediate between interest groups more effectively. In almost all these aspects the current NPC system showed insufficiency; due much to its unawareness of its own role, it doesn't have sufficient institutional protections. However, we need acknowledge the legitimacy of Politics First principle. An Executive Procedural Law should be promulgated to improve government information disclosure and improve the quality of public participation. Aside from institutional democratization at the NPC level, spontaneous democratization at the grassroots level should also be given greater priority. Here we must point out a trend of increasing preference of a descriptive portrayal based on the finest Western samples such as the American Constitution as a replacement for original rigorous thinking. Our understanding of constitutionalism has a structuralist trait whose origin can be traced to the 1789 *Declaration of the Rights of Man and of the Citizen*, according to which "A society in which the observance of the law is not assured, nor the separation of powers defined, has no constitution at all." The notion of separation of powers was conceived by Montesquieu, which offers a scientific solution from within, with its logical proof was provided later by Immanuel Kant. The concept of "rights" was first put forward by John Locke in his liberalist government theory, whose central idea is that state power should be limited; rights were used to demarcate the boundary between state and society – here right is construed not only as a passive defense of the citizens against the state power, but forms the foundation for social self-governance. Today the academia often talk about human rights in the context of constitutional review techniques, but I think human right is also extremely significant concept in terms of separation of power between state and society, which is critical to liberty and modern constitutionalism. The essence of social construction is that society be regarded as a subject, rather than an object, and the only criterion that can be applied to measure whether the society is treated as a subject is the level social self-governance. However, this is not the case in our social development, which has been placing its emphasis on people's living conditions and distribution of social wealth, while denying to accord society the necessary autonomy, which is a main defect in the guidelines of our socialist construction. As a result, despite the government constantly talking about improving economic wellbeing, large amounts of resources (estimated to have exceeded national defense budget) were allocated to "social stability maintenance". This indicates that we are not developing a "society" in the true sense of the word, for the development lacks spontaneity. The real stability can only be achieved in society's spontaneous operation within the bounds of law without political interference. Only through open democratic deliberation and self-governance, can we have a rational mature democracy and develop a social public domain, which is also the best way to avoid social order crisis in the process of democratization and transformation towards constitutionalism.

To a good measure due to the barriers between academic disciplines, interaction between Political Constitutionalism and related jurisprudential fields have been limited. However, given the urgency of China's constitution reform, research in

Political Constitutionalism has gained considerable interest from constitution theorists and government alike, resultant in the emergence of a new field of study called Legal Politics Study.[30] The rise of Political Constitutionalism presaged the rationalization of China's transformation legal system reform and must be treated as a new interpretative angle. Also noteworthy is that new development of building a "rule of law government", which put an emphasis on ensuring citizens' "right to know", "right to participate", "right to express and supervise"; political and legislative processes are becoming increasingly open to democratic participation; government's accountability improved; measures are undertaken to reinforce democracy within the Party and rule of law reform. Although these don't normally fall into the purview of Judicial Constitutionalism study, or jurisprudence comparison study, they are nonetheless part of the Chinese practice of Political Constitutionalism. In terms of implementation of constitutionalism, Political Constitutionalism is undoubtedly a valuable direction to explore.

5.3 Rule of Specific Law: From Private Law Taking Precedence to Rise of the Public Law

Compared with the lack of progress in constitution reform, much has been accomplished on the front of normal laws, mainly in the form of what I would refer to as specific law or department law self-governance. Criminal law and civil law were promulgated shortly after the Cultural Revolution due to the urgent need to recover ravaged social order and to regulate the burgeoning "commodity" economy. The two laws served their purpose well in stabilizing social and maintaining market order during the first two decades. However, as the reform reached its third decade, cracks began to show in the relationships between government and market as well as government and society. Starting in 1980, there arose the need for an administrative law. Given China's goal of building a market economy and implementing rule of law, administrative law posed a new possibility for China's governance model reform, and resulted in a period of fast development of public law. Some other main developments of department law self-governance during the period are: (1) A self-governed academic discourse system emerged, which has great implications to legislative and judicial practice; the academia exerts increasing influence over the legislation of normal laws and judicial policy formulation, while the public participation showed little improvement; (2) A judicial community was formed. Through education and training, interaction with legal professionals, and consultation, academia was able to exert greater influence on normal laws and adjudication-related matters. (3) A fast growing lawyer community, whose active participation in "charity public interest lawsuits" effectively checked the government's violation of the

[30] Professor Gao Quanxi's *Political-legal Thoughts Anthology* is a typical example in this regard, see Tian Feilong's *China Political-legal Cause and Responsibility – the Ideals of Political-legal Thoughts Anthology*, Economic Observer, book review special issue, August, 2011.

laws. (4) Lack of effective communication with constitution, and its legitimacy overly relies on idealistic norms that are impossible to be proven empirically. As for the self-governance phenomena, a balanced view is highly recommended – while it is the most concrete and practical achievement in the reform era in terms of normal laws, and has huge implication to public awareness, resolving social disputes, as well as exploring government governance models, however, due to the lag on the constitution development, the structural defects of China's legal system remained. As for the overall direction during the reform era, a basic pattern is clear: The focus has shifted from private law to public law; public administration and government-public relationship is the current focus. Because there are many department laws, we will primarily focus on three of them.

5.3.1 Criminal Law: From "Procedural Self-Governance" to Public Opinion's Involvement

Criminal Law and *Criminal Procedural Law* were both promulgated in 1979. *Criminal Law* was enacted first and was given higher priority due to the urgency to hold trial against the four culprits of the Cultural Revolution; moreover, the social order, badly damaged during the Cultural Revolution, needs to recover. In the early days of the reform era, the old "movement-style governance" thinking continue to reign supreme in the judicial system, as a result, throughout the 1980s, despite procedures introduced by the two laws, breaches of proper procedures and violations of suspects' basic rights were commonplace. As social order stabilized, the focus of the judicial system was shifted from curbing crimes to safeguarding human rights; it has become a consensus that legal procedures should be the main recourse to ensure human rights. During the reform era, in response to increasingly vocal demands from criminal law academics and public, two new developments took place, namely Procedural Supremism and Procedural Self-governance.

In 1997, revision was undertaken to revise *Criminal Law* and *Criminal Procedural Law* to better reflect the decade worth of legal practice. As a result of the revision, crimes such as "anti-revolution" were removed; penalty system was also adjusted in compliance with the principle of "proportionality of crime and punishment"; procedural protections of suspects were strengthened; "no penalty without a law" principle was upheld as the primary principle of criminal law, while "procedural justice" became the primary principle of criminal procedural law.

To a good measure due to the effort of academia and law professions, a normativist criminal law system took shape. However, criminal law department's demands for autonomy often clash with the existing political and social norms. On one hand, it contravenes the "victim justice" convention, and affected the courts' decisions in cases such as the Liu Yong case, Yao Jiaxin case, Li Changkui case; under pressure of public opinion, the courts were forced to succumb to external force and give up their autonomy. Such situation beg the questions – how should the judicial system respond when legal notion of justice contradicts the public's notion of justice, how to bridge the gap between judicial system and the "democracy" factor, or rather the public will. In addition, procedural self-governance also clashes with government's governance model, as indicated by the trial of lawyer Li Zhuang, in which the law scholars and lawyer community expressed great support for Li, presumably a factor that led the Chongqing government to drop the suit.

The tension between judicial system and public will is often compounded by the lack of judicial independence and judicial corruption. Public opinion in China is often disparaged as irrational by law professionals because it often contravenes the "formalist rationality" that law scholars' upheld. However, such a "professionalist" attitude from the law professions has proved to be often counterproductive in softening the conflict between judicial system and the public opinion, which can't be dismissed as totally irrational. The year of 2008 saw two renowned cases, Xu Ting case and Yang Jia case. In the former, the defendant received a reduction in sentence due much to the demand from both law experts and the public in his favor. In the later case, despite the sympathy the public and law profession accorded to the defendant, the Supreme Court upheld a death sentence meted out by a lower court. Although in the two cases, the law professionals largely concurred with the public, this is not always the case, as exemplified in the Liu Yong case. In this case, the court succumbed to the public will and disregarded the law scholars' appeals contrary to the public's. One thing in common among all the cases is that they were highly publicized and garnered much public attention. Nonetheless, they showed that the public's conception of justice and the law scholars' can be radically different.

When we talk about democracy institution in our modern times, we usually refer to representative democracy, which entails a fair election – people are given equal right to choose their representatives who represent their interests in the parliament. The parliament is where the laws are made, and the laws are meant to be observed as the fundamental rules within the society. The soul of modern democracy, many believe, rests on the democratization of legislation. The so-called Rule of Law, put simply, means courts meting out justice in strict compliance with law, only when these requirements are met, implementation of law can be regarded as realization of justice. Through implementing democratic institution, legitimacy is first transferred from individuals to parliament, then to the court of law and finally back to individuals. In this way, law can be regarded as a legitimacy conveyer belt, an indirect expression of the public's will, given that it is formulated through in "indirect" democratic representation system, instead of made by the people directly. Such is how the modern states' democratic legal system works, and is what China's legal system modernization seeks to install. This indirectness can lead to conflict between public will and law. This is in fact clashes of two public wills – on one side, there is the normative public will under the assumption that the representation is full and effective, on the other, the incidental public will from a specific group of people.

As long as representative democracy continues to exist, this conflict will continues. To address this conflict, the West conceived three solutions: election, parliamentary deliberation and public participation in legislation as well as jury system in the judicial process. In China, election has yet been fully implemented; efficacy of parliament is hindered by the uneven quality of People's deputies and these deputies are part-time. The mechanism allowing the public to participate in legislation is not fully functional while the quality and independence of justice can't be taken for granted. To sum up, China's law suffers three hereditary defects: insufficient democracy, insufficient public participation and insufficient judicial justice. As a result, when the public's demand for justice can't be met by the system, they would seek it externally in the form of social movement, leading to frequent protests, petitions, and public letter writing, favored by academics.

This situation led to what is called "individual case justice": Due to the lack of a set of mature and functioning institutions, handling of any individual case can potentially lead to a dispute that requires intervention of legislation and politics, whereas existing legal procedures are often disregarded. Political authority rather than legal institutions or legal rationality is seen as the final solution. Such an environment, marked for frequent public outcries, and lack of a mature order is reminiscent of Rousseau's description about "the sovereign". While the consultation enshrines popular sovereignty, the application of this principle is limited to constitution making and revision, while in everyday life, the task of maintaining state order falls into the hands of the government and its agencies. In this sense, the frequent outcries should be regarded as an alarming signal that requires measures in terms of legal construction.

Regardless of the outcome of these outcries, the risk of public opinion spiraling out of control and hazard state order does exist. For those who have faith in rule of law, an ideal society is one that has a normative democracy and follow normative procedures; it should be a society where common people can expect to receive justice by abiding the law, even it was the state power that they are confronted with; the people and law must always be on the same side rather than against each other. Given the above-mentioned reasoning, people shouldn't held be responsible for frequent "social incidents"; the real culprit of these incidents is the lack of supply of justice.

If the judicial system fail to maintain public confidence in its capacity of delivering justice, then the public would continue to seek justice through channels external of the judicial system, including the political process or social movements, with outcome often more unpredictable. One negative effect of such a development is political authority assumed the role of justice giver, often to the detriment of the health of representative democracy and justice system, and their esteem among the people. If such situation goes unchecked, then China's objective of becoming a "rule of law" country can be hard to realize. Modern politics is first and foremost democratic politics, which presupposes that government stay responsive to people's demands, thought often failing to check the government's inclination to make empty promises and instigate social movements to serve its own agenda.

When we look into the public outcries, it is evident that the only solution lies in strengthening everyday democratic and legal institutions, rather than providing political justice through social movements. The superiority of law as opposed to political movements is the former's ability to break down big convoluted social-political issues into smaller, individualized and compartmented legal issues where judgments can be readily serviced by applying existent obligation-right modules. Justice in the form of judges' adjudications is applicable only affect finite number of cases, therefore the risk of a large scale backlash is lower when compared with a political movements.

There is no such a thing as a perfect democracy or a perfect justice system. Even in the US, there are cases such as the O.J. Simpson trial, which weakened public trust of the judicial system. This sort of confrontation between the public and the judicial system is not necessarily a bad thing to the state stability; what is truly dangerous is when pressure build up without ways to relieve it other than the political way, which carries the risk of escalating the situation into social turmoil. Overall, the frequent exertion of public will should serve as a reminder for us to build a democracy system assessable to the public. Judicial system is the direct manifestation of rule of law, the first defense line of democracy. Given the frequent public outcries, we need to pay extra attention to maintain our rationality, to identify the shortcomings of the existing system, and address them through institutional improvement and increase the capacity of institutionalization; in doing so, it is vital that some guidelines should be observed: (1) Democratic legislation: Improve election and parliament to enhance overall democracy quality; (2) Increase legislation process disclosure, institutionalize public participation and build an effective feedback mechanism to respond to public opinion; (3) Build a composite governance model: In respond to the "Administration Supremism" reality and worldwide trend of democratization, China should build a legitimate governance structure to settle most social disputes that arise in the administration process; (4) Quality justice. Improve judiciary's professional qualification; maintain balance between legal principles and non-legal factors to ensure reasonableness in adjudication.

The public's mistrust of "procedural self-governance" as reflected in some highly publicized cases, revealed problems deeper than "legal formalism"; it concerns the constitutionalist democracy foundation of law and the ill-communication between ordinary law and the constitution. While we have a good reason to be opportunistic, for instance, the victory of legal community in intervening the handling of the Li Zhuang case, we should also have realistic expectations as to China's legal system, which often demonstrated lack of respect for the public and insufficient persuasiveness and even the communication skill in dealing with the public will. Here we should note that neither contempt nor servility is the right attitude for both will certainly damage the value underscoring the legal system.

5.3.2 Civil Law and Private Rights: The Foundation of Civil Society

In February 1949, after Beijing was liberated, CPC Central Committee issued a directive announcing the abolishment of *Six Codes*, including the ROC civil law. Civil law, a typical private law, is a cornerstone in any civil society and has been the most basic and systematic ordinary law since the age of Rome. In comparison, the public law is a recent phenomenon. The emergence of public law coincided roughly with the appearance of modern sovereign states, with many concepts and technologies borrowed from civil law. As the fundamental law of civil society, civil law presaged the arrival of civil societies independent of political states, and provided a set of rules that form the basis enable civil society to govern itself. Lenin once said that socialist country doesn't need private law; the reason is because according to the Marxist-Leninist orthodox, in socialist countries, such independent civil societies no longer exist, thus everything must submit to the state authority. In the socialist countries, the economy was regulated through central planning, rendering civil law, a tool of adjusting economic relationships, useless. Since the civil law ideal contravenes the radical ideal of Marxist Leninist socialism, it is regarded as counterproductive to the socialist ideals. On the other hand, in socialist countries, public law is often reduced to a planning and regulation law.

In 1978 when China began its reform, it was a country ravaged by decades of planned economy and political tumult. Once social order was stabilized, the state priority was switched from "class struggle" to "economic development". A reform to overhaul economic institutions ensued. Between 1978 and 1992, after much vacillation, the government finally fully embraced the market economy. In 1993, a new provision was introduced into the constitution and "socialist market economy" was enshrined as the fundamental economic form. During the reform era, civil law academic study has exerted great influence over the institutional construction. Also in this period, a debate over the relative merit of an economic law and a civil law, spanning the subsequent 7 years, took place. In comparison with the achievement achieved on the front of criminal law, there was weaker consensus regarding the civil law.

On August 7 and 9, 1979, a symposium was held at Chinese Academy of Social Sciences in Beijing where civil law and economic law were discussed. A debate erupted during the symposium. At issue is that some scholars argued that civil law should be promulgated as soon as possible, for such legislation would facilitate adjustment of economic relationships. Others argued that a more specialized economics law would serve the purpose better.[31] Economy law is a new law that was first seen worldwide in the post-WWI Germany, where state-level economy regulation was introduced. Back in the day, the concept of market economy has yet been fully recognized in China, while the officially stated economic form was "a planned commodity economy" – while some old constraints were removed in order to unleash the market force, state control remained tight in sectors of strategic value. Economy law advocates argued that given that planned economy and commodity economy coexisted in China and an economy law is necessary to regulate the "vertical" government-economy relationship, as well as the horizontal relationship between participants of the economy. Civil law supporters, on the other hand, argued

[31] An academic symposium regarding civil law, economic law, Jurisprudence study, issue 4, 1979; Su Qing, Li Yong's *Report on Beijing Political Legal Circles' Conference on Civil Law and Economic Law-related Questions*, Jurisprudence Development, issue 19, 1979.

that the civil law, could do the same, if not better. Among the civil law advocates, Prof. Tong Rou was one of the most prominent.[32]

The promulgation of *General Principles of Civil Law* in 1986 is another milestone in China's legislation history. The Article 2 of the law states that the law "shall adjust property relationships and personal relationships between civil subjects with equal status". Such provision limited the law's applicability to "vertical" economic relationships. It not only earned the law greater independence from governmental intervention, but also provided legal support for further economic reform. The law garnered great attention from overseas scholars as well, some lauding it as a symbolic achievement – China's "Chapter of Private Rights". From 1986 to 1992, despite a hybrid pricing system and disruption caused by the 1989 Tian'anmen Incident, the Civil Law retained its critical role in the process of China's marketization and private rights protection. In 1993, "socialist market economy" was written into the constitution, which is followed with China's civil law legislation's increasing independence and a new period of "expert legislation" and "precise legislation". Around this period, a number of related new laws were enacted, including *Contract Law* (1999), *Property Law* (2007), and *Tort Liability Law* in 2009. Considerable achievements were made in terms of civil adjudication reform, civil law-based social culture construction, and law community development. Up until 2009, China had promulgated a comprehensive packet of laws and the priority of legislation had been shifted to codification of existing laws. Through the systematization of the existing laws, the legal system to certain extent achieved reconciliation with the legal tradition of the Republic of China era and even the Roman Law tradition. Such a development would facilitate China's marketization reform, private rights protection, public right awareness enhancement and establishing a "culture of contract".

Overall, civil law development during the reform era is driven more by CPC leadership's will, especially its commitment to "economic reform", rather than constitution or civil society tradition. Had the economic reform stopped, as many worried, after the Tian'anmen Incident, the civil law development as we know today would haven been inconceivable. Hence we say that a more fundamental driving force of civil law development is the strong national consensus in favor of reform. However, as the reform deepened, such consensus split,[33] and new problems arose such as how to handle the relationships between civil law and constitution, administrative risks, social order and traditions.

The first problem concerns civil law's constitutional basis. The legitimacy, aside from government's will, is also derived from the "natural law proof" work undertaken by law theorists to prove the intrinsic values upheld by civil law. We had mentioned previously China's constitution revisions have taken an "additionist" approach, which led to inner instability. Without a systematic interpretation system, confusion is inevitable. The promulgation of civil law was a result of political deci-

[32] See Yang Lixin, Sun Peicheng's *Tong Roumin's object adjustment theory originality*, The Jurist, issue 6, 2004.

[33] See Wu Guoguang's *The end of reform and continuation of history*, twenty-first century, Hong Kong, issue 6, 2002.

sion hence its constitutional basis was weak. This is corroborated in the constitutionality debate over the *2006 Property Law Bill Draft*, mainly caused by the contradiction between the "socialist economy" provisions and the later introduced "market economy principle". Due to this incompatibility, both sides of the debate could find direct support from the constitution to defend their claims and attack the other. It is unfortunate that in spite of the debate, no interpretation system was introduced to address the problem; the final solution was a political one rather than jurisprudential. At the heart of the issue is the civil law's positivist constitutional proof being overlooked. The answer to such a issue should not be based on textualist analyses, or citing some individual provisions, but a holistic interpretation theory that systematically interprets the entire constitution and effort to make civil law consistent with the constitution. To achieve this end, civil law scholars should engage in building a constitutional positivist foundation, finding a third road in addition to political endorsement and natural law proof; second, constitution theorists should take initiative in bridging the gap between their position and the position of the civil law scholars; they should work together to develop a constitution interpretation theory to iron out the kinks inside the constitution.

Another problem is how should civil law respond to the modern administration-related risks. One often-unsaid assumption underlying the civil law is its preference of smaller government. Such liberalist ideal might be true in the free capitalism era or in the pre-sovereign state era city-states, but when the world entered modern times, such an ideal has been rendered obsolete. Modern industrialized society and the ingrained high risks could not be envisaged either by the Roman law-makers or other pre-modern civil law composers. In fact, only half a century after the French Civil Code established three principles – contractual liberty, absolute ownership and fault liability, new problems arose in the process of urbanization and development of cartel capitalism. To address these new problems, "contractual, restricted ownership" and "strict liability" were introduced into the civil code. When the world entered the twentieth century, a new trend emerged that greatly influenced civil law development, which is greater degree of socialization and increasing convergence with the public law. As a result, the external environment that today's civil laws face is drastically different from those of the autonomous city-states, or the freewheeling market economy enshrined by near-modern constitution and civil code; more sophisticated state systems are called for to cope with the high risk nature of modern economy.

A third issue is the conflict between civil law and traditional customs. Contractual liberty and property right are central concepts in the civil law, these concepts are often contradictory to local traditions and customs. One such conflict, for instance, is the civil law's apparent contradiction with the traditional Chinese matrimonial institutions. One example is the "Luzhou Mistress" case, which demonstrates the conflict between inheritance right guaranteed by the civil law and traditional conception of what is morally acceptable: Should the man's property bequeathal to his mistress be annulled on the grounds of its immorality or regarded as his legal right? Another example is the "Husband paying wife for not coming home at night", which raised the question whether husband and wife can revoke their obligation of fidelity and responsibility to care for their children by signing a contract.[34] A juridical interpretation of the marriage law was issued amidst much controversy. The interpretation upheld one's right to property is criticized by many for having weakened the convention regarding married couples' common property, which may undermine domestic harmony and social stability.[35] Similar conflicts also arose over cases concerning same sex marriage, partner swapping and other activities that contravened traditional conception of morality.

To recap, civil law has achieved considerable progress during the course of China's reform era. Like criminal law, civil law contributed greatly to form a solid foundation for social and economical stability. However, it is likely that the conditions that civil law's long-term prospect depends on may change. The value system that civil law upholds has been increasingly accepted by the political-social system, leading to backlash such as complaints over "civil law imperialism".[36] After the priority of the reform shifted from economic development to social-political reform, the condition that civil law departments' self-sufficiency and self-governance rely on may diminish. Caution must be applied in handling the relationship between civil law with constitution as well as social convention and customs.

5.3.3 Administrative Law and Implementation: Administration First or Procedure First

Unlike civil law and criminal law whose purpose is to maintain market and social order, the Public Law (mainly Administrative Law) is primarily concerned with adjusting government – public relationships. During the course of the reform era, administrative law pursued a different route from civil Law and criminal Law. As the basic department laws, civil law and criminal law have been centered around "litigation", which makes it reliant on the courts of law when it comes to execution. This was also the model that administrative law originally adopted – both the administrative litigation law and several "single laws" placed their emphasis on administrative litigation. After 2000, a new trend emerged. Within the academia, interest gradually shifted from the continental legal system emphasizing on administrative litigation to Anglo-American tradition that focuses on administrative procedures and judicial review system. In 2004, State Council issued a directive called *Comprehensively Promoting Legal Administration Guidelines*. The directive is

---

[34] See Tian Feilong's *Misuse of Contract Concept – Analysis and Field Study of the First "Empty Bed" Case in China*, Beijing University Law Journal, issue 49, May 15, 2007.

[35] See Zhao Xiaoli's *Trumpet of Chinese Families' Capitalization*, Cultural Review, issue 2, 2011; Qiang Shigong's *On Supreme Court's Interpretation of Marriage Law*, Cultural Review, issue 2, 2011.

[36] See Miao Lianying, Cheng Xueyang's *Civil Law Imperialism Fantasy and Confusion of Constitution Study – A Third View of Dispute Regarding Law's Constitutionality*, Sichuan University Journal (Philosophy and social science edition), issue 2, 2008.

widely regarded the first step towards full implementation of "rule of law" principle, which was first recognized by the constitution in 1997. Such a directive echoed the academia's increasing demands for change regarding the government administrative law. The directive ushered in a new era of "rule of law government". In the following part, we will try to draw a sketch of the three decades-long trajectory of the administrative rule of law process.

Even in the Mao era, there were still some administrative norms functioning, such as the 1958 "Population Ordinance", which to this day remains effective. However, the "administrative law" back then was essentially a Soviet style management law, whose main purpose is to serve and meet the requirements of managing a planned economy, rather than restraining the government's power, as modern administrative laws try to do. China's transition from planned economy however raised the need for administrative law. The development follows the paradigm of "subject – behavior – responsibility": The first step was the promulgation of an organic law, which resulted in *Organic Law of the Local People's Congresses* and *Local People's Governments of the People's Republic of China* (enacted in 1979, has henceforth been revised four times), *Organic Law of the State Council* (enacted in 1982, no revision). Today, these laws are often criticized for granting the administrative departments too much power; however, one should not overlook the rational side of such arrangement under the circumstances when these laws were made, which has drastically changed as today China is striving to "build a rule of law state".

The main function of Administrative Organization Law is assigning administrative legal liabilities. Over the past three decades, in spite of the progresses made, China's "rule of law" level remains slow. This is corroborated by: (1) Administrative reforms were mostly initiated by political decisions; (2) Institutions designed in compliance to the "administration supremism" guideline failed to adapt itself to development of democratization, resultant in concentration of power in the hands of administrative agencies. (3) No breakthrough achieved in the reform of the central – lower governments relationship. (4) Redundant and ineffective government agencies not up to the task of social risks management; (5) Despite initiative undertaken by the government to transform itself from a "management" government to a "service" government, neither "limited government" nor "social self-governance" have been recognized or implemented, and the government remains an "all-controlling" one.

The success of *Administrative Organization Law* hinges on three conditions: First, increase NPC's role in policy making regarding administrative organizations and increase "institutional supply"; delegate more power to lower governments, encourage them to take more initiative in carrying out administrative reforms; adopt "limited government" concept and social self-governance in the reform, while relieving the government the burden of being "all-controlling". Second, further promote development of the administrative litigation law. The 1989 *Administrative Litigation Law* granted citizens' right to sue the government. Such a law, aside from great thought-liberating value, also helped transforming the government-public relationship from one of one-sided "suppression" to one of "equal contestation".

However, in practice, qualification standard for administrative litigation is unreasonably high, limiting the law's applicability only to cases where infringement of citizen's personal rights and property rights were involved, whereas violation of social rights and political liberty rights are often denied of legal relief. This is due to underlying assumption of citizens being "private" entities, hence in theory, legal relief should only be provided in case of violation of their private rights. One exception is that citizen's right to education was violated as indicated in the Qi Yuling case. In 2008, the *People's Republic of China Government Information Disclosure Bill* was enacted, which extended the right to litigation to cases involving violation of citizen's right to know. Overall, administrative litigation's benefit to promote constitutional rights are limited; the court system are more restrained and "conservative" in handling administrative litigations in comparison with civil law or criminal law litigations. This is corroborated by a 2009 Zhejiang Supreme Court's rejection of a man's request demanding government to disclose information according to the law; the rationale behind the ruling is that no infringement on personal rights and property rights was incurred.[37] Finally, administrative litigation only promise to provide legal relief to victims of specific administrative misconduct, whereas such protection was denied for those whose rights were infringed by abstract misconduct – a defect that needs to be mended. Also worth noting is the development of administrative "single laws", exemplified by the administrative behavior laws, such as the 1996 *Administrative Sanction Law*, *Administrative Review Law* (1999), *Administrative License Law* (2004), *Administrative Compulsory Enforcement Law* (2011). These highly specialized laws provided more detailed description of administrative misconduct and blameworthiness; some innovative institutions were introduced, for instance, the 1997 Administrative Sanction Law incorporated an American-style hearing system. Overall, between 1979 and 2000, the development of administrative law largely followed the Continent Law tradition, laying its emphasis on legality of administrative organizations and culpability of administrative misconduct. Since the promulgation of *Administrative Litigation Law* in 1989, China's administrative jurisprudence and litigation system, centered around the "judicial review" principle, rapidly matured. Later, with the promulgation of "single laws" such as *Administrative Sanction Law*, *Administrative Review Law* and *Administrative License Law*, greater achievements were made on the front of administrative behavior laws. The development of classification of administrative behavior further perfected adjudication technology. A rigorous normative framework was established that reflects the principle of "administration by law", resultant in an administrative law "formalistic" legal system underpinned by judicial review principle and administration by law principle. However, legal formalism is grounded in Western separation of powers structure and passivist administrative power. Although such theory enhanced the public awareness regarding the administrative laws, and supported the infrastructure development of China's administrative law,

[37] See Zhejiang Province People's Court special study group's *Study regarding government information disclosure administrative litigation case*. Administrative Jurisprudence Law Study, issue 4, 2009.

yet its insufficiency in terms of openness and democracy elements as well as incompatibility with constitution prevented it from providing a reasonable interpretation system and better guiding China's administrative agency reform. From 2000 onwards, some fundamental change occurred. First, great academic efforts were undertaken to the study of administrative procedural laws, where Anglo-American influence was strong. Although the administrative procedure law received NPC's support, it finally miscarried due to opposition from government agencies, uneven local conditions and insufficient research preparations. Despite the temporary setback, certain progress was later achieved due to State Council's initiative aimed to promote administrative procedural construction. Lower level governments in general showed more enthusiasm for such a law. In 2004, the State Council issued a directive urging governments of all levels to "comprehensively promote law-abiding administration". Two concepts, namely "scientific administration", "democratic litigation" were highlighted in the directive; thanks to the directive, the administrative decision-making also places its emphasis on legal compliance, scientificness, and democratization; to realize the three ideals, public participation, experts consultation and the government decision making were implemented. Several guidelines outlined in the law includes: Firstly, procedural openness. Disclose "item, rationale, and result" to the public; second, establish expert deliberation, public participation and legality review procedures for major government decisions. The directive further demanded establishment of a post-decision making tracking, appraisal and accountability system; it is noteworthy that through the separation of decision-making, execution and supervision, the directive intended to bring a check and balance tripartite system into the government. In 2008, the State Council issued another directive urging to improve compliance in municipal and county-level governments' administrative process. The directive lists six key procedures that must be adhered to in the decision-making processes, including opinion solicitation, hearing, legality check, collective consultation, post-implementation review and accountability review. In the same year, the state council implemented a set of rules regarding government information disclosure, which reiterated citizens' right to know. In the same year, Hunan provincial government released its provincial level administrative procedural guideline; the guidelines, which place an emphasis on information disclosure and public participation, is the first such guidelines released by a provincial government. Shortly afterwards, Shangdong Province announced a similar set of guidelines. As more legislation and practice regarding administrative procedures are carried out at local level governments, China's administrative law construction has been carried to a new height in terms of openness and public participation. Progress has been achieved in academia too. One example is the discussions over the new administration law. Among the participants, Prof Wang Xinxi was one of the most prominent. In Wang's *Public Participation and Administration Process* published in 2007, a brand new reasoning was given. Using "openness" and "democracy" as the entry points, the author conjectures that "public participation" should be upheld as the spirit of new administrative procedural law. Wang also argued that the administrative procedural law should be regarded as an interpretation framework for administrative activity legality, hence its validity has to be tested by everyday practice. The public participation model that Wang proposed is an integrational administrative legal framework, which not only addresses traditional demands such as parliamentary control and judicial review, but also advocates democratization of the administrative procedure. The new administrative law framework that Wang advocated represented several major innovations and breakthroughs. (1) Democracy is upheld as a key value along with rule of law. (2) A series of institutions aimed to increase information disclosure and public participation were implemented; (3) Legality is not only set as a goal in the adjudication of individual cases, but for the entire system, including legislation, decision-making, execution and justice; moreover, different interest groups are allowed to openly express their concerns by transforming the administrative legal system into a limited, effective democratic forum in the view of solving the democracy deficits in the modern administration process; (4) In terms of participants, remove the distinction of subjects and objects, all the participants are treated equally; in doing so, turning the public into a integral part of the administration process, and establishing an inter-subjective ethical basis to facilitate "cooperative administration" and "citizen participation"; (5) Enhance procedural awareness in the exercise of legislative and judicial powers; (6) Recognize and respond in a rational and structured fashion to demands for scientificizing policy-making both from within the political system and without; involve experts, the public and the government in rational, specific project-oriented and labor-divided decision-making system. Of course, this is only a preliminary framework, which leaves much to be desired regarding how to bridge the gap between the current institutions, how to design and build a system that ensures governmental information disclosure and democratic participation, how to transform the so-called "China-specific" institutions such as Party Secretary, People's National Congress, and CPPCC into legal norms, how to extend support to political democratization and construction of a judicial review system, how to effectively utilize Internet as a platform to promote transparency and enhance public participation. Such exploration inevitably poses challenge to the formalist theory and its underlying principles. By incorporating the concept of democracy into modern administrative and judicial process, a question is raised concerning democratization of the administration legal system, which suggests a possibility of "tolerable growth". Two things of note: First, the administration law's republican tendency – openness and public participation are derived from republicanism tradition, as well as the republican normative assumption that presuppose citizen's inherent decency. Such republican point of view demands democratization in the administrative legal process, through which, the public's decency and capacity would be further enhanced. Secondly, the "re-division of powers" concept. The traditional division of powers is mainly about separation of three branches of public powers, which is guaranteed by the constitution, and division of state and society power, where citizen's access to politics is limited to election, and the state is operated by elites chosen through a representation system. The new way of division is superior to the traditional one in two respects – first, in terms of public power division, it recognizes the actual change of power division structure, to which it provides procedurally sound normative defense; secondly, in terms of division of powers between state and society, it transcend the traditional simplistic public domain/private domain dichotomy, and rethinks the relationship between state and society in terms of administrative power and judicial power. Although the administration legal reform is primarily concerned with problems within the purview of administration law, these problems also has great constitutional implications.

The Administrative law is traditionally a highly technical law, hard to be codified for involving too many government agencies, and not closely related to constitution. Yet the new administration law under the "procedure first" principle, greatly increased democratization by reflecting the constitutional provision regarding public participation. Such democratic participation in the administration process compensated the lack of direct public participation in the political system. By simulating and replicating parliamentary democracy in the administrative process, a sub-parliamentary system was formed and to some extent supplements the ill-functioned parliament. Today, as China still in the middle of transformation; its democratization level too low to provide a basis of legitimacy for the administration power; yet with the development of administrative democracy, this gap is closing. However, as a complimentary democracy tool, administrative democracy can easily lose its constructive value, as shown in the public's increasing mistrust in the administrative hearing system. This indicates that any real progress must be achieved across the system, because progress in a specific field is unlikely to succeed without support from proximate departments. We should understand that both litigation-based department self-governance and administration-dominated procedural self-governance build better channels to communicate with the constitution and obtain constitutional support. Thus we concludes administrative procedural law democratization can't replace true political democratization; while it might have its constructive value at this stage, vital to institution of disclosure system and public participation system, in the long run, a more comprehensive progress in terms of public law can only be achieved through a political reform.

Chapter 6
Review and Outlook

China's modernization began as part of the national effort in response to the Western provocation. It has two objectives: building a modern nation state and cultivation of a modern citizenry. Effort towards the first objective started a little earlier and received greater priority,[1] though both played significant roles that contributed to the generation of China's modern legal system.

The late Qing dynasty constitutionalist movement – led by reformists Kang Youwei, Liang Qichao, Zhang Jian, as well as legal modernization movement led by Shen Jiaben, were the first attempts seen in China that actively sought to better its jurisprudential and legal system. During the period leading up to 1949, great strides were made on the front of legal modernization, resultant in the promulgation of a comprehensive body of laws. However, the process was impeded and at moments, halted due to a number of reasons, among them foreign invasions, domestic tension, and civil wars. In 1949, CPC took over Mainland China. With the abolishment of the *Six Codes*, KMT-dominated legal modernization came to its end.

Despite crises at home and abroad, the Manchu ruling class originally rejected the idea reform with great intransigence, barring the possibility of other political forces from sharing the state power. Mighty it once was, the dynasty had its Achilles' heel – It was founded by a non-Han Chinese ethical group, a weakness that was exploited by the revolutionaries who sought to bring about a "racial revolution". Trying to stem the crisis, Qing government made a dash to implement a constitutionalist reform. This effort led to the birth of *Imperial Constitution Outline* in 1908 and *Nineteen Creeds of Constitution* in 1911, yet they were cut short by the outbreak of revolution.

From the ruins of the empire rose two Han-Chinese political stars, namely Sun Yat-sen and Yuan Shikai. Although they sent China into a new era, neither brought about constitutionalism. Although today highly revered in Mainland China and Taiwan alike, Sun Yat-sen had a rather questionable claim on being China's first

[1] Li Zehou calls this "saving the nation over Enlightenment".

Q. Gao et al., *The Road to the Rule of Law in Modern China*,
Research Series on the Chinese Dream and China's Development Path,
DOI 10.1007/978-3-662-45637-8_6

republican activist, as Kang Youwei and his comrades were as republican as Sun in all but name.

The failure of the late Qing constitutionalism efforts led some to question whether a British Glorious Revolution-style constitutionalist movement was possible for China. Some scholars aligned themselves with the British conservative theorists, criticizing the revolutionary radicalism for its role in China's failed attempt to install constitutionalism. Valid perspectives they may be, there need to be backed up with specific case studies.[2] Moreover, scholars tended to exaggerate the difference between Sun Yat-sen and Yuan Shikai, neglecting that both Han Chinese political leaders shared great commonality, which contributed to the speedy armistice between the North and the South. Had Yuan been a Manchu aristocrat, some argue, the Qing emperor might be spared of the abdication. Some compared the Qing royal family with the English one, and wonder why did the English monarchs, descendants of foreign conquerors as well, faired so much better than the Chinese counterparts. They overlooked Britain's long tradition of constitutionalism; even though that they didn't have a written constitution, the representative democracy and common law tradition offered great protections to the crown and moderated the revolution.[3]

After the Republic of China was established, sympathy for the failed Constitutionalist Movement grew fast; this is true even within the revolutionary camp. The shift of sentiment prompted the revolutionaries to ditch their original anti-Manchu stance and introduced provisions allowing other ethnic groups including the Manchus to participate in the new government. Around the same time, within the revolutionary camp, a small group led by Song Jiaoren, sought to further reform to adapt the KMT from a "revolutionary party" to a "political party"; they demanded rigid implementation of constitutionalist procedures outlined by *Provisional Constitution*. Yet after Song's assassination, such plan didn't achieved the desired result.

The following years saw a concatenation of "revolutions". In 1914, Sun Yat-sen reorganized KMT. Although by that time "party rule" had yet been elevated to a party doctrine, a heavy emphasis was placed on absolute loyalty to party leader. The purpose of the restructuring was never to turn the party into a constitution-abiding parliamentary party, but to seize the state power through more violent revolution with a view to transform China into a modern state through measures outlined by Sun's three phase state building theory. Yet this movement too failed to achieve its objective, which would be left for its successor to solve. As it turned out, CPC's solution was in many ways similar to its predecessor's.[4]

---

[2] See Gao Quanxi, *The Constitutional Moment: On the Imperial Edict of the Manchu Emperor's Abdication*, Guangxi Normal University Press, 2011.

[3] Even for Britain which has a great constitutional tradition, its political modernization took over half a century since the Glorious 1640, during which there were radical Cromwell Tyranny and protracted conflict between the two sides.

[4] Historian Yuan Weishi said that China constitutionalism was ruined by Yuan Shikai and KMT both, although differed from mainstream point of view, remained a solid theory nonetheless. See

The Constitutionalist effort seen in late Qing dynasty went through two stages. The first stage lasted until KMT's First Congress was convened. During this stage, Han Chinese political forces joined hands and forced Qing emperor to abdicate. Yet following the abdication, conflict arose among the coalition; with Yuan Shikai's demise, the last checking power was gone and internal fights amongst his Beiyang clique exacerbated, leading to a short-lived restoration of the former Qing emperor. Behind the failure of the restoration, there was not only elite Han Chinese intellectuals' strong identification with republican ideals, but also the warlords who felt threatened by the emperor. During the second stage, Sun Yat-sen adopted a pro-Soviet Russian and pro-CPC policy, which led to the first cooperation of the two parties. Enamored of Bolshevik revolution's rapid success, Sun adopted some Leninist principles to bolster discipline of his revolutionary force. These measures contributed to the success of the North Expedition, in which both parties joined forces in their military campaign and finally vanquished their common foe. Despite their ideological differences, both parties shared great common ground: Both believed in control of the military and government. Sun's Three People's Principles was agreed upon by CPC, thus formed the foundation of their first cooperation. Constitution-wise, the 1911 *Republic of China Nanjing Provisional Government Organization Outline* and *Republic of China Provisional Constitution* were promulgated around this time. There were also several constitutional documents that didn't see the light of the day, the Beijing parliament's *Tiantan Constitution Draft*, Yuan Shikai's *Republic of China Provisional Constitution*, as well as the one produced during the presidency of Cao Kun. Although during the period, practice of constitutionalism and parliament politics were not entirely successful, constitution was generally recognized as a symbol of political legitimacy; as a result, every new administration took power, making a constitution would be the first thing to do. Around 1924, China achieved territorial unification, the political stability led to a boom era. Despite collapse of KMT-CPC cooperation, ensuing military conflict, as well as the Mukden Incident, the country experienced a prosperous decade that was called *Golden Ten Years*. It was also a golden decade for the legal system development, which culminated in the promulgation of the *Six Codes*. This legislation development however was brought to a halt by the Japanese Invasion. Following the success of the Anti-Japanese War, the KMT, disregarding its previous oath to democracy, took constitution making into its own hands. Around this time former Harvard Law School dean Roscoe Pound was invited to China to advise on its legal reform, however, such efforts failed to achieve substantial result with civil war fast escalating.

Overall, although during the late Qing dynasty and ROC era, China's legal system modernization proceeded at an excruciating slow pace, some ideas managed to achieve mainstream recognition. Today, we are indebted to our predecessors, both for their intellectual bequeathal and empirical experience.

Yuan's Yuan *Shikai and KMB*, Taste and Classics, issue 1, 2011, Pp 40–59; can also be seen on his Netease blog.

The abolishment of *Six Codes* set forth the New China legal system modernization. Despite the abolishment, CPC inherited much of its political institutions from the ROC, including the conception regarding the relationship between the revolutionary party and state. Thus the New China's legal system was not completely new. Later, with revolutionary passion fading, there is increasing tendency to reconnect with the past. The 1949 revolution was also called New Democracy Revolution; aside from the difference in terms of outlook and social class basis, it has a lot in common with Sun Yat-sen's Old Democracy Revolution. Once CPC obtained state power, it faced the task of transforming party rule into rule of law as well as superseding party leader's individual will and party discipline with constitution and law.

The first three decades of New China is often called Mao era. Due to international hostility and frequent political movements, normalization of legal system stalled during this period. Up until the end of Cultural Revolution, a legal framework was so lacking that rights can't often be distinguished from power, which was particularly evident in the Cultural Revolution. Overall, Mao era didn't entirely steer clear from the ROC twin revolution themes of state-building and citizenry cultivation, but assorted to an more extreme radical socialist approach.

After Deng Xiaoping took office, China entered the Reform era. During this period of time, the state development saw a shift from radical idealism to empirical pragmatism; economic development had replaced class struggle as the new priority. Due much to the reflection over the Cultural Revolution experience, the government actively engaged to reinstate the bureaucracy system torn down during Mao era. Despite occasional disputes and setbacks, a stable political environment was created and maintained. From the promulgation of criminal law in 1979 to enactment of the new constitution in 1982, as well as codification of civil law and commerce law and the rise of administrative law in the late 1980s, for three decades, a constantly improving socialist legal system with Chinese characteristic took shape. Aside from reform of the legislature, judicial system reform is another direction of the legal system modernization. Although due to political and social interruptions, progress was sometimes slow, but this reform had irreversible shaped public's consciousness regarding the law, and built channels of communication between judicial system and the political - social system. Judicialization of constitution was regarded as the highest goal of law self-governance movement, but due to lack of political commitment and constitutional support, this goal failed to achieve desired outcome. Overall, the three decades of reform era was remarkable for stability and uninterrupted development. In the field of constitution development, judicial constitutionalism lost momentum to political constitutionalism. In terms of normal laws, self-governance became the trend, but the communication between constitution and normal law remained to face institutional hurdles, which affected China's overall rule of law development.

As we said at the onset of the book, China solved during 170 years the problems that took the West several centuries. Yet as we are standing at a point where West stood in the eighteenth century, today we are facing a world drastically different from the one of the eighteenth century. Hence, we can't completely rely on the old Western experience for guidance. Today, China's modernization faced a dilemma –

on one hand, we need to fulfill our mission of building a modern nation state and a constitutional liberal democracy. On the other, we need to respond to the new trend of "desovereigntization" as a counteraction to the flaws of the world order as well as modern constitutionalist state founded on the principle of liberty and democracy. That is to say that while half-way into our modernization journey, we are now facing post-modernization challenges, which put the legitimacy of our modernizing endeavor to test. In addition, China is a civilized ancient country with three thousands of years of tradition, a heavy baggage that we have to handle with great delicacy. Circumstances demand us to take a balanced view towards the Chinese characteristics as well as world order, modernity model and pluralism, historical tradition and universal value, indigenous resources and foreign institutions. All these problems couldn't be expected to be solved through a century worth of reform and will likely to become more pronounced when our government finished its transformation from an "all-controlling" one.

Overall, an incremental improvement route has taken over the past three decades, which is a fundamental departure from the country's previous revolutionary radicalism. Such a change has enormously implications to institutions, social value, technology, and its interaction with external environment. Today work had been undertaken to create a division of legislative, judicial and executive powers; as a result, the trinity of party-government-legislation is dissolving. There have also been talks about concepts such as "people-oriented" governance, judicial review, rule of law, political civilization, and world order shaping; we see China is assuming increasingly important responsibility as a world power,[5] while trying to maintain peacefulness in its rise. Through China's legal system modernization, we see a rational China that handles domestic and foreign affairs in keeping with modern conception of rule of law emerging - we should acknowledge that these are great remarkable progresses. If there is such a thing as China experience, then this experience is about reform, legal system modernization and state building based on Deng-style realistic and pragmatic rationality, in Deng's words, "seek truth from facts".

A few more things that I would like to say here about China's three decades of modernization and its future:

First, continue to apply a pragmatic transformative rationale in China's legal system reform. The essence of the principle is captured well by the famous slogan: "Practice is the sole criterion for testing truth". Without an inclusive, open attitude

[5]Zheng Bijian believes that China's reform has to take a route that centered on economic development, and pursuing its socialist road through increasing its integration level into the economic globalization process. Economic globalization facilitated China's peaceful rise, hence, CPC has no intension to challenge existing international order; neither did it want to break it in violent means. Economic globalization provided resources globally, therefore one doesn't need to wage wars to obtain them. All the resources that China needs for its modernization can be obtained through globalized market. Since late 1970s, China has launched onto a route of peaceful rise, and CPC has been firmly stay on the course of developing a socialist market economy, a socialist democratic political system, a rule of law country, and an advanced culture and a harmonious society. See Zheng Bijian's *CPC's Direction in the 21st Century*, People's Daily (overseas edition), November 22, 2005.

for trials and errors, it would have been inconceivable that China's legal system reform to achieve what it has. From "benign unconstitutionality", "precedent system", to "petition in accordance with law" – all of these developments show how the rationale was applied in everyday legal practice and achieved different degrees of success. Given the different nature of the problems that China faced, to address them, China had to be practical-minded, exploratory, and fearless for mistakes, ready to get hands dirty as a way to gain valuable experience.

Secondly, continue to promote its integration into the world order, bringing itself up to the world standard of rule of law and build a sound modern legal system accordingly. By integrating into the world order, we don't mean that China should copy the Western institutions or forsake its own characteristics; on the contrary, it should actively take measures to retain and develop China's own characteristics. This is not to say that China should seek answer of everything from its tradition. The old moral legal and academic standards were already destroyed in the Opium War and would not be revived. Hence what we are talking about here is our living tradition, instead of the dead one. The tradition can be classified into four types: First, the conservationist tradition represented by Shen Jiaben; second is Kang Youwei and Liang Qichao's radical reformist tradition, third is Sun Yat-sen's Three People's Principles that and the *Six Codes*, and the last being CPC's proletariat tradition. In the future, China should look beyond the narrow communist revolution narrative and recognize itself as part of hundreds of years of continued effort, during which four waves of reforms took place, and conscious that it was the fifth wave to attain the goal that the previous four failed.

Thirdly, innovate to adapt to changes. One achievement in the three decades of legal system reform is its effective effort to integrate China into the world order and adjust our system to meet the world standard. We should be aware that we are living in a world where significant changes are taking place – globalization, new round of technology revolutions, world economic integration – all these pose challenge while bring opportunity. China's three decades of reform was not in an isolated environment, but through constant interaction with the external world in all possible respects. Because of China's ties with the world grew tighter all the time, our legal system must modernize itself to adapt to the new condition. Although we still can't boast that we had implement the political institutions that a major world power deserves, but at least we have done enough to demonstrates China's openness to the world through the three decades of legal system reform.

As much as we are proud of our achievements, we should not overlook our drawbacks: First is the polarization of rule of politics and rule of law; second, inner contradictions within China's legal system as a result of failure to implement constitutionalism, third, doctrinarism in China's jurisprudent theories. These three owed their origin to the same fundamental problem – China's political form. This is why after three decades of reform we have to return to the starting point and now is the time for we to resume our political institution reform; if this political institution reform can't be implemented then the space of improvement for China's economic and legal reform would likely be limited. To a good measure, the future of China's road towards rule of law hinges on what is going to happen to China's political system.

By returning to the starting point, we are not saying that this round of reform has been futile, that what it achieved was nothing other than proving that modern rule of law doesn't suit China or that China should take an anti-modern route and return to its own tradition; on the contrary, China's rule of law for three decades broke the shackles of tradition, and eased the constraints imposed by a party-state system. However, it is evident that the reform is incomplete. The rule of law and modernity are universal, but this universality is manifested through the success of West as individual countries and their ability to shape the world order. For China, it also needs to prove itself through the success of creating a rule of law model with its own characteristics.

Today, the Chinese society had gone through great changes; and they were not limited to economy and legal system; even China's political form is changing, albeit at a much slower pace. It is impossible that that China's political system stayed unchanged while its economy and legal system undertook great transformation. If China's political system has changed, then why do we still demand a "return to politics"? Why do we urge political institution reform, and say that the political factor was affecting China's economic and legal development? When we examine the relationship between political institutions and the legal system, we should ask ourselves what makes a sound political system. Although great changes happened, overall, the reform had yet touched the core of China's political system; the old party-state authoritarian model remained intact and the spirit of rule of law has yet been fully reflected in political institutions. Hence, the "return to politics" is not to return to the state of three decades ago, or to casually install some "rule of law" features to the existing political system; what we are calling for is a comprehensive reform, to achieve both the rule of fundamental law and normal laws; in doing so, a sound public political platform should be installed to facilitate China's transformation to modern society.

Return on politics is mainly about two things, namely rule of the fundamental law or constitution and rule of normal laws. This corresponds with two human political states, namely everyday politics and extreme politics. In a mature society, everyday routine politics is the norm, people go about their lives, free from state intervention as long as they abide the law. Such is what normal laws try to achieve. But not all societies can attain such a state; neither do those who attained it could maintain it all the time.[6]

Since the Opium War, China has been in a state of extreme politics. Throughout the subsequent 170 years, despite much effort, a sound constitutionalist political

[6] See Bruce Ackerman's *We The People: Foundations*, Harvard University Press, 1991. There are two theoretical modes regarding these two political states and their interpretations; one is German public law scholar Carl Schmitt's absolutization of extreme politics; the other is American constitution law scholar Bruce Ackman who posited a theory of transformation from extreme politics to daily routine politics. Carl Schmitt, trans Liu Zongkun, *The concepts of the political*, Shanghai People's Publishing House, 2004.

form failed to emerge. So when we talk about returning to politics, what we mean is that we should uphold constitution as a rulebook to guide political activities; to achieve a condition that every political decision is strictly in accordance with constitution. We should point out that three decades of legal system reform is not driven by constitution, neither the split between political institutions and rule of law a product of constitutionalism. The stalling development of constitutionalism has already led to slowdown of legal system reform, which caused a full array of problems. When we demand returning on politics, what we mean is to acknowledge the extreme political condition that we are in and introduce a political reform, uphold constitution as a guide for the state and party, to make constitution a true tiger, instead of one made of paper.

The road towards modernization is rarely smooth; otherwise it wouldn't take the West three centuries. China had only been half way down the road. If we choose the Opium War as the starting point then we had just completed half of the course that the West traveled; if we take the latest round of reform as the starting point, then our modernization had just took three decades. Hence we should not overlook the difficulty lying ahead by wishfully thinking that everything can be done easily at one stroke. In a way, this "return to politics" is not a problem unique to New China, but a problem that has been dogging China since the late Qing Constitutionalist Movement. China has a long traditional dynastic tradition, but it also has a rich constitutionalist tradition. It is vital to connect with this constitutionalist tradition in our effort to solve problems related to constituent power, political legitimacy, revolution and reform, transformation of revolutionary party to the ruling party, etc.[7]

There is another route to achieve "returning to politics", which we call "rule of normal laws". By rule of normal laws we mean to make the judicial system truly independent of political intervention; try to ensure people's rights in everyday life, return law its true authority, to make every ruling just and adhere to every specific procedure. There is no question that constitutionalism is important, but it is not the end. Constitution is great only when it is applied in everyday life, and there needs a way to transform constitutional ideals to daily politics. In a way, China's modernization of politics resembled those of Germany and France. For a century and half, we often found ourselves in revolutionary upheavals, as a result, not only constitutionalism remains unaccomplished, but daily politics failed to take control. All we have is strong political power, hence we need to construct everyday routine politics, which is what normal laws do. To strictly distinguish the boundary of political power and individual rights. Here we may have to learn from the British and American experience, for they enjoyed mature politics only because, according to

[7] See Xia Yong's *Govern the Country by Law – State and Society*, Social Sciences Academic Press, 2004 and *Constitutionalist construction – regime and people*, Social Science Academic Press, 2004; Yu Keping's *Contemporary China Political Institution*, Lanzhou University Press, 1998 and *Sound Governance,* Social Sciences Academic Press, 2004; Lin Shangli's *Contemporary China political form study*, Tianjin people's publishing house, 2000; Li Lin's *Rule of law and constitutionalism Evolution*, China Social Sciences Press, 2005.

Ackman, they always found a route transforming the constitution ideals to everyday routine politics.[8]

Today's after three decades of reform, all the achievements notwithstanding, problems were becoming increasingly entangled. To further promote the transformation, we need to return to the political reform route. The difficulty is that such a return can go two directions, extreme politics and everyday routine politics. How to balance the two, to help China complete its constitutionalist transformation is a question that is in front of both the politicians and legal scholars, as well as "We the Chinese people".[9]

[8] See He Weifang's *The Detailed Rule of Law*, China Legal Institution Press, 2002; Bruce Ackman's *We the People: Volume 2: Transformations*, Sun Wenkai, trans, China Legal Institution Press, 2003.

[9] To pay homage to Ackman's "We the people", I would use "We the Chinese people" here. Yet question remains as to how to deal with the relationship between different expressions in the constitution related to the people – Chinese people, Chinese people under the leadership of CPC, Chinese people of all nationalities, etc. See Chen Duanhong's *On fundamental principles of the Chinese constitution and its rhetoric devices*, from Constitutionalism and sovereignty, China Legal Institution Press, 2007; Chen Duanhong's *On constitution's as the fundamental law and advanced law*, Zhongwai Jurisprudence, issue 4, 2008; Gao Quanxi's *On republican political form – contemplation over the political form of People's Republic of China*, from *Five Arguments on Modern Political Institutions*,, China Legal Institution Press, 2008.

References

Chinese Language Monographs

Ai, Yongming, and Lu Jinbi (eds.). 2004. *Yang Zhaolong law writing anthology*. Beijing: China Law Press.

Bruce Ackman. 2003. *We the People: Volume 2: Transformations*. Trans. Sun, Wenkai. Beijing: China Legal Institution Press.

Carl, Schmitt. 2004. *Political Concept*. Trans. Liu Zongkun. Shanghai: Shanghai People's Publishing House.

Carl, Schmitt. 2005. *Constitution Theory*. Trans. Liu Feng. Shanghai: Shanghai People's Publishing House.

Carl, Schmitt. 2008. *Protector of Constitution*. Trans. Li Juntao and Su Huijie. Beijing: The Commercial Press.

Central Research Institute. 1982. *China near modern reform – Law reform and constitutionalism symposium*. Taipei: Central Research Institute near Modern History Institute.

Chen, Xiqi. 1991. *Sun Yat-sen chronology*. Beijing: Zhonghua Books.

Chen, Yongsen. 2004. *Bid goodbye to the identity as Monarch's subject*. Beijing: China Renmin University Press.

Chen, Duanhong. 2007. *Constitutionalism and sovereignty*. Beijing: China Law Press.

Chen, Duanhong. 2010. *Constituent right and fundamental law*. Beijing: China Legal Institution Press.

Chiang, Kai-shek. 1943. *China's destiny*. Nanjing: Zhongzheng Books.

Cohen, Paul A. 1991. *American Historical Writing on the Recent Chinese Past*. Trans. Li, Rongtai and others. Taipei: Linking Books.

CPC Central Literature Study Department. (ed.). 1993. *Significant post-1949 archives selection*, vol 4. Beijing: Central Party Literature Press.

Deng, Ye. 2003. *Coalition government and one party rule*. Beijing: Social Science Literature Press.

Ding, Xuliang. 2011. *On China model*. Beijing: Social Sciences Academic Press.

Ding, Weizhi, and Chen Song. 1995. *Between China and West Ti and Yong*. Beijing: China Social Sciences Press.

Feng, Xianzhi, and Chongji Jin (eds.). 2003. *Mao Zedong biography 1049–1976*, vol. 1. Beijing: Central Party Literature Press.

Gao, Quanxi. 2008. *Five arguments on modern political institutions*. Beijing: China Legal Institution Press.

Q. Gao et al., *The Road to the Rule of Law in Modern China*,
Research Series on the Chinese Dream and China's Development Path,
DOI 10.1007/978-3-662-45637-8

Gao, Quanxi. 2009. *From extreme politics to daily routine politics – On contemporary political judicial system*. Beijing: China Legal Institution Press.
Gao, Quanxi. 2011. Constitutional moment: *On Qing Emperor's Abdication Decree*. Nanning: Guangxi Normal University Press.
Gu Zhun. 1994. *Gu Zhun anthology*. Guizhou: Guizhou People's Publishing House.
Han, Dayuan (ed.). 2008. *1954 constitution and China's constitutionalism*. Wuhan: Wuhan University Press.
Harvey, Mansfield. 2005. *Taming the Prince*. Trans. Feng Keli. Nanjing: Yilin Press.
He, Weifang. 2002. *The detailed rule of law*. Beijing: China Legal Institution Press.
Hegel, G.W.F. 1989. *Shorter Logic*. Trans. He Lin. Beijing: The Commercial Press.
Huan, Yanpei. 1982. *The recent 80 years*. Beijing: China Literature and History Press.
Huang, Kewu. 2000. *The rationale of liberty: Yan Fu's understanding and criticism of John Stuart Mill's liberty thinking*. Shanghai: Shanghai Book Store Press.
Huang, Zhangjian. 2007. *Hundred Days Reform history research*. Shanghai: Shanghai Book Store.
Ji, Pomin. 2007. *Constitutionalism and the essence of state – Reflection and review on new democracy and common program*. Hong Kong: Strong Wind Publishing House.
Jin, Zhiren. 1984a. *China constitutionalism*. Taipei: Linking Books.
Jin, Chongji. 1984b. *20th century China: A brief history*. Beijing: Social Sciences Literature Press, 2009.
Jin, Chongji. 2004. *Different stages of Sun Yat-sen's thoughts on people's livelihood over half an century*. Beijing: Central Party Literature Press.
Kong, Xinfeng. 2009. *From natural man to citizen* – Hobbes political thoughts reinterpretation. Ph.D. thesis. Beijing: Beijing University.
Li, Jiannong. 1930. *China's political history in the recent three decades*. Shanghai: Pacific Bookstore.
Li, Jiannong. 2002. *China's political history in the recent century*. Shanghai: Fudan University Press.
Li, Buyun. 2005. *Towards rule of law*. Changsha: Hunan People's Publishing House, 1998.
Li Lin. 2005. *Rule of law and constitutionalism evolution*. Beijing: China Social Sciences Press.
Liang, Qichao. 1989. *Hundred Days Reform*. Beijing: China Bookstore.
Lin, Yifu. 1999. *China miracle – Development strategy and economic reform*. Shanghai: Shanghai People's Publishing House.
Lin, Shangli. 2000. *Contemporary China political state study*. Tianjin: People's Press.
Lin, Laifan. 2011. *From constitution normativism to normativist constitution – A preamble of normativist constitutionalism*. Beijing: China Law Publishing House.
Lin, Zhihong. 2005. *"Minguo is our enemy": Qing Loyalists and Near-modern Political Transformation*. Ph.D. thesis, Taipei: Taiwan University.
Liu, Junning. 1998. *Economic democracy and economic liberty*. Shanghai: Shanghai Sanlian Bookstore Press.
Liu, Shaoqi. 2005. *Writings since the establishment of PRC*, vol. 4. Beijing: Central Party Literature Press.
Liu, Yiqing, and Zhang Qinde (eds.). 2007. *Gong Xiantian Whirwind report – A discussion over property law bill*. Beijing: China Finance and Economics Press.
Lu Xun. 1984. Lu Xun's *Lu Xun complete works*, vol 4. Beijing: People's Literature Press, 1989.
Ma, Yong. 2001. *Transcend revolution and reform*. Shanghai: Shanghai Sanlian Bookstore.
Mao, Zedong. 1991. *Mao Zedong's selected works*, vol. 4. Beijing: People's Publishing House.
Mao, Haijian. 2005. *Hundred Days Reform facts investigation*. Beijing: Shenghuo-Dushu-Xinzhi Joint Publishing Company.
Mark, Tushnet. 2012. *Why Constitution is Important*. Trans. Tian Feilong. Beijing: China University of Political Science and Law Press.
N/A. 1997. *Zhou Enlai chronology 1949–1976*. Beijing: Central Party Literature Press.
Peng, Ming. 1984. *History of May 4 Movement*. Beijing: People's Press.
Qin, Xiao. 2009. *Contemporary China: Modernization or modernity*. Beijing: Social Science Academic Press.

Qin, Xiao. 2010. *On China's modernity solution*. Beijing: Social Science Academic Press.
Qiu, Yuanqiu, and Zhang Xibo. 1997. *History of ROC laws*. Beijing: Capital Normal University.
Sieyès, Emmanuel Joseph. 2004. *On Privilege: What is the Third Estate?* Trans. Feng Tang. Beijing: The Commercial Press.
Tang, Degang. 2003a. *70 years of late Qing (vol 1): A review of China's social culture transformation*. Taipei: Yuan-Liou Publishing House.
Tang, Degang. 2003b. *70 years of late Qing (vol 3): First Sino Japanese War and Hundred Days Reform*. Taipei: Yuan-Liou Publishing House.
Tang, Zhijun. 2003c. *Hundred Days Reform history*. Shanghai: Shanghai Social Sciences Academy Press.
Tang, Degang. 2004a. *70 years of late Qing (vol 5): Yang Shikai, Sun Yat-sen and Xinhai revolution*. Taipei: Yuan-Liou Publishing House.
Tang, Degang. 2004b. *Yuan Shi-kai's reign*. Nanning: Guangxi Normal University Press.
Wang, Qisheng. 2010. *Revolution and counter revolution*. Beijing: Social Science Literature Press.
Xia, Yong. 2004a. *Govern the country by law – State and society*. Beijing: Social Sciences Academic Press.
Xia, Yong. 2004b. *Constitution construction – Regime and people*. Beijing: Social Sciences Literature Press.
Xu, Shishen. 1984. *List of nationalist government positions*. Beijing: China History Press.
Xu, Chongde. 2005. *History of PRC constitutions*. Fuzhou: Fujian People's Press.
Xu, Jilin. 2006. *Shi Huaci's commentary on China*. Beijing: Xinxing Publishing House.
Xu, Zhangrun. (ed.). 2010. *Ratio status*, historical jurisprudence, vol. 4. Beijing: China Law Press.
Yan, Fu. 1986. *Yan Fu anthology*. Beijing: China Book Store.
Yan, Quan. 2007. *Failed legacy – China's first parliamentary constitution 1913–1923*. Nanning: Guangxi Normal University Press.
Yu, Keping. 1998. *Contemporary China Political Institution*. Lanzhou: Lanzhou University Press.
Yu, Keping. 2004. *Sound governance*. Shanghai: Social Sciences Academic Press.
Zhang, Yufa. 1984. *Early ROC political parties*. Taipei: Central Research Institute Near-Modern Department.
Zhang, Qianfan. 2000. *Western constitution system – American constitution*, vol. 1. Beijing: China University of Political Science and Law Press.
Zhang, Qianfan. 2001. *Western constitution system – European constitution*, vol. 2. Beijing: China University of Political Science and Law Press.
Zhang, Pengyuan. 2007a. *Constitutionalists and Xinhai revolution*. Jilin: Jilin Publishing Group.
Zhang, Pengyuan. 2007b. *China's democratic political dilemma 1909–1949*. Jilin: Jilin Publishing Group.
Zhang, Pengyuan. 2007c. *Liang Qichao and ROC politics*. Jilin: Jilin Publishing Group.
Zhang, Ming. 2011. Xinhai, *A Rocking China*. Nanning: Guangxi Normal University Press.
Zhu, Yunhan, et al. 2012. *Taiwan democratic transformation – Experience and revelation*. Beijing: Social Sciences Literature Press.
Zou, Dang. 2002. *Chinese revolution reinterpretation*. Hong Kong: Hong Kong Oxford University Press.

Chinese Language Papers

Cao, Siyuan. 2010. Taiwan constitutionalism transformation and revelation. *Changcheng Monthly Journal*, Beijing, issue 3.
Chen, Duanhong. 1992. A tentative argument on constitutionalism. *Comparison Law Study*, Beijing, issue 4.
Chen, Hongyi. 2007. Taiwan and Hong Kong constitutionalism development. *Academia Sinica Jurisprudence Journal inaugural*, Taipei, issue.

Chen, Duanhong. 2008a. On constitution as a fundamental law and advanced law. *Zhongwai Jurisprudence*, Beijing, issue 4.

Chen, Duanhong. 2008b. On constitution as the basic law and advanced law. *Beijing University Law Journal*, Beijing, issue 4.

Gao, Quanxi. 2010a. American political "Secret" – Review from the perspective of political philosophy perspective. *Strategy and Management*, Beijing, issue 5 and 6.

Gao, Quanxi. 2010b. On revolutionary jurisprudence. *Beijing University Post Graduate Magazine*, Beijing, issue 1.

Gao, Quanxi. 2010c. Revolution and constitution and China's constitutional institutions, Beijing, issue 2.

Gao, Quanxi. 2010d. Western early modern thought history and its China questions. *Dushu*, Beijing, issue 4.

Gao, Quanxi, and Tian Feilong. 2011. Political constitutionalism's question, identification and method. *Suzhou University Journal* (Philosophy and Social Science Edition), Suzhou, 3rd issue.

Han, Dayuan. 1997. Social change and constitution's adaptiveness – An Mr. Hao and Mr. Tong's debate over benign unconstitutionality. *Jurisprudence*, Beijing, issue 5.

Han, Dayuan. 2006. Multiple constitutional problems related to property law bill. *Jurisprudence Magazine*, Beijing, issue 3.

Hao, Tiechuan. 1996a. On Benign unconstitutionality. *Jurisprudence Study*, Beijing, issue 4.

Hao, Tiechuan. 1996b. Limitation of social reform and written constitution, *Legal Study*, issue 4.

Huang Songyou. 2001. Constitution judicializaton and its implications. *People's Court News*, August 13.

Jiang, Yongjing. 1982. *Revolutionary party's criticism of the late Qing constitutionalist movement – Min Pao and Xin Min Cong Pao's analysis of constitutionalism debate*, published as part of the anthology *Chinese near modern reform*. Beijing: Central Research Institute Near Modern History Institute.

Li, Shenzhi. 2000. Five decades of Tumult. *History Monthly*, Beijing, March.

Liang, Huixing. 2007. Property law bill and multiple problems. *China Jurisprudence*, Beijing, issue 1.

Mao, Zedong. 1964a. *New democracy theory*. Selected works of Mao Zedong. Beijing: People's Publishing House.

Mao, Zedong. 1964b. *New democracy constitutionalism*. Selected works of Mao Zedong. Beijing: People's Publishing House.

Mao, Zedong. 1964c. *On coalition government*. Selected works of Mao Zedong. Beijing: People's Publishing House.

Miao, Lianying, and Cheng Xuyang. 2008. Civil law imperialism fantasy and confusion of constitution study – A third view of dispute regarding law's constitutionality. *Sichuan University Journal* (Philosophy and Social Science Edition), Sichuan, issue 2.

Qiang Shigong. 2011. On supreme court's interpretation of marriage law. *Cultural Review*, Beijing, issue 2.

Su, Qing, and Li, Yong. 1981. Report on Beijing political legal circles' conference on civil law and economic law-related questions. *Jurisprudence Development*, Beijing, issue 19, 1979.

Sun, Yat-sen. 1956. *State building strategy*. Selected works of Sun Yat-sen. Beijing: People's Publishing House.

Tian, Feilong. 2007a. Property law bill unconstitutionality debate points review and reflection. *Jiangsu Police Academy Journal*, Nanjing, issue 1.

Tian, Feilong. 2007b. Misuse of contract concept – Analysis and field study of the first "Empty Bed" case in China. *Beijing University Law Journal*, Beijing, issue 49, May 15.

Tian, Feilong. 2010. Tian Feilong's administrative adjudication white paper system: Construct a dialogue system between legal construction rational powers. *People's Court Journal*, Beijing, January 15.

Tian, Feilong. 2011a. *China political-legal cause and responsibility – The ideals of political-legal thoughts anthology. Economic Observer* (Book Review Special Issue), Beijing, August.

Tian, Feilong. 2011b. Conservative constitutionalism and hundred years of republicanism. *Strategy and Management,* Beijing, issue 5–6.
Tian, Feilong. 2013. Political constitutionalism in China's constitutionalism study, *Xuehai*, Nanjing, issue 2.
Tong, Zhiwei. 1996. Benign unconstitutionality should not be recognized. *Jurisprudence Study*, Beijing, issue 6.
Tong, Zhiwei. 1997. Constitution flexibility's bottom. *Jurisprudence Study,* Beijing, issue 5.
Tong, Zhiwei. 2006a. How can property law bill pass the gate of constitution – Comment on a constitutionality dispute caused by a public letter. *Jurisprudence Magazine*, Beijing, issue 3.
Tong, Zhiwei. 2006b. Second comment on constitutionality problems in property law bill. *Jurisprudence Study*, Beijing, issue 7.
Wang, He. 2004. Economic legislation and economic jurisprudence. *Social Sciences*, Beijing, issue 1.
Wang, Renbo. 2005a. The Chinese characteristics of constitution – The background of 54 constitution. *21st Century* (Online Edition), Hong Kong, issue 46.
Wang, Renbo. 2005b. Created public ritual – Reading and interpretation of 75 constitution. *Comparison Law Study*, Beijing, issue 3.
Wang, Liming. 2007a. Property law is the foundation of the law Edifice, *Democracy and Law*, Beijing, issue 1.
Wang, Liming. 2007b. Why the equal protection provision is completely constitutional? *Bright Daily*, Beijing, January 22 issue.
Wang, Taisheng. 2009. KMD's party rule experience in China – Impetus and impediment of democratic constitutionalism. *Academia Sinica Jurisprudent Journal*, Taipei, issue 5.
Wu, Guoguang. 2002. Reform's end and continuation of history. *21st Century*, Hong Kong, June.
Xiao, Gongqin. 1995. Re-reflection on Hundred Days Reform – On cultural roots of early political radicalism. *Strategy and Management*, Beijing, issue 4.
Xiao, Beisheng. 2003. Behind the constitution-making ritual – From common program to 1954 constitution. *Contemporary China Research*, Beijing, issue 2.
Xue, Jianfu. 2010. 54 constitution and Chinese democratic political model's construction. *Northeastern Normal University Journal* (Philosophy and Social Sciences Edition), Changchun: , issue 3.
Yang, Zhaolong. 1957. Distinction between party and non-party in the law profession, *Wenhuibao*, May 8 issue.
Yang, Zixuan. 2004. *Making economic law suits the four modernization needs*. Collection of economic law-related papers compiled by Southwestern Political Science and Law University. *Jurisprudent Theorist*, Beijing, issue 6.
Yin, Tai. 2007. Construction of imperialism in China – Case study of civil revolution in 1920s. *International Relationship Academy Journal*, Beijing, issue 3.
Yu, Yingshi. 1998. Wuxu reform rereading, *21st Century*, Hong Kong, issue 2.
Yuan, Weishi. 2011. Shikai and KMB. *Taste and Classics*, Beijing, issue 1.
Zhang, Taiyan. 1911. Zhang Taiyan and destruction of party views. *Takunpao,* Tianjin, December 12 issue.
Zhang, Qianfan. 2005. What the constitution should not stipulate. *Jurisprudence Forum*, Beijing, issue 3.
Zhang, Qianfan. 2006. The use and misuse of constitution – How to treat the constitutional problem in property right law. *Jurisprudence Magazine*, Beijing, issue 3.
Zhang, Qianfan. 2007. What the constitution should not stipulate, *Jurisprudence Forum*, Beijing, issue 3, 2005.
Zhao, Xiaoli. 2011. Trumpet of Chinese families' capitalization. *Cultural Review*, Beijing, issue 2.
Zheng, Bijian. 2005. Zheng Bijian's CPC's direction in the 21st century. *People's Daily* (Overseas Edition), Beijing, November 22.
Zhu, Guang. 2001. Mao Zedong and Huang Yanpei on historical cycle. *Bright Daily*, January 20, 1993.

Foreign Language

Ackerman, Bruce. 1991. *We the people: Foundations*. Cambridge: Harvard University Press.

Bellamy, Richard. 2007. *Political constitutionalism: A Republican defense of the constitutionality of democracy*. Cambridge: Cambridge University Press.

Gierke, Otto. 1958. *Political theories of the middle age*. Boston: Beacon Press.

Kahn, Paul. 2005. *Putting liberalism in its place*. Princeton: Princeton University Press.

Plamenatz, J. 1992. *Man and society: Political and social theories from Machiavelli to Marx*, 2nd ed. New York: Longman.

Teng, and Fairbank. 1954. *China's response to the west: A documentary survey, 1839–1923*. Cambridge: Harvard University Press.

Internet

Ma, Ying-jeou. 2010. Remember Mr. Chiang Jingkuo. *21ccom.net*. http://new.21ccom.net/plus/view.php?aid=16479. 3 Sept 2010.

MIX
Papier aus verantwortungsvollen Quellen
Paper from responsible sources
FSC® C105338

If you have any concerns about our products,
you can contact us on
ProductSafety@springernature.com

In case Publisher is established outside the EU,
the EU authorized representative is:
Springer Nature Customer Service Center GmbH
Europaplatz 3, 69115 Heidelberg, Germany

Printed by Libri Plureos GmbH
in Hamburg, Germany